Royal Navy Actions: Africa, 1914-18

Cruiser "Königsberg"

Royal Navy Actions: Africa, 1914-18

The Rufiji Delta, Lake Tanganyika,
Lake Victoria Nyanza

ILLUSTRATED

The "Königsberg" Adventure
E. Keble Chatterton

The Destruction of "Königsberg"
W. L. Wyllie

LEONAUR

Royal Navy Actions: Africa, 1914-18
The Rufiji Delta, Lake Tanganyika, Lake Victoria Nyanza
The "Königsberg" Adventure
By E. Keble Chatterton
and
The Destruction of "Königsberg"
By W. L. Wyllie

ILLUSTRATED

First published in the titles
The "Königsberg" Adventure
and
Sea Fights of the Great War (Extract)

Leonaur is an imprint of Oakpast Ltd
Copyright in this form © 2025 Oakpast Ltd

ISBN: 978-1-917666-28-2 (hardcover)
ISBN: 978-1-917666-29-9 (softcover)

http://www.leonaur.com

Publisher's Notes
The views expressed in this book are not necessarily those of the publisher.

Contents

Preface	7
Prelude to Adventure	9
The Deed and Its Consequence	17
The Chase Begins	27
Secret Intelligence	35
Clearing the Clues	42
The Dar-Es-Salaam Incident	53
The Rufiji Delta	61
Discovered	71
Running the Gauntlet	78
Blocking up the Enemy	88
The Enemy at Bay	96
Within the Blockade	103
The Sky Service	113
The Relief Ship Comes	124
Over the Delta	131
The Monitors Arrive	139
The First Attack	148
The Second Attack	162

From Sea to Lake	178
Establishing Command	191
Tanganyika Tactics	202
Victors on the Lake	214
Dénouement	222
The Final Phase	231
Down the River to Death	241
The Destruction of "Königsberg": A Synopsis	249

Preface

The following chapters represent the first attempt to publish a full and separate account of a rare adventure. Shortly after the War began, considerable public interest was aroused by the escape and concealment of the German cruiser *Königsberg*, but in those censored days it was never possible to get a clear account of what really happened; and not till very recently have all the complicated facts, the explanatory details, the missing motives, become available for a proper understanding of a difficult and fascinating campaign.

I have been fortunate to be given access to a considerable amount of invaluable information belonging to that period; and to have the personal records of those who played conspicuous parts in solving the *Königsberg* riddle. On such original matter of the greatest historical importance, supplemented by verbal communications, I have for the most part constructed the following narrative. Most manuscripts nowadays are, more accurately, typescripts, and this is the first age when irreplaceable documents have begun to fade at an alarming rate. The old days of pen-and-ink written MSS. have departed, yet there was a far greater permanence in their production. Today, after only seventeen or eighteen years, typewritten records and letters of the War period become fainter as the months speed by; and for that, if for no other reason, it is the duty of this generation to extract the truth before too late.

I cannot sufficiently express my sense of obligation to the immense assistance which has been given me by Vice-Admiral Sidney R. Drury-Lowe, C.M.G., who carried out the great task of organising the search for the *Königsberg* and bottling her up inside the African river. To Group-Captain J. T. Cull, D.S.O., R.A.F., I am very greatly indebted for the information covering the work so brilliantly performed by the Air Service, which caused the enemy to abandon their ship after the hottest duel. A list of further authorities will be found on another page.

It is a pleasure once more to acknowledge the courtesy of the Imperial War Museum both in regard to many of the photographs here reproduced, and in other respects. Both Admiral Drury-Lowe and Group-Captain Cull have also been good enough to allow a number of their illustrations to appear in the following pages. The opportunity has been appreciated all the more, seeing that in some cases these are the only pictorial records, and the original negatives do not all exist today.

E. Keble Chatterton.

CHAPTER 1

Prelude to Adventure

One of the most fascinating studies is to watch the effects of suspense and uncertainty on human mentality. In the theatre the dramatist well realises nothing is so sure of maintaining his audience's attention as that which incites curiosity by keeping the result of some great issue in a state of delay. In the realm of the Press is appreciated the fact that few items from day to day so hold the readers' interest as the search for one who has committed a daring deed and got clean away, leaving behind only the slenderest of clues. And the enormous consumption today of what is known as "detective fiction"; the anxiety to know the result of some important athletic contest; can be traced to the psychological characteristic that we remain ill at ease and unsatisfied until convinced of ultimate solutions. Inquisitiveness is less a failing than a desire to be relieved of further uncertainty.

Now one of the most prolonged instances of suspense afloat, combining mystery and doubtful fate right till the end, embracing also the frailest clues and the wildest of rumours, with the threat of great possibilities impending all the time, had for its scene the East African coast. And we have before us as fine a mystery narrative as ever the imagination could demand, with the most uninhabited and little-known scenery for the background, where few ships had ever steamed and little cartographical knowledge had ever been obtained. Contrasted with all this primitive environment of mangrove swamps, reefs, islands, uncharted channels and dense jungle, there come the modern developments of fast ships, airplanes, wireless; together with the intrigues of spies and the performance of most heroic adventures.

The story begins on July 27, 1914, when the Cape of Good Hope Squadron, under the command of Rear-Admiral Herbert King-Hall, during its cruise chanced to be at the island of Mauritius. Such were the alarming reports which arrived of the approaching European sit-

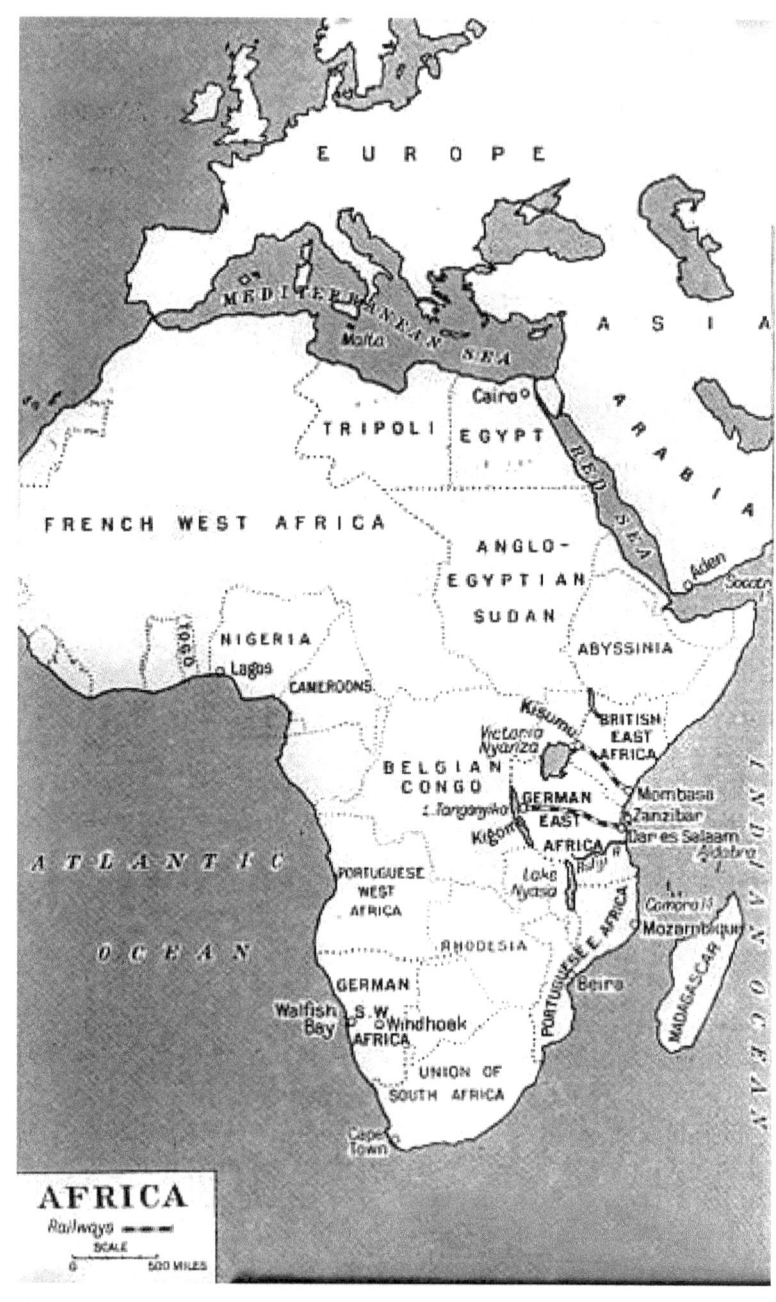

uation that Admiral King-Hall took his ships to sea that afternoon bound for Zanzibar. These units were but three in number, and were neither fast nor modern. His flagship was the *Hyacinth*, a cruiser of 5,600 tons that was already thirteen years old and had never done better speed than 21 knots. She was armed with eleven 6-inch and eight 3-inch guns. The *Astraea* was older still, having been completed as far back as 1894. She was of 4,360 tons, but armed with two 6-inch and eight 4.7's, and her best speed was less than 20 knots. Finally, there was the *Pegasus* of only 2,135 tons, 20 to 21 knots, and an armament of eight 4-inch. She dated from 1899.

There was thus no homogeneity about this old-fashioned trio, but the pre-war situation had not required that the latest and best British cruisers should be allocated to a station which extended as far west and north as St. Helena; as far east and north as to include the whole of East Africa and its outlying islands. Within this area were only two German men-of-war: the gunboat *Eber* and the protected cruiser *Königsberg*. The former was of but slight fighting value, and just before the declaration of war she steamed away from South Africa across the South Atlantic. Her subsequent career has already been noted, and we need not trouble to think of her again. (See my *The Sea-Raiders*.)

But the *Königsberg* was a reason for serious consideration. She was only seven years old, had been known to steam at over 24 knots, and was armed with ten 4.1-inch guns. This 3,350-ton cruiser was a sister ship of the *Nürnberg* which was to be one of von Spee's squadron at the Battle of Coronel, whose 4.1-inch guns sank H.M.S. *Monmouth*. At the Battle of the Falklands, she was in turn sunk by H.M.S. *Kent*, but only after a hot chase of 200 miles and her 4.1-inch guns had consistently outranged the 6-inch guns of *Kent*. There can be no question as to the *Königsberg* 's superiority over any of the three British African cruisers: she could have kept them at her chosen distance in any engagement, and then outranged them. Alternatively, she was possessed of at least 3 knots higher speed which would enable her to decline battle.

Based on Dar-es-Salaam, the capital of German East Africa, which was not merely an important military station but a great trading centre, the *Königsberg* with her three tall funnels and lithe slim hull was a source of pride to German colonials, and of no little awe to the natives. But to the British naval mind her situation so close to the steamship routes, running up from Capetown and Natal to Zanzibar and the Suez Canal, was to suggest a grave menace. Further eastward, well out on the Indian Ocean, there is a veritable spider's web of shipping lines from Australia, Java, Malacca Straits, China, Singapore, Calcutta, Ceylon, Bombay, Mauritius; whilst at the north and west the approaches to Aden were ripe possibilities if the *Königsberg* escaped to go raiding. And for this precise purpose she was particularly suited.

It was quite obvious, then, that before war should be declared the British cruisers should definitely locate *Königsberg's* whereabouts, and be ready to counteract her future hostile activities. Zanzibar, by reason of its proximity to Dar-es-Salaam, was clearly the station to make for at present, and on the voyage there was an opportunity for Admiral King-Hall to get the Cape Squadron into fighting trim. Hands were busy, in spite of the awkward heavy swell of the Indian Ocean, changing the beautiful white enamelled topsides to a dull flat colour of naval grey paint. It was farewell to leisured steaming, to pleasant visits, hospitable entertainments, picnics: the political situation was already tense. The fatal wireless signal might come through at any moment now.

But cruising means coaling, and it was a peculiarity of the Cape station that the use of Welsh coal for His Majesty's ships was forbidden: by an Admiralty order the fuel was to be either patent blocks or else coal from the Natal collieries. Neither of this was satisfactory, for it fouled the ships' boilers and caused considerable loss of speed to a squadron already slow enough. A call was made at Diego Suarez, which is at the north end of Madagascar and on the route to Zanzibar, but here no coal was available, so the latter stage of this voyage found the cruisers all too short of the wherewithal for chasing any fast German raider, whether genuine man-of-war or converted merchantman. The steamers of the German East Afrika Line that might chance to be in Dar-es-Salaam would certainly be expected to be sent along the trade routes waylaying British and French liners.

There was enough cause for anxiety during these last of the preliminary days, but the first thrilling moment arrived after sunset on July 31. Admiral King-Hall crossed the intervening sea between Madagascar and the African continent, and his voyage was nearly completed. He had detached the *Astraea* and *Pegasus* with orders to watch Dar-es-Salaam where the *Königsberg* might probably be at anchor, though this could not be certain. The *Hyacinth* was now steaming alone, and news came from the *Pegasus* that *Königsberg* was somewhere at sea. Darkness fell upon the tropical waves, the moon rose, and suddenly on the *Hyacinth's* starboard bow a strange vessel loomed up in the faint light.

Steamer of sorts! Warship! German—definitely the *Königsberg* herself! The occasion was rich in suspense. What was about to happen? Night action? And the *Hyacinth* short of coal? Had war been declared? Both the *Hyacinth* and *Königsberg* thought it possible the other knew hostilities had begun: yet each hesitated to open fire. Both cruisers were darkened, with crews at action stations; and the first ship to fire its salvo would break the uncertainty. Those were exciting, breathless moments, for the two silent foes-to-be passed each other at only 3,000 yards distance.

But the tension passed almost as quickly as it had begun. The *Königsberg* was playing only the first episode in a long game: she was required for other duties presently than to fight a duel with the *Hyacinth*, and she took full advantage of those extra knots which she so splendidly possessed.

"On sighting us," relates Admiral King-Hall, 'she bolted off at full speed and soon disappeared out of sight."

So, what with the British flagship being by nature slower, short of fuel, and allowed only inferior coal at that, it was impossible to shadow her. This statement cannot be stressed too heavily. We were within four days of the Great War, the one German cruiser off the whole East African coast had been sighted, and we had three cruisers to dog her steps. Instead of being able to blockade her or sink her on August 5, we had allowed her to get away into space, sink our ships, create immense anxiety, and keep our forces at sea for month after month hunting her down. The material and strategical cost was beyond all calculation. At a time when overseas shipping was being endangered by raiders and our light cruisers were so badly needed for escort and ocean patrol, the elusive *Königsberg* was able to keep them on the alert day and night for the one purpose of her destruction; whereas two of our modern cruisers, with plenty of good coal, during those fateful four days could have settled the *Königsberg's* career and saved the British nation millions of pounds.

Early in the morning of August 1 the *Hyacinth* reached Zanzibar, coaled, and then hurried south to the Cape of Good Hope, as the only naval strength there consisted of two torpedo-boats already thirty years old. The *Astraea* and *Pegasus* were left behind, though it is difficult to imagine what good they would have been collectively against the *Königsberg* except at close range; and this the fast German would never have permitted. Individually, the two British cruisers would not have had even a sporting chance: the enemy would have done what she liked with either.

However, whilst the *Astraea* a busied herself on August 8 at Dar-es-Salaam destroying the German wireless station, she was luckily not fallen upon. She certainly caused alarm to the enemy in bombarding that port, insomuch that the Germans sought to protect themselves by now sinking their floating dock across the harbour entrance. But whilst this afforded a measure of security, it not merely robbed the *Königsberg* of the very base outside which she had been sighted a week previously; but it shut in several fine German steamers, of which one was the 8,000-ton East Afrika Company's *Tabora*. This was a typical Teutonic liner of the multiple-deck type, with one funnel and two masts, and had arrived off the coast only a few days since. She was thus prevented from being employed as an auxiliary cruiser.

The *Astraea* and *Pegasus* during the first part of August both continued to steam about in the hope of finding the *Königsberg*, but without success; for the latter had indeed vanished right away from this region and cleverly gone north up the coast till she reached that approach to the Gulf of Aden where so many lanes of steamship traffic—from Karachi, Bombay, Colombo, and East Indies, China, Australia and South Africa—meet the traffic coming down the Red Sea from the Suez Canal. That is to say the German cruiser chose out a focal point where she could be absolutely sure of finding a victim merchantman, though it would be dangerous to hang about in such a busy locality for too long.

On August 6 she was rewarded, when 280 miles east of Aden, by the appearance of the British S.S. *City of Winchester* (6,601 tons) bound from Colombo to England, and thus the very first capture during the War of a British merchant vessel by the enemy took place within two days of hostilities commencing. But the incident was kept secret for a fortnight, and the *City of Winchester* had not been immediately sunk. A whole week passed during which the raider helped herself to coal and provisions, then finally scuttled her, and, after placing the prisoners in other German steamers, once more made her disappearance.

By August 24 the *Astraea* had been called away from the East African area and was engaged in convoying duties, thus leaving the *Pegasus* alone. If, therefore, the *Königsberg* should decide to revisit her peace-time region that was so familiar to her, she would have quite a fair chance of wiping out the sole British cruiser provided a certain amount of trouble were taken. Perhaps by means of careful staff work and sound naval intelligence based on espionage it would be possible to employ darkness for springing a surprise. In any case her ten modern 4.1-inch guns and superior speed would be more than a match for the eight-year-old 4-inch guns of the obsolete *Pegasus*.

It is undeniable that the *Königsberg* played her role with ability. She had created a crisis, as sudden as it was disturbing, by demonstrating the necessity for our cruisers in the protection of trade routes; and she had then resumed her cloak of mystery. What had become of her? Whither had she steamed? Week after week went by, and still she was unreported. On what plan of campaign was she working? The most reasonable appreciation seemed to suggest that she would continue to harry merchantmen but probably many hundreds of miles further to the east—perhaps near Sumatra—and all sorts of rumours concerning her having been sighted soon began to be spread. But would she reappear off the Zanzibar neighbourhood? On the whole, having regard to the loss of her Dar-es-Salaam base, it was far more likely that she would frequent Oriental trade routes and keep well distant from East Africa. Her normal coal capacity was 400 tons, and her maximum. stowage was more than twice that amount. She could go on refuelling from her prizes and maintain a normal radius of more than 5,000 knots. It is true that she had over 300 officers and men to feed, but here again the well-stocked merchant steamers would supply her needs.

September came and still there was no information of *Königsberg*, but on the 10th began those startling raids by the German cruiser *Emden* in the Bay of Bengal, whereby within five days half a dozen vessels had been captured and before the month's end more were to follow. Such exploits still more seemed to indicate that the *Königsberg* was somewhere on the trade routes awaiting similar opportunities: it was in fact rumoured that she was co-operating with the *Emden*.

But all theories and suppositions were with dramatic suddenness swept aside when, after seven weeks' mysterious silence, the *Königsberg* in the early morning of September 20 showed herself—not at the eastern side of the Indian Ocean, but in her original waters, and not far from where she had been sighted in the moonlight of July 31.

So, with no little skill, her captain had kept her foes badly guessing and (when least expected) he pounced upon the *Pegasus*, destroyed her without delay, and once more vanished utterly into the unknown. The *City of Winchester*'s loss had been a material disaster of some hundreds of thousands of pounds: but the sinking of even an obsolete cruiser belonging to His Majesty's Navy, and under such special circumstances, was a moral misfortune that called for immediate and drastic action. The necessity of finding the *Königsberg* and wiping her off the sea became of paramount importance, and no expense was to be spared, no relaxation permitted, until this culprit should have been hunted to death.

This, then, is the high adventure that we are about to follow through all its complexities and ramifications, the false and true clues, the checked chase, till the final kill. The culprit is the *Königsberg*, the victims are the two vessels just mentioned, the detectives and police are the naval officers and men aboard fast-steaming cruisers called in to concentrate on a difficult and hazardous quest. All sorts of supernumeraries join in the exciting drama, and from small beginnings great happenings develop, culminating in one tremendous climax.

But first let us see for ourselves exactly the circumstances of that tragedy which occurred on September 20.

CHAPTER 2

The Deed and Its Consequence

The poor old *Pegasus* this morning belied her name: there was not much in common with the "winged horse," for she was in a state of immobility. After all this steaming about during the last few weeks seeking out the missing *Königsberg*, and consuming indifferent coal, the time had come when the cleaning of boilers and the repairing of engines could be no longer delayed. So, she put into Zanzibar and began her overhaul. Before he had left for the south, Admiral King-Hall had given orders that steam was always to be ready in one engine at least; and, foreseeing certain possibilities, he had represented to the Admiralty the danger of withdrawing *Astraea* from co-operation with *Pegasus*: but the Admiralty deemed the risk slight and, in any case, to be accepted.

Commander J. A. Ingles, R.N., was *Pegasus's* Captain, and whilst there was every reason to suppose that the *Königsberg* was many hundreds of miles away, precautions against a surprise attack were not forgotten. An armed tug named *Helmuth* was kept patrolling in Zanzibar's South Channel to give warning of a stranger's advent. Within the port also was the Admiralty collier *Banffshire*, and this was fortunate. Just before 5.30 a.m. the *Helmuth* sighted a long lithe vessel approaching by the South Channel. She had three funnels and a beautiful hull with a cruiser stern. Evidently, she was of bigger tonnage than the *Pegasus*, and fifty or sixty feet longer.

The *Königsberg* at last!

But before the tug could get a signal through to the *Pegasus* at anchor off the Eastern Telegraph Company's office, the German began shelling the British cruiser at 11,000 yards, though this range came down to 7,000 yards presently, and by 6 a.m. the dawn visitor departed in a southerly direction. It all happened as quickly as that: a short quick raid, but with a fierce result. Evidently the *Königsberg* was

THE S.S. *PRÄSIDENT*

Lying up the Lukuledicreek, Lindi. It was this German liner which pretended to be a hospital ship. Documents found aboard her proved she had aided the *Königsberg*.

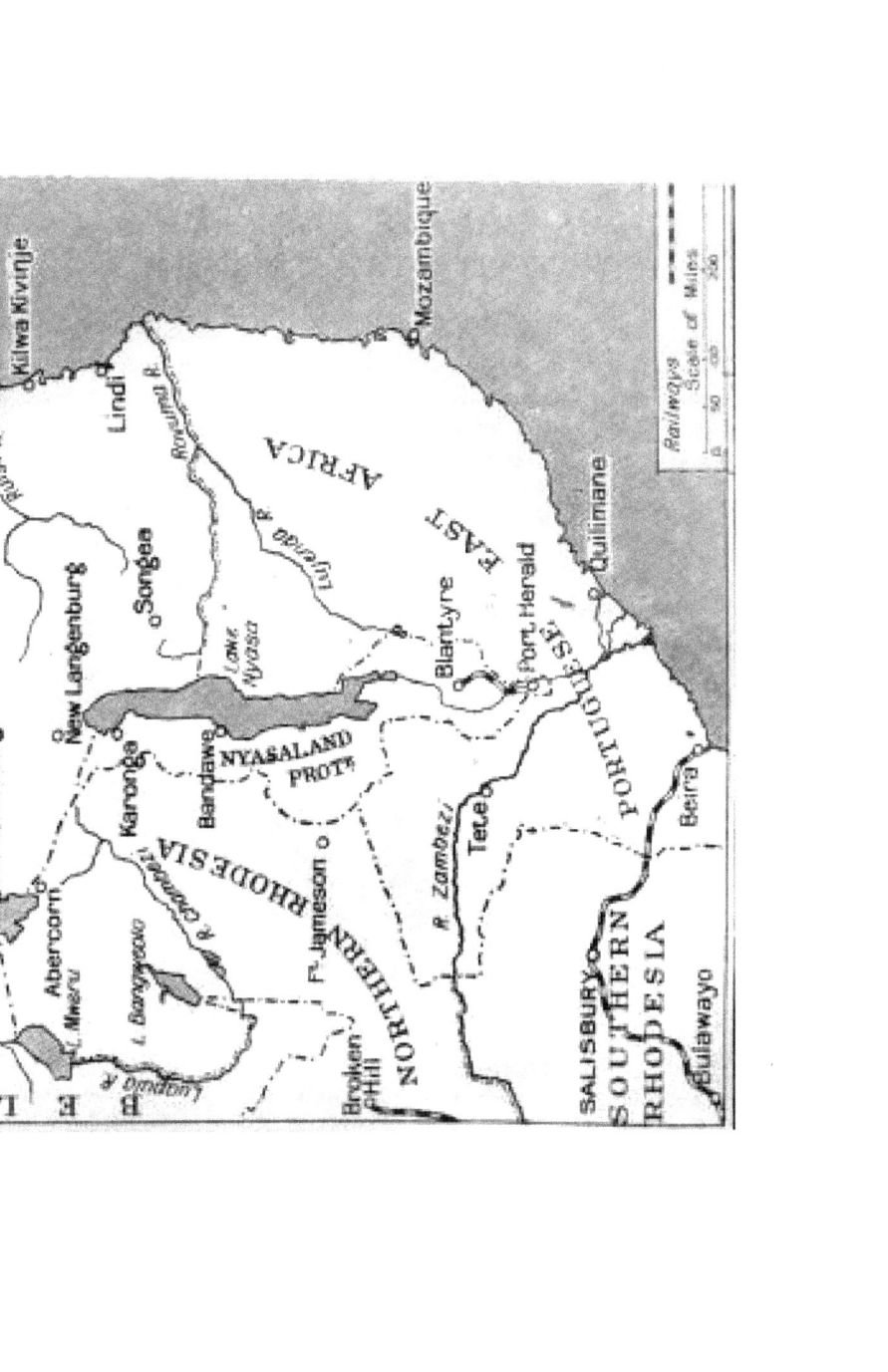

nervous, and in a hurry to escape again. Had she chosen to remain, the whole place was hers. The big *Banffshire* with all those tons of coal would have been a welcome prize, and the Germans had only to have landed an armed party, cut the ocean cables, destroyed the wireless station, blown up the Government buildings, and thus created a severe moral effect.

Still, the situation after the stranger's departure was quite bad enough. The *Pegasus* having been both surprised and outranged, made ineffective attempts with her 4-inch guns against the more modern 41-inch. Within ten minutes the British cruiser was knocked out of the contest. The *Banffshire* was lying only four hundred yards from *Pegasus*, and the collier's boats were luckily able to perform rescues: but the casualties numbered over eighty. At 2 p.m. the *Pegasus*, having turned over, sank, and the tragic episode ended. Certainly, the enemy had, by means of his excellent spy system, obtained accurate intelligence as to the present condition of Commander Ingles' ship; and, acting on this, had chosen the time well. It was the hour when human nature is about at its weakest and is least alert.

But the fortunate feature was that the event could at once be telegraphed to the British Admiralty, and immediate steps be taken towards a fitting revenge. This was essential, for two reasons. Firstly, the sinking of the *Pegasus* was an ugly national blow to political prestige in the East; but secondly, it seemed as if the *Königsberg* was going to become as serious a menace on the trade routes as the *Emden*.

It is illustrative of the great assistance to be found in telegraph cables and wireless that at 4 a.m. the next day (September 21) an urgent message sparked into the wireless-room of H.M.S. *Chatham*, who chanced to be steaming down the southern end of the Red Sea. She now received orders to search for the *Königsberg* "with all despatch," first calling at Aden for coal and further instructions. But, for the reason that this British cruiser will during the ensuing chapters considerably demand our close attention, let us first become acquainted with some more details.

This lovely vessel, built as recently as 1912, was armed with eight 6-inch and four 3-pdr. guns. Her displacement of 5,400 tons, and speed of 26 knots complete the list of features superior to those of Königsberg. In command of *Chatham* was Captain Sidney R. Drury-Lowe, R.N., with Commander Raymond Fitzmaurice, R.N., as second-in-command. And here let us note the wonderful manner in which some seem predestined for high adventure. One of the world's best-known sea stories is that concerning the hurricane of March 15, 1889, at Apia, Samoa, when six out of seven warships of various nationalities, also a German trading barque together with seven coasters, were all driven ashore. The naval vessels consisted of H.M.S. *Calliope*; the United States cruiser *Trenton*; the corvette *Vandalia*, and the sloop *Nipsic*; the German corvette *Olga*, and the two gun-vessels *Adler* and *Eber*. These seven were all single-screw, and belonged to the days when steam had not utterly ousted canvas from the world's navies.

Commanding the corvette *Calliope* was Captain H. C. Kane, R.N., and during this dreadful night the ships began to drag and collide in the most alarming manner. Both the *Vandalia* and the *Olga* drove down on to *Calliope* so that she looked like becoming a total loss. Captain Kane was a plucky and determined seaman of the old school, who took a great gamble. His engineers provided him with the utmost steam, and at the gale's height he slipped his cable, began steaming into the monstrous wind whose force was such that the *Calliope* was making good at no better speed than 1 knot, although ordinarily she could do her 14 and 15 knots. Ship-rigged, with three masts, this 2,770 tons steel and iron craft with her square yards and high freeboard created considerable windage. But gradually, after a most trying suspense, she drew ahead and got away safely to sea. No fewer than 130 lives were lost by the other vessels.

Such cool courage and masterly seamanship could not fail to impress all the young officers serving under Captain Kane, and the names of her eight midshipmen are as follows: The Hon. Horace Hood, after a distinguished career, ended his life as Rear-Admiral, and went down to a gallant death at Jutland in the battle-cruiser *Invincible*; Frank Brandt rose to be Captain of the *Monmouth* and perished when she was sunk at the Battle of Coronel; Wilmot S. Nicholson became Captain of the *Hogue* and was in her when she was torpedoed by a German submarine that sank the three *Cressys*, but fortunately he was saved; John C.T. Glossop became Captain of the *Sydney*, and sank the *Emden*;.

Cecil H. Fox was in command of the *Amphion* and destroyer flotilla which sank the German minelayer *Königin Luise*, but the next day the *Amphion* foundered on one of the German's mines, though Captain *Fox* was saved; Sidney R. Drury-Lowe became Captain of the *Chatham* and is now an Admiral; the other two midshipmen, Edmund Prendergast and Hugh Hopkinson, had left the service before the war but came back and served again. Thus at least six of the eight junior officers in the *Calliope's* gun-room made history.

But how the *Chatham* happened to be in the Red Sea on September 21 may briefly be explained. During the year preceding the Great War she had been stationed in the Mediterranean, and on August 2 left Malta with orders to ascertain whether the *Goeben* and *Breslau* were at Messina. After steaming through Messina Straits next day, and finding no enemy there, she returned to Malta and began patrolling off Pantellaria, capturing a German steamer which was now sent into Bizerta. After the *Goeben* and *Breslau* had escaped inside the Dardanelles, the *Chatham* was one of the units sent to concentrate off there, but was soon required at Port Said. It was whilst on her way thither that she captured the fine 8,000-tons S.S. *Marienbad* of the Austrian-Lloyd one night off the east end of Crete, and took her into Alexandria.

There was great joy aboard the cruiser at such a useful prize, but happiness was turned into disappointment when under the "Days of Grace" agreement the *Marienbad* was ordered to be released.

From Port Said the *Chatham* went to Suez in order to guard the southern entrance of the Canal, and in the last week of August escorted the two British transports *Dongola* and *Somali* to Aden. Either of these steamers would have been most welcome captures to the *Königsberg*, for they were full of officers returning to India from leave, and in the *Dongola* alone there were 600 of them including 13 generals, besides numerous colonels and majors. During this voyage the *Chatham* was to experience—what was to manifest itself in other seas during this war—the disadvantages not inseparable from the use of wireless.

It was August 28, a day before reaching Aden, that the Dutch S.S. *Kawi* near the southern end of the Red Sea called up the British cruiser and transmitted through the ether the following quaint message:

From *Kawi* to *Chatham*.
Have very bad news. Germans took nearly whole Belgium. Troops landed at Ostend and badly beaten. This is sorry news. Hope people German are beaten, but they have a very large army. As for British Fleet nothing was said. Hope they will have victory else we are lost. What are you thinking about? Where are you now? Do you think your *commandante* will come on board see papers? Can't tell you where we are or anything. You will know when you see us. That will be soon enough.

This was exactly the kind of chatter which was not to be desired, and more especially when it is remembered that the *City of Winchester* had been captured in the locality where the *Kawi* now happened to be. And, when the Dutchman again began to be communicative, he was promptly told to shut up.

At Aden there were reports that the *Königsberg* was off Socotra, but these were immediately followed by totally irreconcilable statements that she had been sighted off Sabang on August 28, and off Madagascar on August 30! But it was just this sort of uncertainty which was making the work of escort so very necessary. So, from Aden the *Chatham* continued with her two troopships until a position half-way across the Arabian Sea towards Bombay had been reached; and then she took over seven transports bound from Bombay westwards.

During these first weeks of the War, when so many troops had to be moved across the ocean, the time-honoured use of convoying was to prove its value as it had in previous wars. Then for many months convoys were somehow no longer employed, until the U-boat campaign during the last phase made this system an essential revival. But it was not long before Captain Drury-Lowe this first September discovered (as other Convoy Officers were eventually to learn) that lack of homogeneity is a most tantalising failure. Of the seven units the best could steam at 14 knots and the slowest at 10 knots, which of course became the rate for all. But when a sea got up, the slower ships at once dropped astern so that the formation tailed out, and dawn might find the last steamer five miles to the rear; thus, making her an easy victim for the *Königsberg*.

As everyone is aware, the prevailing strong winds of the Red Sea from the days of the ancient Egyptian sailing ships that went to Somal*i*land to fetch apes and incense back to the Nile, have always been northerly; and against these head breezes the convoy's steaming speed fell to 8 knots at the best. But the navy was now in process of learning many things, including the surprising fact that whilst military signalmen aboard the transports were good at helio, they were very slow at Morse, and seemed to have no knowledge of using semaphore or flags. Still by the night of September 13, the *Chatham* had safely brought her transports to Suez, and next came an order to come south again, cross the Indian Ocean to a secret rendezvous, where she was to help in escorting the much bigger convoy of forty transports. She had, however, in the early morning of September 21 arrived off Perim and not yet got clear of the Red Sea, when the urgent order to seek out the *Königsberg* switched her on to quite different duties.

At Aden, whilst hurriedly coaling, the *Chatham* learned all that was known about the *Pegasus* disaster of the day previous. Inasmuch as the East African coast was now bereft of a single British man-of-war, it looked as if the German cruiser would for a few days at least be able to spend a high old time destroying merchantmen, bombarding such places as Zanzibar and Mombasa. There was no time to waste, so by midnight the *Chatham* had finished coaling and at 1 a.m. on September 22 was leaving Aden astern bound for the British East African port of Mombasa.

Down to the south-west this good-looking warship with the four funnels and the raking masts, the sweet lined body and the razor bows, sped along the dark continent. Stokers toiled below in the heat, and turbines hummed their hymn. Speed! Speed! The British colonials were at the enemy's mercy. Even now it might be too late, yet what good fortune that so able a match for the *Königsberg* should have been available within a mere two thousand miles of the German's last reported position! But two adverse factors united to prevent the *Chatham* from making the fastest time.

Firstly, it was still September, and the south-west monsoon, which does not end till the next month begins, was still blowing. But secondly, there was the northerly set of the current, which used to be such a kindly friend to the old slow sailing ships of three centuries ago and onwards, when outward bound from England to the Indies; but was to the *Chatham* a grave drawback. The net result of these two forces was that until crossing the equator she lost 80 knots a day. Meanwhile there was plenty of time for conjecture, for discussion, for planning. Before leaving Aden Captain Drury-Lowe had arranged that any further tidings should be wirelessed. But by the time his ship had passed out of the radius, nothing had reached him, and he had closed down the *Chatham*'s wireless so as not to give away her approach. For, be it remembered, in German East Africa were several wireless stations which could keep the *Königsberg* informed.

As *Chatham*'s captain pondered over the picture which he expected to find at the end of these few days, he could find little consolation. Mombasa and Zanzibar would certainly be gutted, and the Admiralty colliers (which were the sole means for replenishing our naval forces) would assuredly have been captured or sunk. There seemed but three possibilities:

1. The *Emden* and *Königsberg* might be working more or less together over a wide area, but on the trade routes.

2. The *Königsberg* might be operating alone on the trade routes to Capetown, using some secret base for her collier and store ship.

3. She might elect to remain off German or British East Africa, and must have known that Mombasa as well as Zanzibar were practically defenceless.

"We arranged," says Captain Drury-Lowe, "to arrive off Mombasa at daybreak on September 27, ready for immediate action and hoping to find the *Königsberg* there." But when the *Chatham* at 6 a.m. slowed down, she was disappointed to find no sign of the enemy, and that all the few available British troops were either up country, or along the coast frontier engaging numerically superior forces. For Mombasa was relying solely on (*a*) the Town Volunteers and a few King's African Rifles, (*b*) a weak Harbour Defence which comprised two old 40-pdrs. (muzzle-loaders) which had a few locally manufactured shell together with some round shot. These antiquated guns had been mounted near the lighthouse and were capable of throwing the projectile perhaps 1,000 yards—provided the gun did not burst. Mombasa's harbour had not been mined, and from a certain bearing could have been shelled by the enemy cruiser with grave results.

Not quite twenty-four hours did the *Chatham* remain at Mombasa, but within this period she landed a couple of Maxims for the defence of Makupa railway bridge (which connected Mombasa with the mainland and was expected to be blown up by the German military), erected wire entanglements, and mined the approaches with charges of gun cotton. Captain Drury-Lowe was surprised to find Mombasa full of Germans, so telegraphed to the Governor of British East Africa at Nairobi to have them all interned and removed up country. Then, steaming off southward, the *Chatham* having filled her bunkers from the *Banffshire* collier, looked into all the bays along the coast, and reached Zanzibar late that same afternoon.

It had been stated by observers that when the *Königsberg* on September 20 was leaving Zanzibar after shelling the *Pegasus*, the German in the Southern Channel dropped a number of mines overboard. This assertion, however, was inaccurate though the mistake was natural under the circumstances. On the way from Mombasa to Zanzibar Captain Drury-Lowe says that *Chatham* sighted "several suspicious-looking objects in the water, which were at first taken to be mines, but on investigation were found to be the long cylindrical zinc cases used in the German Navy" for cordite charges. These were the supposed mines and had been carried all the way from the Southern Channel by the strong northerly current a distance of 90 miles in eight days. Perhaps the *Königsberg* had deliberately intended to deceive, for as she steamed away from Zanzibar she had wirelessed *en clair*, "Keep clear of the Southern entrance." It is interesting here to mention that during the Falklands battle the German cylindrical cases were, on being thrown overboard, carefully avoided by Admiral Sturdee's battle-cruisers who were under a similar delusion.

CHAPTER 3

The Chase Begins

It was no small relief for the *Chatham* to find Zanzibar intact, though so much damage could have been effected if only the German cruiser had not been so hasty. There was a weak garrison consisting of some native soldiers under a subaltern with a couple of Maxims, and it cannot be doubted that the *Königsberg's* captain was aware of these details. Ridiculous to relate, many of the German residents up till now had been permitted to remain in Zanzibar, and the valuable intelligence that the *Pegasus* had come in for repairs, which would need forty-eight hours, was readily conveyed to our enemy.

But whilst the Germans were able to keep in wireless communication with Berlin, the Zanzibar wireless station was good for only 150 miles even at night. Actually, it received no damage on September 20, for it was well hidden by trees from the South Channel, and the *Königsberg* blazed away at what was a dummy wireless erected in full view of the town. But the remarkable fact still obtruded itself that the *Königsberg* had not waited to cut our cable.

The latter, which reached Zanzibar at Bawi Island, connected with Aden, the Seychelles Islands to the eastward, Mombasa to the north, and Mozambique to the south. The *Emden* showed by her activities at Cocos Island that she appreciated the importance of cutting telegraph communications, and it will always seem extraordinary that the *Königsberg* did not make use of the perfect opportunity for isolating the whole of British East Africa in one act. Thus, so easily could she have long delayed the time when Aden and London should learn of the *Pegasus* catastrophe: thus, too, would the arrival of *Chatham* have been indefinitely postponed.

Captain Drury-Lowe could obtain no information at Zanzibar as to where the enemy had betaken himself. Over there the mastheads of *Pegasus* were just visible even at high water, though only 17 feet had been her draught before the sinking. News now came that the British Admiralty were sending along the sister ships *Dartmouth* and *Weymouth* to help *Chatham* in the search, and it began to be obvious that sooner or later the *Königsberg* would be in for a hot time if only she could be tracked down. But at present there was no reliable evidence, though there were innumerable rumours, conjectures and some intentional lies.

She had, however, been heard talking at night across the sky. Thus at 8.30 p.m. on September 22 she began calling up DSF, at first very weakly and then loudly. But at 8.35 p.m. she called up DNG, who answered AKO, whereupon AKO wirelessed to DNG a code message. Commercial ships and others listened in. At g.12 p.m. AKO was again talking to DNG.

The messages actually heard were as follows:

DSF .DSF .DSF .HIER .NEX .AKO .DE .AKO .AKO. AKO. DNG .DNG .DNG .DE .AKO.AKO .AKO .*KAWID* KAMILDIRES.KAMILDIRES.KIRANOPUMI.KIRANOPUMI. AKO.NNN. KKK.

It should be mentioned that AKO was the *Königsberg's* own call sign. DSF and DNG were evidently two German steamers to whom she wished to give instructions. Now there is no such thing as an immaculate code: sooner or later its secrets can be discovered by those endowed with a particular kind of intellect. It may take months, weeks or merely hours, but the revelation comes at last. (The reader who is interested in this technique will find some striking examples in an indiscreet book entitled *The American Black Chamber*, by H. O. Yardley). And the war provided one important lesson, which we are only now beginning to appreciate: that wireless, like propaganda, can become a most dangerous boomerang. For, now that we are no longer in the sailing-ship age, the very life of a warship depends on her fuel supplies; and, when a cruiser has to keep moving about, she must needs call up her colliers or oilers every few days to appoint rendezvous.

But herein lies the weakness of modern conditions, for the ether is free to all, and no respecter of nations' secrets. That was how the *Dresden*, after escaping from the Battle of the Falklands and for three months eluding the most diligent search by British cruisers, was at last discovered. She was short of coal and began calling up on her wireless. This message was intercepted by H.M.S. *Kent*, who could make nothing of it, but re-wirelessed it to H.M.S. *Glasgow*, whose captain tells me that one of his lieutenants having worked at the puzzle for most of a week elucidated the meaning. The *Dresden* was ordering some vessel—evidently one of her supply ships—to meet her at Juan Fernandez. The result was that next day the British cruisers surprised *Dresden* at that island, and before sunset she was no longer a scourge of the ocean but lying beneath the water never to rise.

Commander Ingles after the loss of his *Pegasus* had certainly not lost heart, but became extremely busy, as we shall presently notice, and after devoting his attention to the above messages evolved that the *Königsberg* was appointing a rendezvous for Thursday, September 24, at 6.30 p.m. The unfortunate and exasperating feature was that the locality of this meeting-place could not be elucidated, and in any case the *Chatham* did not reach Zanzibar till the 28th, so it would have been impossible to have brought off a coup such as was to happen next March at Juan Fernandez. On September 25 yet another code message from AKO calling up DTM was plucked out of the air, which indicated that the *Königsberg* was calling up a German steamer.

The duty now was to make such complete plans as would bring about the ultimate destruction of *Königsberg*, whilst at the same time doing what could be effected in strengthening the weak defences of the two British bases at Zanzibar and Mombasa. At the latter a system of patrol boats was therefore properly organised, signalmen and lookouts placed in the lighthouse, and the Eurasian wireless operators at the station displaced by naval ratings. All this was to prevent a recurrence of the previous surprise. From the survivors of the *Pegasus* artisans were selected for employment in the workshops ashore to fashion gun carriages that would be used on the mainland, whilst the rest of the sunken ship's crew formed a much-needed reinforcement of the local army.

All the remaining German subjects were rounded up, interned and sent to join their fellows at Nairobi, whence they were later transported to India: so, a stop was put to a most obvious method of spying, though a highly efficient organisation still remained, as we shall presently understand. Under Commander Ingles' direction salvage operations started on the *Pegasus*, in the hope of recovering her eight 4-inch and eight 3-pdr. guns. This was no small undertaking in the absence of a suitable salvage ship with gear, but appliances had to be extemporised and it was found that a small local steamer possessed a strong steam cable windlass.

Most fortunately, likewise, the *Pegasus*, in the act of heeling over, had thrown all her 4-inch guns and mountings clear of deck and hull into the water. The result was that when the divers went down, they were able to secure *Pegasus's* chain cable in turn to each gun and mounting, which were then hoisted up, taken alongside the wharf and landed. Thus, by the end of November two of these useful weapons had been sent to Mombasa and there mounted for defensive purposes, whilst the others were put on the field carriages manufactured in the Zanzibar workshops. The best had therefore been made of a sad job.

But there still remained the primary necessity to ascertain through every likely source whither the *Königsberg* had betaken herself; and this was a most complicated affair. Commander Ingles was placed in charge of our Intelligence organisation at Zanzibar, which included the employment of native spies; but the arrangement was never satisfactory and the results were very disappointing. There was no lack of applicants, yet scarcely one could be trusted. Reports came in that were mostly vague and generally inaccurate. Of the agents which had been landed in German East Africa to gather facts on our behalf some never returned at all, having been done in by the enemy who ruled the whole coast line with a hand of terror.

It was impossible to obtain any clear notion from the medley of reports which arrived, and in order that the reader may have before him the problem as presented to the *Chatham*'s captain on reaching Zanzibar from Aden, let us present all the available clues whether possible, probable or doubtful in value. Zanzibar Island was from a strategical consideration strangely situated, for it was so close to German territory that Dar-es-Salaam was only 40 miles away from the Zanzibar anchorage; but at its narrowest the sea which separated the Island of Zanzibar from the African continent was no wider than the English Channel between Dover and Calais. Even from the German port of Bagamoyo it was a mere 23 miles across to the *Pegasus* wreck.

Thus, it was easy enough for the enemy both to obtain up-to-date information and to spread false news, especially since among the Arabs at Zanzibar he had quite a number of his agents. There was little difficulty for a native to get across from the continent by night in a dhow, or even a dugout; and, notwithstanding all our patrols, this occurred constantly. It must be remembered, too, that within Dar-es-Salaam were (besides the sunken floating dock) the three German steamers *König*, *Feldmarschall* and *Tabora*; and that on her way from Mombasa the *Chatham* had observed within Tanga the S.S. *Markgraf*.

Straightened out, then, from a strange and contradictory medley there emerged such reports as these: Our spies asserted that there existed a system of watch fires and mounted patrols all down the coast of German East Africa; that the *Königsberg* was up the Rufiji River and using the village of Salale there as her base, that she was going in and out of that river followed by one small ship. Other statements were that she had been with the German S.S. *Somali*, (not to be confused with the previously mentioned British troopship of that name), that she had provisioned from the German S.S. *Präsident* at Dar-es-Salaam on September 20 and thence proceeded to Salale. In view of what will later be made known, these facts should be kept in mind.

But at the same time the *Königsberg* was reported to be working from a base in the Comoro Islands, which are a French group situated between the northwest of Madagascar and the south-east of German East Africa. She was, on the contrary, supposed to have been seen at 8.30 p.m. on September 24 off Dar-es-Salaam steaming fast towards the south-west, searchlight and rockets being also observed. A searchlight was reported also to have been seen at 9.20 p.m. on September 27 south of Mombasa. And, during the first week of October, she was said to be anchored behind Casuarina Island, off the coast of Portuguese East Africa. There was still another allegation that at the beginning of October she had been located at Jeddah, up the Red Sea, in the act of coaling.

All this diversity was most confusing, and it was quite possible that before many more weeks of mystery should pass there might come the startling news that *Königsberg* had joined hands with *Emden*. It was indeed not improbable that the former was keeping quiet until the latter was able to extend her operations further westward; and but for the fact that *Emden* met her fate at the hands of H.M.S. *Sydney* (commanded by Captain Drury-Lowe's old shipmate of *Calliope* days) on November 9 off Cocos Island (which lay less than a fortnight's steaming to the eastward of where *Königsberg* actually did hide herself) this co-operation might well have been accomplished and another grave crisis have arisen.

In the meanwhile, the truth had to be faced that the geographical formation of the East African coast was most favourable for a ruthless raider. The *Emden* during her victorious cruise had established the unpleasant principle that no fixed base was requisite, but that out-of-the-way anchorages could be made of supreme utility for a time. Whilst the immediate vicinity of Zanzibar would be regarded just now as too risky, there were to the southward, even as far south as the limits of Portuguese East Africa, such a number of small harbours, creeks, islands, reefs and little-explored rivers that light cruisers, supply ships, colliers, merchant steamers improvised as men-of-war, could find cover in localities so sparsely populated that secrecy was almost certain.

Thus, it became manifest that from as far north as Mafia Island (see map) to as far south as at least the Zambesi, the littoral must forthwith be combed carefully. Not merely that, but the sea area to the eastward (which included the Comoro Islands and the Mozambique Channel) must be patrolled and kept examined in order both to afford protection to allied shipping and to test the tidings which were coming in almost daily from native fishermen and others. Could there be any reliability in those slender intimations of "a warship with dark hull, number of funnels uncertain"; "three-funnelled warship"; "vessel thought to be anchored off island, but impossible to distinguish vessel"; "German coasting vessel left port suddenly yesterday on receipt of information from the north. . . said to be communicating with *Königsberg*"; and so on?

The *Chatham* was soon under way again. By 1.30 on the afternoon of September 29, that is to say within less then twenty-four hours of her arrival, she was steaming from Zanzibar to make a preliminary investigation of the coast as far as Mafia Island, proceeding down the north and east coasts of Zanzibar and down the mainland. It was noticed that the Dar-es-Salaam lighthouse was still working, notwithstanding that the sunken dock made the harbour useless; but the Germans evidently had their good reasons for not dowsing this beacon when her shipping remained active.

And now the *Chatham* was to become visually acquainted with what Captain Drury-Lowe considers to have been a "most efficient Intelligence system all along their coast, as well as an extremely well-organised Defence Force." Not merely were there numerous signal stations posted in a chain down the littoral, but they were connected up by a land wire. Various islands, protected by dangerous reefs, likewise had their signalling apparatus. By this series of links, the movements of every vessel were reported and telegraphed to the four German inland wireless stations at respectively *Tabora*, Muanga, Bukoba and Mgau Mwania, who in turn were able to flash the news aboard the *Königsberg*. *Tabora* could also communicate across the African continent to the high-power wireless station at Windhoek in German South-West Africa, and Windhoek—for the South-west campaign had still to be fought out—was able to talk with *Berlin* direct.

In short, then, by meticulous organisation the German Admiralty was in touch with even its minutest outposts, and able to watch our sea activities. Both Captain Max Looff (commanding officer of the *Königsberg*) and his superiors at home were able, almost immediately, to learn that a British cruiser of the "Town" class had now become busy off the coast, and further developments could not fail to be signalled through.

The foresight and thoroughness with which these coastal signal stations had been placed was typically Teutonic. When once the *Chatham* realised that there were so many single lights and such a string of fires that the cause was other than a coincidence, the obvious thing to do was to patrol during the dark hours; but the coast was fringed with coral reefs, small islets, and in many places an outer line of reefs. The charts were by no means exhaustive, the various channels capable of passage were unmarked, and they were invisible at high water. Altogether these waters were as nearly a "navigator's nightmare" as the most hardened could select. Captain Drury-Lowe says:

> Wherever *Chatham* steamed within sight of the coast, signal fires sprang up along the hills inland, and these would accompany or precede us along the coast like a *feu de joie*. The only way to defeat it was to move at night, but it is not pleasant to navigate with no lights of any sort to guide one, and the currents are very strong.

Further details of the signalling show how easily these stations combined primitive methods with practical utility.

> On passing some of the numerous islets among the coral reefs along the coast we had noticed a small white flag showing from some tree or other, sometimes two or three of these, very similar to a native's shirt. As these islands always had natives on them, we at first regarded them without suspicion, and probably as signals of neutrality; for the natives were obviously very much frightened on the approach of a man-of-war, and we could always see them watching us from the beach or amongst the trees.

> On September 30, after passing amongst several reefs and searching the channels west of Mafia Island, vigilant eyes suddenly sighted among the trees what looked like the figure of a man clad in khaki.

That was significant; for it could be only a European, Whilst the British Navy was serving afloat so near to the equator, the custom was to dispense with the usual uniform and for officers to wear jackets, "shorts" and helmets—all of khaki. The men wore vests, khaki "shorts," or whites stained, and khaki helmets; white hats being found to be hopeless. But Germans also wore khaki, so this must be one of the enemy and the matter needed investigation. The time was 9 a.m. and the locality Komo Island; course was altered towards the shore, and two or three white men in khaki carrying rifles were seen on the beach in company of some natives.

When the *Chatham* was observed to approach, instantly panic seized the island, and there was a general *sauve qui peut* from the beach in the direction of a dhow which was at the other end of Komo. In order to cut off their escape, the British cruiser loosed off a few shells from her 3-pdrs., ran round to the north side, anchored, and sent an armed boat's crew in pursuit. The party having landed took part in the kind of exciting chase that is familiar to those who watch such a spectacle from the comfortable seat of a cinema theatre: it was more in keeping with melodrama than actual war. The blue sea, the brilliant sunlight, the grey cruiser in the background, the sailors leaping ashore, the eagerness of human hounds not to be cheated of their hunt: here was a picture reminiscent of those double-page illustrations which nineteenth-century artists used to sketch for the weekly newspapers.

The pursuers won to the extent of returning after two hours with one *dhow*, one catamaran, and some personal effects belonging to German military officers. A force was then landed to capture the latter as well as to destroy signal masts, and at 2 p.m. came back with a man who was dressed in khaki uniform and was found armed with a revolver. Two tents on the island were destroyed, and at 3 p.m. *Chatham* resumed her cruise, calling next day at Zanzibar.

CHAPTER 4

Secret Intelligence

This little incursion, so invigorating for a ship's company that had been sorely tried with the monotony of the Mediterranean and the slow convoying through the Red Sea heat, had illuminative consequences.

Contained in a couple of tin cases were discovered private possessions which included a diary, and clearly indicated that the owner had been well chosen for this coastal job, as he was a reservist of the German Navy. The entries also proved that at the outbreak of hostilities the enemy had expected a British Expeditionary Force to land at Dar-es-Salaam, to which place therefore the writer was first appointed. Thus:

1 August. News of war. All naval reserves called up, which meant my going to D.E.S. (Dar-es-Salaam). I arrived D.E.S. 7 Aug. 14. At first, I was treated as an ordinary reserve (in spite of my being a naval reservist)....

8th August. English man-of-war bombarded town of D.E.S. with sharp shell. I went as ordered to the station. From there it was arranged we should go to Pugu (a station in the hills about 23 kilometres from D.E.S.) as arrangements were made to resist the enemy here. Eventually we proceeded to Pugu and encamped. We remained there two days but, as no Englishmen appeared, we returned to D.E.S.

Apparently, this colonial German had rather bad luck, since he had barely begun new duties on Komo than the *Chatham* came along and took him away. For the diary ends with:

26 Sep. Island Komo. Have been called in for service on the Island Komo with two other Europeans.

A very interesting clue was available under the date of September 25, though perhaps its full import at the time was not fully appreciated during this period of wild rumours; though, with all the information now before one's eyes and every card face upwards, it is possible to discern something of great worth. For the *Königsberg* is here mentioned as being definitely at a certain place. What was the name of that place?

Well, on the day of the Komo incident the metaphorical fog which hung over the East African naval war was still very dense; and the *Chatham* having only just arrived on the scene was groping about among reefs, rumours, flares and facts single-handed; with a vast responsibility, a long coast line, and everyone doing the work of two men. It was the same strenuous existence for the shipless people of the *Pegasus* at Zanzibar. The *Königsberg* was "at. . ."—somewhere that was spelled with six letters. For an Englishman translating the German diary, and not yet so deeply acquainted with jungle geography as to know the name of a certain remote African village (someday to become historic), it was naturally impossible to say quite surely whether the word was Falalo, Galalo, or Salalo: the foreign handwriting might mean any one of these three. Actually, it was the latter: otherwise known as Salale. It was, we can now clearly perceive, another of those hidden clues, one of those slender threads, only waiting to be woven into the complete garment.

But apart from the diary were some documents as valuable as if one of the German code-books had been obtained, and as incriminating as the instructions of one wrong-doer to another; for here was positive proof of abuse by the white flag, and here was the whole secret signalling system of the coast divulged, with the post at Komo specifically cited. That which the *Chatham* had seen was now confirmed and expanded.

The first document was merely a telegram of September 18 calling up military reservists and inviting volunteers to form a third battalion for coast defence at Kissiyu. Nine days afterwards comes from the latter a message to Komo Island from First Lieutenant von Geldein reporting on the practice test which had been made of signalling from Komo:

> From Kissiyu 27th Sep. 1914 to Post Komo. Lieut. v. Neuenstein.
>
> Your note reached here yesterday afternoon. The signals in Komo are now clearly seen here. It seems as if your signals were recognised on your side. This *dhow* shall, as the *nahoza* (captain)

says, proceed to Kilwa by order of a European. In Kivale there are a large number of *dhows* who came here today. Can I release the men? I am sending to you during the day by another *dhow*, which is being used by our station. The arranged signs will be tried again; please do not send any new ones. The arranged signals are:

Signal No. 1 ——	Look out.
" No. 2 ——	From the North.
" No. 3 —— .	From the South.
" No. 4 —— ——	Seen. Believed to be the enemy.
" No. 5 +	Landing on Komo.

Fire signals at night. `Last trial 9 p.m.

sd. Von Geldein
1st Lieutenant.

The signals between watch station and signal station were:

Signal for 'Look Out'	Wave white flag backwards and forwards 3 times.
" 'Mistaken'	Wave white flag backwards and forwards many times.
" 1 Steamer from North	One white flag.
" 1 Steamer from North, enemy	One white and one red flag.
" 1 Steamer from South	2 white flags.
" 1 Steamer from South, enemy	2 white flags and one red flag.
" 2 Steamers from the North, enemy	2 white flags and between them one red flag.
Signal for 2 Steamers from the South, enemy	3 white flags and one red flag.

Further Signals:

Enemy from North	1 white flag, and waving one red flag.
Enemy from South	2 white flags and waving one red flag.
Enemy attempting to land	1 red flag.

Komo, 28 Sep. 14.

Such, then, was the method by which the enemy hoped to keep the signal stations along the hills of the mainland informed concerning the comings and goings of British vessels: of its ingenuity and practical simplicity there could be no doubt, and it was likely for a long time to assist the *Königsberg* during her efforts to keep out of our cruisers' tracks. But it was a corrupt practice, and by the standards of civilised warfare quite unjustified so far as the white flags were employed. Captain Drury-Lowe therefore caused a communication to reach the Governor of German East Africa to the effect that white flags seeming to be employed on signal stations would in future be fired on at once without further warning.

'The gentleman captured first of all stated he was a planter proceeding on his own business to Kilwa Kivinje, but the following morning owned to being an ex-army officer enrolled in the Coast Defence force for the war. This was no doubt because he was liable to be shot as a civilian in arms. A week later I received a letter from the governor confirming his position and hoping that he had not been shot as a civilian.

Thus, a beginning had been made in the hunt for *Königsberg*: it was the first effort to sever her line of communications, and the search had to proceed on logical rather than casual principles. The weighty problem could be solved not by guesswork but by collecting evidence over a wide area, deducing a conclusion from gathered facts. And in most detective stories it is just the clever, clear, analytical deduction from miscellaneous clues which gives the investigator the right to success. Poe, Gaboriau, Conan Doyle, and their literary followers of today, provide their readers with certain details—some invaluable, some valueless, the essence of the detective art being the ability to recognise what is important under the external disguise of the trivial. And the great danger of failure occurs when the inquiring pursuer bumps up against some fact which seems to have no relation to motive.

Whether by reasoning deductively; or inductively, that is to say from the particular to the general; or using both alternatively; there must gradually be built up in the imagination a definite theory of what is happening to the pursued, and why. It was Poe who insisted that the analytical reasoning is oftenest the identification of the reasoner's intellect with that of his opponent. And, indeed, for the captain of the British cruiser the most obvious and natural attitude of mind was to place himself imaginatively in the position of the German cruiser's captain.

What followed?

Three considerations: (1) The *Königsberg* would require to be supplied with information, and to give news of herself. (2) She was dependent on coal, engine oils and other ship's stores. (3) She must have for her people large stocks of food coming in with certainty and moderate regularity.

Captain Looff's policy could be only one of two alternatives: sea-raiding along the trade routes, or concealment in some lonely locality. But the former—however much the truth were delayed in release—would after a few weeks become known. Moreover, the more miles the *Königsberg* cruised, the more colliers she would need to capture; and the list of missing ships would give some hint of the raider's operational area. On the other hand, if she hid herself and remained inactive so as to preserve her engine-room efficiency and take care of limited fuel supplies against the great day, she must still be thoroughly dependent on others. She must arrange for a number of supply ships to reach her; she must tell them where, when and how to come; and she must take meticulous precautions for covering both herself and this supply traffic with a cloak of secrecy. Thus, she could listen-in on her wireless, but it would be safer to keep as silent as possible. By the employment of moderate-sized and small steamers, such as tugs and dhows, both intelligence and stores could be obtained from friendly parts of the African coast.

In the days of the Anglo-French wars secrecy and independence were far easier. The sail-driven frigate needed no fuel, there were no cables or wireless stations to give her away, she carried practically all the stores she required covering a period of some months; and when she needed new masts or yards, she sent ashore to cut them from the trees. Salt beef and biscuits sufficed to feed the crew, and the ship could be watered by the boats bringing their barrels to a convenient stream. In calm weather it was even frequently possible to careen and scrub the ship at sea.

But, nowadays, the cruiser is not self-reliant, and in the absence of docks or bases she can under favourable circumstances create havoc for even a long time: yet it is to a definite period such activities certainly are restricted. It was now the beginning of October and two whole months had passed since first she had been sighted in the moonlight, yet she had not sunk any more merchant ships than the *City of Winchester*. Therefore, it seemed daily most reasonable to suppose that her policy of raiding the routes must be dismissed, and that she was in hiding. But where? From the knowledge that she had been off Zanzibar on September 20, and the persistent though contradictory rumours of her being to the southward of Zanzibar, it appeared quite probable that she had taken shelter in some portion of the African waters which even before the war were so well known to her. The deciphering of her wireless—sent to her supply ships, strengthened this theory.

So, then, if the waters off the mainland, as well as among the outlying islands could be kept persistently patrolled, and surprise visits maintained, would it not become utterly unsafe for colliers, store ships, tugs and dhows to venture forth? Surely that would be a tedious and expensive way of still further cutting off the *Königsberg's* means of communication, but in the end, it was likely to succeed in the same manner that a blockade eventually brings starvation to the beleaguered country. There was, however, a weakness to be weighed: all this fast steaming over such immense sea areas could not be carried on by one cruiser alone. She must occasionally be permitted to lay off, replenish her bunkers, remedy her engine defects and clean her boilers, even if there was no chance of resting her crew. In a sentence, the situation demanded at least two more cruisers, together with an elastic and abundant coal supply.

All this the British Admiralty now provided. The "Town"-class cruisers *Dartmouth* and *Weymouth* were assigned to help their sister, and arrangements were made for an adequate number of colliers to arrive. In the meanwhile, *Chatham* was just ending her preliminary investigation and, after touching at Zanzibar (following the Komo incident), proceeded up the coast with a view to meeting the *Dartmouth* at Mombasa. It was not improbable that the enemy or some of her ancillary craft might be active by night, so the *Chatham* was making a search between the west coast of Pemba Island and the continent. The weakness of Mombasa, and the possibility that the *Königsberg* might make a spectacular visit to sink our colliers, had also to be borne in mind: another catastrophe of the *Pegasus* type would have an unhappy effect on the public.

Soon after 11 p.m. on October 1 the *Chatham* observed lights inshore, and also a strange sail, apparently a dhow, so altered course to investigate, but at 11.58 p. m, the cruiser grounded on a reef off Mombasa where she remained hard and fast. It necessitated taking 662 tons of weight out of the ship, but everything went well, and at 11.55 p.m. of the following night—exactly twenty-four hours after the accident—she floated off. It was just a piece of bad luck that she happened to have got ashore at high water, but this was one of the conditions which had to be accepted in wartime off an inadequately surveyed coast. In the early hours of October 3 she steamed into Mombasa, re-embarked her stores and cables, and sent down divers to make an examination of her bottom. Happily, there was not too much serious damage.

By October 6 the British naval strength in these waters had become transformed by the arrival of three light cruisers: H.M.S. *Dartmouth*, *Weymouth* and *Fox*. The first-mentioned at the beginning of hostilities happened to be in dockyard hands at Bombay, but after a few days was ready for sea. She found herself employed in convoy duties and during the last week of September, in conjunction with the *Fox*, escorted from India some transports destined for Mombasa. *Weymouth* at the beginning of war had been serving in the Mediterranean, left Port Said on September 25, Aden on October 2, and four days later was at Mombasa.

Captain F. W. Caulfield, R.N., in command of the *Fox*, now took over the duties of Senior Naval Officer at Mombasa and vicinity, so at last this port with its colliers was well protected; marine defence patrols and lookouts were arranged, and everything got ready for the Expeditionary Force that was shortly to arrive from India escorted by H.M.S. *Goliath*. The three "Town" class cruisers, under the command of Captain Drury-Lowe, thus formed a force devoted solely and entirely to rounding up the *Königsberg*, and from now we enter upon a most interesting phase.

CHAPTER 5

Clearing the Clues

With three such able modern units, each individually about two knots faster and, at least nominally, of greater gunnery strength than the German cruiser, it remained now only to employ this squadron in the best manner.

For the purpose of conducting the search on systematic lines, the ocean was divided into four areas, W, X, Y, Z. The first extended from Zanzibar south to Cape Delgado (at the frontier between German and Portuguese East Africa); the second from Cape Delgado to Mozambique; the third from Mozambique to Kilman Bay; and the fourth from Kilman Bay to Delagoa Bay. The magnitude of the task may well be appreciated. It consisted of some 1,700 miles of coast taken in a straight line, but of course it meant far more than that: for there were the Comoro Islands and Madagascar to the eastward, there was the Mozambique Channel with its 500-miles width, whilst to the north there was that difficult and ill-surveyed area between Mafia Island and the continent. The Mafia section measured about 30 miles by 40 miles, but it was so full of islands and uncharted coral reefs as to make its good anchorage quite a possible locality for *Königsberg* to play some tricks.

Captain Drury-Lowe's orders to his squadron may be summarised as follows:

> The Admiralty have ordered *Chatham*, *Dartmouth* and *Weymouth* to act as a detached and separate squadron under orders of captain of *Chatham*, to be exclusively employed hunting *Königsberg*, and direct that on no account are ships to be diverted from their sole object, namely, capture of *Königsberg*, by any pretence like capture of tugs or enemy's merchant ships.
>
> We know that *Königsberg* has been and is being helped in her movements by an extremely well-organised intelligence sys-

tem, including look-out stations along the coast, and that the information so obtained is sent to her by the German Wireless Stations inland. Included in this intelligence system is the use of certain tugs and steamers, which have been reported and named from time to time as operating with *Königsberg*....

The capture of any of the above, if met with, should be effected as a means of helping to corner *Königsberg*, but on no account is time to be wasted by taking or sending any captured ship into port, unless special circumstances necessitate so doing. Captains will exercise their own discretion in this, keeping in mind the spirit of the Admiralty instructions quoted above. ...

It is important that we should all present an appearance similar as possible. Ships are therefore to cover their names on stern with wood, and all funnel bands are to be painted out.

Should the *Emden* come to East Coast of Africa, she may possibly make Madagascar first or Comoro Islands. Ships proceeding to Mayotta to coal should bear this in mind.

The *Königsberg's* assistant ships mentioned above were: the two sea-going tugs *Adjutant* and *Leutnant*; the two steamers *Somali* (2,550 tons) and the *Präsident* (3,335 tons). But the Admiralty collier *Burbridge* was destined to sight at Mozambique two other German ships. It was decided that until the *Königsberg* was definitely located the *Dartmouth* and *Weymouth* were to be based on the French-owned Comoro Islands at Mayotta, where there was a convenient wireless station, whither also the first available collier was to be sent from Mombasa. Whilst these two cruisers were to search the areas X, Y and Z, the *Chatham* was looking after the area north of Cape Delgado.

The distances being so considerable, and the importance of one ship being able to pass on news from as far north as Mombasa to another abreast of Delagoa Bay, or off the coast of Madagascar, demanded some careful staff work. The cruisers could communicate with the wireless stations at Durban, Diego Suarez (northern end of Madagascar), Majunga (western side of Madagascar), in addition to Mayotta Island. When the *Chatham* was no longer in wireless touch with the other two ships, she could call up Zanzibar, who in turn would send messages by cable to Mozambique, thence by another cable to Diego Suarez, thence by wireless to the nearest cruiser. Whilst the *Chatham* was away at sea, the *Fox* was always at Zanzibar or at Mombasa so as to pass on telegrams by wireless. But there was the difficulty that wireless in those latitudes was frequently subjected to considerable hindrance by very strong atmospherics, and in any case the Mayotta station was of a weak character.

At this date all merchant shipping off the east coast was running as usual, though along special routes. Little or no intelligence could be obtained therefrom, for in those days only a few liners were fitted with wireless. True the French *Messageries* steamers running *via* Aden, Mombasa, Zanzibar and Madagascar were so fitted, and did their best to co-operate: doubtless, too, they might have been able to flash a valuable warning had they sighted a German cruiser. It was quite within probability that one of these liners might also notice one of the *Königsberg's* supply ships. It is, however, to be noted that undisciplined enthusiasm on the part of one's best and well-meaning friends can become a dangerous embarrassment: Consider the following instance, which occurred to the *Chatham* early in the search.

Captain Drury-Lowe explained:

> About a fortnight after our arrival, whilst coaling at Mombasa and previous to finding the *Königsberg*, I received a polite wireless message from a *Messageries* Maritimes steamer *en clair* presenting the captain's compliments and begging to state that off Socotra he had passed 40 British transports; escorted by H.M.S. *Swiftsure, Duke of Edinburgh*, and others. He was then told to shut up, but next morning, when apparently only about three miles off the entrance, he commenced again with his compliments and quite unnecessarily informed me that he noticed the leading marks into the harbour had all been altered. These messages were of course most interesting news for the German wireless stations. After that the French were requested to shut down their wireless entirely.

Unfortunately, the *Chatham* was not able to resume her searching immediately: in consequence of having grounded on the reef already mentioned, it was not until October 14 that she had completed repairs to her oil fuel tanks, stopped the leaks in the damaged frames and bottom plating by putting on cement over the outer plating. (In addition to their coal, these light cruisers carried a certain amount of oil fuel.) But on the afternoon of October 15 she left Mombasa, called at Zanzibar, searched to the southward off Mafia Island thence to the German port of Kilwa Kivinje, where a good deal of trade used to be carried on in peace time. *Chatham* now observed several large dhows on the beach immediately under a large white house flying a Red Cross flag.

A little to the southward of Kilwa Kivinje lies Kilwa Kisiwani, this German harbour being entirely landlocked and extending many miles into the land, carrying as much as 3 to 12 fathoms for a distance of 17 miles. The *Chatham* made an examination but there was no sign of the missing *Königsberg*. Further south still came Lindi, another landlocked German port much used by traders. Here, too, the river extended for several miles up country and then branched off into several arms. But it was already nearly half-past nine in the evening of October 17 when the British cruiser entered the anchorage outside, and she had to be content with an investigation by searchlights. Nothing transpired, and she went on that night to Tunghi Bay which is in Portuguese territory. Here for a moment, we will leave her at the end of her southernmost limit, having obtained nothing but disappointment. The only choice accordingly was to go north again and examine the coast in greater detail.

In the meanwhile, the *Dartmouth* and *Weymouth* had begun their tasks of combing out the areas assigned to them off Portuguese East Africa and Madagascar. Two important items of news on October 8 became available, and led to increased vigilance down here. One was that the 250-tons seagoing German tug *Adjutant* had left the port of Beira the previous night ostensibly bound for Mozambique, each of these harbours being in neutral territory of Portuguese Africa. A few hours later came the statement that *Adjutant* was most likely bound beyond Mozambique for Lindi, where (it was suggested) the previously mentioned *Präsident* was lying at anchor. It was reported that both *Adjutant* and *Präsident* were in communication with *Königsberg*.

These two announcements contained the germs of a most exciting development—if they were not based on mere rumour. There was reason to suppose that the tidings this time was unquestionable: and so, it was soon proved, for on October 10 the *Dartmouth* sighted the *Adjutant* near to Mozambique and promptly captured her. In the accompanying illustration from a German photograph which fell into our hands and shows her flying the German ensign, it will be recognised that whilst her high fo'c'sle with lofty bridge made her quite suitable for working along the coast even during heavy weather, she was of just that moderate draught which would make her very handy for crossing bars, navigating tricky channels, and entering shallow African rivers. She was not destroyed, but was destined to fly the British naval ensign during the next few months and perform most useful service as we shall presently observe.

Another bit of news came through on October 12, this time to the *Weymouth*, which stirred every officer and man to great hopes. It was reported that the *Königsberg* was at Hurd Island, a small spot about 150 miles south of Mozambique. Full of enthusiasm, end of a fast passage came steaming up to Hurd Island at dawn of the 14th, only to realise that she had been led away on a false trail. It was no small disappointment to her people, but such are the misguiding scents which must form part of any great mystery hunt. So, this cruiser had to content herself with an examination of every river and inlet throughout her sphere, during most of the time being compelled to trust the eye rather than her inaccurate charts.

The capture of *Adjutant* was of an importance far greater. than could immediately be appreciated. Here, indeed, was the first of the essential clues: and if we may regard the three cruisers as analogous to the "Big Three" sent forth from Scotland Yard after a much-wanted man, they had made a decided advance by arresting one of the culprit's accomplices. From one fact is deducible a second item. If the tug had been bound for Lindi, then there must have been some important motive: and if the *Präsident* should really be found up that winding harbour, it would be an additional reason for presuming that the *Königsberg* was not very far away.

Lindi was clearly the next locality to demand attention. On October 17, owing to the bend of the river to the west and the obstructing trees on the mainland, the *Chatham* from her outside situation had been unable to look up the inner harbour and river; so, at 6.45 a.m. on the 19th, picture this cruiser once more arriving and halting off the entrance. No little excitement buzzed about on land, binoculars were focussed on to the British man-of-war, about fifty German troops were hurriedly collected at the small fort by the town, and the colonials waited in suspense.

The *Chatham* lowered one of her steamboats into the water, and in charge of her went Commander Fitzmaurice, who carried with him a letter which was to be delivered to the local German governor, provided a certain fact were established. The little steamboat with her khaki-clad sailors sped over the intervening sea past the fort, rounded the corner, churned the calm waters of the river, and not a shot was fired by either side. At the end of about 3½ miles the boat came alongside a German steamer that was moored alongside the northern shore.

She was of 3,335 tons but was so high out of the water as to indicate the emptiness of her bunkers.

On her side was painted a white cross, and from her masthead she was flying the Geneva Cross: but the hull was red and not painted in accordance with the international regulations proper for hospital ships. The name of the ship was *Präsident*. At 9.45 a.m. Commander Fitzmaurice shoved off down the river: that which he had just seen justified delivering Captain Drury-Lowe's letter. Having on his way back again arrived near the fort, he stopped engines and was met by a boat flying a white flag. In this boat was the German Governor's Secretary, and to him Commander Fitzmaurice handed the following:

H.M.S. *Chatham*,
19th October, 1914.

The Governor,
Lindi,
German East Africa.

Any steamers now in harbour are to be sent out at once.

Commander R. Fitzmaurice, Royal Navy, who bears this letter has my full authority to act for me.

Should the above demand not be complied with within half an hour, I shall take such steps as I consider necessary to enforce them.

(Sd.) S. R. Drury-Lowe,
Captain, Royal Navy.

The steamboat carried on back to her ship, and it was noticed that a white flag was hoisted at the fort: whereupon the *Chatham* likewise hoisted one at the masthead. Little time was expended, Commander Fitzmaurice made his report to the captain, who now furnished him with a second letter, and at 10.45 a.m. the steamboat was once more sent off. On this trip she carried a number of engine-room artificers who were to disable the *Präsident's* machinery. The short passage was accomplished as before, but the governor's secretary came out bearing his chief's answer to the first letter. Written in German, it read thus:

Lindi,
19th Oct., 1914.

Imperial District Officer.
No. 9388.
To The Commander of H.M.S. *Chatham*.

In answer to the letter, you sent today in relation to the steamer lying in Lukuledicreek, I beg to inform you that the S.S. *Präsident* (of the G.E.A. *i.e.*, German East Africa, Line) has since the outbreak of war been converted into a Hospital Ship (by order of the district officer). Since war has broken out, we have considered it necessary to remove our sick and women to a place of safety in Lindi. This is only possible on board the ship *Präsident*. The ship is not capable of putting to sea as the machinery is not entire. Therefore, I am not in the position to bring the ship out, and therefore must leave the matter to you.

District Officer,
(Sd.) Wends.

The secretary was given Captain Drury-Lowe's second letter, but informed Commander Fitzmaurice that he as secretary had no authority to decide the question involved. Thereupon the Commander replied that he would have to take the necessary action forthwith, so promptly hauled down the white flag which was flying in the steamboat, and proceeded up the river. Captain Drury-Lowe's second letter is appended:

From the captain of His Britannic Majesty's Ship *Chatham*.
To the District Commissioner, Lindi.
Date... 19th October, 1914.
I am informed by Commander Fitzmaurice that the steamer *Präsident* is flying a Geneva Hospital Flag and has a white cross painted on a red side. If this is intended to indicate that she is a Hospital Ship I cannot recognise it, as her name has not been communicated to His Britannic Majesty's Government or to me, and neither is the hull of the ship painted white with red or green band in accordance with the articles of the Hague Convention, (1907), (Copy attached).
I am therefore sending an armed party on board to have the ship brought out if possible, and if this is not feasible, to take the necessary steps to disable her.
I must request you to give an immediate reply to Commander Fitzmaurice, and, if satisfactory, I shall keep the white flag flying, and request that you will do the same. If it is not satisfactory, I shall haul down the white flag and take whatever steps I consider necessary.

(Sd.) S. R. Drury-Lowe,
Captain.

S.M.S. *KÖNIGSBERG*
This photograph was taken at Dar-es-Salaam before war broke out.

THE S.S. *PRÄSIDENT*
Lying up the Lukuledicreek, Lindi. It was this German liner which pretended to be a hospital ship. Documents found aboard her proved she had aided the *Königsberg*.

There can be no question about the duplicity which was being employed to deceive us, and that the *Präsident* was not a genuine hospital ship. It was laid down by the Hague Convention of October 18, 1907, that: "Hospital ships shall be distinguished by being painted white outside, with a horizontal band of green about a metre and a half in breadth"; and that the names of such ships were to "have been communicated to the belligerent powers at the commencement or during hostilities, and in any case before they are employed."

Now, firstly, not one of these conditions had been fulfilled. But note, secondly, that when the demolition party from *Chatham*'s steamboat went on board, they found there was nothing which in any way suggested a hospital ship: no sick, no doctors, no medical stores, no special fittings. There were not even women or children. Contrariwise, some highly instructive documents were revealed, from which there was conclusive evidence that on September 15—that is to say, five days before the *Pegasus*' sinking—coal had been supplied in lighters from the *Präsident* at Lindi to the *Königsberg* at Salale. So here was still another clue that the missing cruiser was on the coast, and the vague village somewhere up the scarcely known Rufiji River yet again received mention. Nor did matters end with that.

After the party had done their job of disabling the *Präsident's* engines, ensuring that she should not render further aid, there were also removed five compasses, one chronometer, and a set of charts. Amongst the latter was one of the Rufiji, and this was a glorious find; for it afforded that hydrographical information which the British Admiralty charts did not possess. The discovery was akin to finding the key of a secret room, and (in a minor degree) is comparable to that incident of the year 1592 when the Elizabethan sailors after capturing the carrack *Madre de Dios* unearthed among the captain's personal treasures his "Compass, map and astrolaby," together with his secret documents ("enclosed in a case of sweete cedar wood, and lapped up almost an hundred fold in fine calicut cloth, as though it had been some incomprehensible jewel").

In the midst of such heavy business as the directing of three cruisers, together with the necessity of always being at hand to calm the British colonials when alarms demanded that the *Chatham* should reappear off British East Africa; amid all this constant steaming through regions that bristled with reefs; perhaps the deductive faculties have not the opportunity of obtaining their requisite quietude. This visit up the Lindi River had emphasised the probability—almost the cer-

H.M.S. *CHATHAM* IN ACTION
The British cruiser is seen bombarding the enemy's positions at the Rufiji delta.

THE GERMAN COLLIER *SOMALI*
shows her minus foremast, and her hull burnt out, after being shelled by H.M.S. *Chatham*. The *Königsberg*'s supply ship is seen lying on the Rufiji mud, a hopeless wreck.

tainty—that if a similar trip were made up the Rufiji it would disclose the *Königsberg* at Salale; the German chart would show the way in.

But there was no possibility of making immediate use of the invaluable data which the *Präsident's* papers had yielded: for no vessel of the *Chatham's* draught could casually attempt entrance of such a difficult river. Except at top of high-water springs (that is to say for about two days a fortnight) the *Chatham* would not be able to approach the Rufiji nearer than six miles. That is a longish distance for even naval steam-cutters, let alone open rowing boats, and who knew whether the mouth would not be lined with guns and troops? It was always an anxiety for the cruiser's commanding officer when his boats had disappeared out of sight round the corner into one of these African rivers, so that not even from the ship's masthead could the boats' fate be known till at last they were on the way back. It was a risk, indeed, at Lindi, and the enemy might well have shelled the steamboat to destruction.

After departing from Lindi, the *Chatham*, in her northward cruise of re-investigation, anchored off Kilwa Kisiwani, sending in her armed steamboat and cutter, but the cruiser's guns could afford cover only till the moment when the land intervened. Nothing was discovered, and a few hours' steaming would have brought the cruiser to the Rufiji Delta, the principal branch of which was (according to our Admiralty charts) unnavigable except for small coasting steamers; and no Englishman or English ship had visited this German delta for about ten years.

But, even had it been deemed prudent then and there to have risked steam-cutters and men's lives without reconnaissance or special preparations, such a possibility was instantly ruled out by an urgent communication from the Resident, Zanzibar.

CHAPTER 6

The Dar-Es-Salaam Incident

It was October 20, and news came that there was increased activity at Dar-es-Salaam: native reports had just reached Zanzibar that the *Königsberg* was already inside Dar-es-Salaam landing guns.

Obviously, the German cruiser could not be in two places simultaneously, and all the evidence derived from the *Präsident* seemed suddenly to slump. Now Dar-es-Salaam was from the beginning of hostilities always a thorn in the side of Zanzibar's Resident: the two places were so adjacent that at any time a German force might attempt a landing on the island—notwithstanding a truce which H.M.S. *Astraea* had made, and the enemy still professed to respect. Captain Drury-Lowe wrote:

> I found the latter were in the habit of sending a German doctor in a *dhow* to Zanzibar about once a week to enquire *re* the health of the few prisoners there. Of course, this charitable habit was stopped at once!
>
> To settle the matter definitely as to *Königsberg* we arrived off Dar-es-Salaam on October 21, after calling at Zanzibar, and from our masthead it was just possible to make out the mastheads of two ships close together to the left of the town, and another one close to the town flying the Hospital flag. All three had wireless aerials up, and the mastheads of one certainly appeared very like the *Königsberg's*. No white flag was flying on the lighthouse or elsewhere. We fired a gun and hoisted signal for them to send a boat and, as no notice was taken after twenty minutes, opened fire with the 6-inch at the supposed *Königsberg* the range being 13,000 yards.
>
> Ten minutes of this produced several white flags and the governor's motor-boat, with governor, secretary and harbour master.

Great show of indignation on the part of the Germans, with the exception of the harbour master, who was an old seaman and kept his eye on some bottles of beer I had on a table on the quarter-deck.

In order thoroughly to appreciate the local British nervousness, it must be stressed that the prevailing belief in Zanzibar still existed that on the morning when *Königsberg* had arrived to sink *Pegasus* the German cruiser came direct from Dar-es-Salaam. But why had *Chatham* been several weeks on the coast and waited till now before making her first visit to this enemy centre? The answer is that hardly anything (so Captain Drury-Lowe had been told) could be seen from outside the bay of the harbour, or of the three steamers *König, Feldmarschall* and *Tabora* which were inside.

I had, also, no intention of risking my ship by taking her inside the bay, owing to the reported mining of the entrance.

When this afternoon the *Chatham* let go anchor in 20 fathoms, 14 miles to the north-east of Makatumbe lighthouse, it was very difficult to see anything above the tree-tops which so effectually hid the harbour. Only after a while were the masts of the two steamers made out, the one bearing S. 54° W., and the other S. 36° W.: the former distant 4½ miles, and the latter 6 miles. From this second ship's position she seemed to have been specifically placed so as to command the whole stretch of the harbour. Surely this must be a man-of-war?

On board the *Chatham* was a photograph of *Königsberg* taken quite recently at Zanzibar, and on referring to it there seemed good reason for believing that the second ship's masts were those of the German cruiser. Two features now visible seemed especially to tally with those of the photograph. Firstly, the wireless aerial had apparently been brought direct to a yard on the mainmast head, instead of using the span-and-spreader arrangement customary in merchant vessels; but secondly, there seemed to be on the foremast head a crow's nest similar to that carried by the *Königsberg*, and most clearly indicated in the illustration.

The *Chatham*, after the interval mentioned, opened fire very deliberately, one gun at a time, at the second ship's masts. No hull being visible, it was necessary for the fire to be directed from aloft over the trees. It was when the first ship (4½ miles off) hoisted the Geneva cross at both mastheads, and the local signal station hoisted a white flag, that the British warship ceased fire. The German officials who came out in the motor boat under a white flag were informed that the shelling had been aimed at what was thought to be a man-of-war. They were further told that all wireless aerials must be at once lowered, and if that were not accomplished by the return of *Chatham*, fire would be resumed.

It was awkward that the German officials spoke and understood very little English, so that evening the *Chatham* weighed anchor and returned to Zanzibar for the purpose of obtaining an interpreter. Owing to the position where the supposed *Königsberg* lay, no damage had been done to Dar-es-Salaam, though the Germans would have had only themselves to blame if the consequence had been otherwise. For when on August 8 the *Astraea* had bombarded Dar-es-Salaam and temporarily disabled the three steamers, a truce was concluded with the German Governor by which the enemy were not to repair steamers, or wireless station, or use the place for any military purpose, or undertake any sort of hostile act in the port. Further, a white flag was to be kept flying from lighthouse and signal station at the approach of a British man-of-war. In return for this the Germans would not be attacked or interfered with.

But this truce, after having been referred to the British Admiralty by *Astraea*, had not been confirmed by the authorities in Whitehall—except that the Germans were to be given due notice before hostile action should recur. Captain Drury-Lowe therefore did not feel in any way called upon to recognise *Astraea*'s truce; and in any case, though *Chatham* had arrived off the port in broad daylight no white flag was flying anywhere. Having regard to the tricks already discovered at Komo Island and in respect of the *Präsident*, it was hardly surprising that suspicion of the enemy's words and deeds remained deeply rooted.

By six o'clock on the morning of October 22 the *Chatham* arrived back and anchored off Dar-es-Salaam in the same spot as yesterday. She had fetched from Zanzibar a Mr. King as interpreter, who was the former British Consul of Dar-es-Salaam; also, Lieut.-Colonel McKye, who had just arrived from India as Military Intelligence Officer ahead of the Expeditionary Force, which it was intended later to land at Tanga as well as Dar-es-Salaam. A preliminary examination of the latter would accordingly be useful for the future.

The British cruiser now fired a blank and hoisted a signal for a German boat to come off. "The same motor-launch came out with the captain of the port, who was informed," by Captain Drury-Lowe:

I required him to take two of my officers and Mr. King into the harbour to search it and the ships. The officers selected were Commander Raymond Fitzmaurice and Lieut.-Colonel Mc-Kye. This was agreed to and carried out under the white flag, which was also hoisted on board H.M.S. *Chatham*. About noon the boat returned and I allowed the two German officials—captain of the port and secretary to the acting governor—to come on board. A conversation was held through Mr. King as interpreter.... I tried to explain to them my opinion that any consideration which attended the truce drawn up between them and the *Astraea* previous to the sinking of the *Pegasus* by the *Königsberg* was entirely out of the question after that event, and that if they wished to avoid bombardment, the white flag should have been shown. Their reply, that a white flag was flying from the flagstaff at the signal station all the time, I simply do not believe. We had it in full view with strong glasses, and there was no appearance of a white flag until about 3.40 p.m.

During this second visit it was noticed that the aerials of the steamers had been now taken down as ordered. The *Feldmarschall* was found to have been hit once by a shell which penetrated two decks amidships, slightly wounding two Indians of her crew. The smaller vessel close to her was the *König*, and the third was the *Tabora*, an ex-liner but at that time alleged to be a hospital ship.

The report of *Königsberg* being in Dar-es-Salaam had now wasted two days, and it would be unavailing if the *Chatham* remained longer. At 1 p.m. she got under way, called at Zanzibar, and thence went on to Mombasa, where she remained from October 23 to 28, coaling and effecting repairs to her condensers. Another false clue had been disposed of, and by the method of exhaustion the inference was that, assuming the *Königsberg* were still afloat, she must be somewhere up the Rufiji.

But, if the *Chatham* by her shelling had created the most angry indignation among the local officials, the master mariners, and the townspeople, she had made it impossible for the imprisoned steamers to transmit any further intelligence across to *Königsberg*: at any rate, it would hardly be worthwhile hoisting up those aerials again. The Dar-es-Salaam visit, however, did cause such a controversy and emphasise such a notable occurrence that I have thought it well to present the arguments of both sides. Below will be found the conversations on board *Chatham*, between Captain Drury-Lowe and the representative of Dares-Salaam's acting-governor, on October 22. It may be added that the officer, who notified on August 8 in writing to the acting-governor the terms of truce, was Lieut.-Commander R. C. Turner, and he had made it plain that this declaration was given only in the name of his superior officer—not in the name of the British Government. Unfortunately, Commander Turner did not survive many weeks, for he was among those afterwards killed in the *Pegasus*.

German Representative. The white flag was hoisted yesterday and though the boat was sent at once, the guns were fired.

Captain of "Chatham." First of all, no white flag was seen until after I had opened fire. Before firing I waited half an hour from the time, I hoisted the signal to send a boat, but saw no answer.

R. That was unavoidable, because the distance was so great it was impossible to send a boat before. The signal could not be read for some time because the ship was so far out, the flags were flying end on.

C. In war, half an hour is the limit I can wait when I considered the ship, I actually fired at had the appearance of a man-of-war by her masts; and that, as regards the other ship with the wireless aerial (*Tabora*), the only reason I did not fire at her was that I might have hit the town.

R. The other two ships were also inside the harbour.

C. They were not in line with the town.

R. I wish to ask whether it is true that as Lieutenant-Commander Turner promised, the arrangement between Dar-es-Salaam and H.M. Ships, to the effect that these ships were prizes and were not to communicate with the shore, was not communicated to the Admiralty. It was promised that this would be done.

C. I cannot say whether the truce arranged with the captains of the *Astraea* and *Pegasus* was communicated to the Admiralty, but I know this: that in any case the Admiralty never recognises any terms of truce arranged by the captain of an individual ship and the local people. They do not bind themselves by any such terms until they have received their formal sanction.

R. Had not the arrangements with the captain of the ship been promised to be communicated to the Admiral Commanding on the East Coast of Africa?

C. I cannot inform you anything about terms of truce being communicated to the Commander-in-Chief or Admiralty, but supposing I now propose any terms of truce to you, although such terms might be binding between me and you, they would not be recognised by the Admiralty until it had received the formal sanction of His Majesty's Government.

R. I cannot accept that point of view. I consider the truce is valid.

C. I do not agree in any way that the truce can be regarded as valid. There has been and can be no possibility of our knowing whether the terms have been or are being kept by you. I had nothing to do with them, but I can express my opinion that it is absurd to consider that such terms of truce could be binding on any one but the parties immediately concerned. For instance, the *Pegasus* was sunk by the *Königsberg* subsequent to these terms of truce; and for all we know the *Königsberg* might have come from Dar-es-Salaam to sink the *Pegasus*.

R. You know the entrance to the harbour is blocked.

C. I do not know that the dock has not been raised.

R. It was communicated in writing to Lieutenant-Commander Turner that the dock has been sunk in such a manner that it was impossible to raise her except with appliances from Europe.

C. It is quite impossible in war to be satisfied with the assurances on such points. The terms of truce arranged with the *Astraea* have nothing to do with me and I do not hold myself bound by them.

R. I wish to know if you will announce to me if this is for your ship in particular, or should I regard it to be cancelled entirely?

C. As far as I am concerned, I do not recognise any terms of truce, and I also know for a certainty that any terms of truce that I make would not be recognised by the Admiralty unless and until I had received their formal sanction of such terms. No terms of truce by captains of individual ships would be recognised as binding by the Admiralty.

Such was the unusual occasion when under the White Ensign and the broiling African sun, loyal sons of two great rival nations contended by word and mind. The training of a naval officer from his earliest years is intended to fit him for something more than a mere fighting machine: he is the deputy entrusted with the welfare of his Sovereign and nation, and in this capacity may be called upon unexpectedly to perform the work pertaining to the diplomatist, the colonial ruler, or even an ocean detective. A young midshipman learns among his first lessons never to be nervous of heavy responsibility; always to be adaptable for any surprising job of work. So, too, the German Emperor could not have been more faithfully served by his representative labouring under the difficulties of a strange environment with a weak case to plead.

The interview ended, Captain Drury-Lowe promised to send the German governor a copy of the above conversations at the first opportunity, and it was eventually despatched in a dhow under a flag of truce. A few days later came the following letter from the governor addressed to the British Resident, Zanzibar:

Dar-es-Salaam,
20th October, 1914.

Lieutenant-Commander Turner, S.N.O., made the following agreement. That all ships of 'the D.O.A. (Deutsche Ost-Afrika) Line in Dar-es-Salaam were to remain untouched and that nothing was to be removed from them. It was further agreed that the crews on board should take no warlike action against England. Both these demands have been obeyed by the Civil Authorities and the crews on board. The carrying out of the first as promised to Lieutenant-Commander Turner, *i.e.* the non-removal of the wireless poles, etc., caused the Commander of an English cruiser to bombard the *Feldmarschall* and *König* whilst some of the crew were on board. Both ships are badly damaged, some of the crew slightly wounded.

This is contrary to the arrangement made between the town of Dar-es-Salaam, the crews of the *Feldmarschall* and *König*; the town of Dar-es-Salaam is unfortified. According to Article I of the Hague Conference, 18th October, 1907, it is forbidden to bombard an unfortified town.

Even if the commander of the English cruiser had suspected the presence of a German warship, according to Article 2 of the same Conference, he could only start bombarding after parley. I protest against the breaking of International Law.

The commander of the English cruiser declared that he did not feel himself bound in any way to respect arrangements made between Tanga, Dar-es-Salaam, and the *Astraea* and *Pegasus*, as since the sinking of the *Pegasus* the arrangement was void.

I have taken note of his views and informed the crews of the D.O.A. Line that they have no longer to keep their promise *re* fighting against England.

I again draw your attention to the fact that Dar-es-Salaam and Tanga are defenceless harbours, and that their inhabitants have undertaken no warlike act. I beg you to inform the Admiralty of the contents of this despatch.

Sd. Hermann.

To the British Resident,
Zanzibar.

At this stage of the world's history, it were useless to prolong the Dar-es-Salaam controversy, or to magnify a minor into a major incident. But before we pass on it may be remarked, in reply to the Governor's criticism, that in the terms of *Astraea's* truce (*a*) there was no mention that the wireless aerials might be allowed to remain up in place aboard the three steamers, but (*b*) on the contrary: "That I shall be allowed to remove and render ineffective the wireless installation of all ships lying in harbour." The question of bombarding an unfortified town was never alluded to by the German official at the time of the interview; and indeed, the *Chatham* had purposely refrained from such bombardment, the supposed *Königsberg* being several miles to the SSE. of the town. According to International Law a ship-of-war in an undefended harbour could be bombarded without notice if the exigencies of war demanded immediate action, provided the guns were not laid deliberately on certain buildings. (See *The Principles of International Law*, by Professor I. J. Lawrence, M.A., LL.D., 4th edition.)

After this diversion let us now come back to the still unsolved problem of the *Königsberg*. The unfounded rumour of her being concealed behind the trees of Dar-es-Salaam having been disposed of; and the African coast line having been so well searched; made it evident that she must either be hiding up the Rufiji, or she must be to the south of German territory beyond Cape Delgado among the islands—perhaps sheltering in the waters of Portuguese Africa. Who could tell?

But the *Dartmouth* and *Weymouth* were still down there "doing more full-speed steaming," considered Captain Drury-Lowe, "than was good for them, and nosing out trail after trail which led to nothing." They had searched as far south as Lat. 22°, obtained a very intimate knowledge of the Mozambique coast, together with the outlying reefs and islands. But the area was so vast, and the possibilities of evasion so many, that who could definitely affirm the enemy was not lurking hereabouts?

Chapter 7

The Rufiji Delta

The modern cruiser, with all her complicated and fast revolving machinery, is as delicate and temperamental a creation as the racehorse; and it was inevitable that days of fast patrolling, of sudden rushes in response to urgent signals, must be followed by occasional intervals at anchor to give the engineering staff opportunity for essential overhauls. By October 28 the *Chatham* in the northern area was again ready for sea, coaled, with defects remedied, and steaming away from Mombasa for the next phase.

The latter presented itself to Captain Drury-Lowe thus:

'Our next move in *Chatham* was now clear, *viz.* to find out if *Königsberg* was up the Rufiji and, failing success there, to join *Dartmouth* and *Weymouth* to the southward. But the Rufiji was a hard nut to crack, as it was impossible to go up the river and equally impossible to see anything from outside.

From the first it had been thought of very slight probability that the *Königsberg* could really be up the Rufiji, and every time the charts were examined the delta made it certain that it was practically unnavigable except possibly at spring tides. So why risk the loss of a valuable cruiser? It is true that vague native reports at Zanzibar had stated the enemy was up these inland waters, but with equal authenticity she was placed up the Rovuma River which is the boundary line between German and Portuguese Africa. On the face of it the latter seemed even more likely, and even as long ago as 1861 Livingstone had explored late in the season (when the water began to fall) as far as 25 miles with the little steamer *Pioneer*. That was in the month of March, but here was October; and in spite of the shoals the *Königsberg* might more credibly be supposed to have entered a short distance up this frontier river than the Rufiji.

Moreover, all local opinion at Zanzibar was firmly agreed that it was impossible for a vessel of the *Königsberg's* draught to proceed further up the Rufiji delta than the mouth of the Simba Uranga, which was one of the various branches.

On the other hand, there was the evidence obtained from the *Präsident* at Lindi; there existed the chit of paper giving a receipt for coal that had been dumped aboard the *Königsberg* by lighters from *Präsident*; and there was that mysterious locality of Salale still to be determined. Another important item was that the Germans had carried out a survey of the Simba Uranga branch at a date later than that shown in the British Admiralty charts. Since the opening of hostilities, the enemy had naturally enough sought to make all navigational difficulties even more awkward still. For instance, at a place named Mwau Mwaimi the leading mark to clear the *Nymphe* shoal (which carried only 15 feet at low water and was therefore a trap for any cruiser) was a conspicuous white Customs House in line with a gap in the hills. The Germans ingeniously levelled this Customs House but painted white a similar building which lay sufficiently to one side as to lead a ship directly on to the shoal. Such tricks had to be kept in mind by a ship's officers who had suddenly been sent from the Mediterranean and Red Sea. Thus, it is not the gunnery experts who alone win campaigns.

It is necessary now to invite the reader's consideration of the Rufiji geography and to concentrate on a part of Africa that was still scarcely better known to Europe than it was when Livingstone marched across to Lake Nyasa, or Stanley came home to write his In Darkest Africa. The very nature of this uncivilised, impossible, region seemed to suggest it to be the last that would ever be suitable for modern cruiser warfare.

Imagine a projection, low-lying, uniform, and overgrown with mangroves, on the continent opposite to Mafia Island. This projection on the coast-line of some 30 miles contains the ten large watercourses, of which eight are always connected with the Rufiji River whilst two are merely salt-water creeks, the ten mouths opening into the Indian Ocean carrying down the mud from interior Africa. It is a remarkable maze of creeks which composes this Rufiji delta, and it is a system comparable only to the labyrinth of canals in Holland.

The Rufiji is a bewildering network of waterways so numerous that east and west, north and south, communication could be carried on by boats without ever having to cross the sea bars at the mouths. The two best entrances are by either the Kikunja or the Simba Uranga mouths. The Kikunja branch of the river is the most northerly and largest, being about a mile wide, where it empties into the sea; but a long island and then a small island soon restrict its breadth which at 9 miles from the ocean becomes narrow and shallow.

The Simba Uranga mouth is some 3½ miles to the south of Kikunja mouth, and this second branch runs inland almost parallel with the Kikunja, the two being joined at several stages by connecting side branches; whilst at the south-western (or innermost) end, less than 10 miles from the mouth, there is a connection whose channel at low water, on being surveyed early in the year 1917, was proved to have a depth of 12 to 19 feet. Thus, the reader will do well to bear in mind a circular route allowing craft to go in at one entrance, penetrate for about 10 miles, and come out by the second exit.

Between the two mouths was formed a peninsula, but at either of these exits to seaward there was a bar. The Simba Uranga used to be visited chiefly by coasters to fetch wood for Zanzibar, but it was an awkward river: for sometimes the ebb tide caused a considerable race, and after 5 miles inland the water shoaled. Even at 3 miles there were several mud banks which only just covered at low water ordinary springs. The Germans used to have a black and red vertical striped conical buoy with a black ball top-mark off the Simba Uranga entrance, from which a south-westerly course could be laid between the low-lying land. This obviously was one of the first things to be removed in war time, and in any case the depths varied from year to year.

There remains for our consideration yet a third of these rivers. Just before the Simba Uranga meets the sea, there sweeps round from upcountry the Suninga, which has likewise been running almost parallel, but is to the south, and also has similar side branches connecting roughly at right angles. It was the combined volume of these two rivers which caused the unpleasant race towards low water. Up the Simba Uranga were two or three villages, of which the least unimportant was Salale. A small tug belonging to the German Colonial Dyeing and Colouring Stuffs Company used, before the War, to be seen towing lighters and dhows from another of the mouths to Salale.

Such was the kind of information to be obtained from the *Handbuch der Ostküste Afrikas* published two years before the war, and every endeavour was made to supplement it from natives that October, but for the most part unsuccessfully. In particular it was desirable to know something about this Salale, yet a native who professed to be acquainted with the district was. as inaccurate as the rest: according to him Salale was a day's journey south of Lindi and on the borders of German and Portuguese East Africa. That was altogether wrong.

From what has been explained above in regard to the Rufiji geography it follows that there were two peninsulas formed where the rivers flowed out: since these projections of land will soon become of importance when we try to visualise certain happenings, we may call attention, (1) to Simba Uranga peninsula between the river of that name and the Kikunja, (2) to the Kiomboni peninsula which was formed on one side by the confluence of the Simba Uranga with the Suninga and on the south side by the River Kiomboni. Off both these projecting areas extended shallows entirely dry at low water and thus forming natural defences.

The current, during the British survey of 1917, was found to average 3 knots, but in places was even 5 knots, the holding ground being indifferent. Add to this inconvenience the fact of the scenery, for some 15 miles inland, being almost entirely covered with one dense mass of mangrove trees in uninteresting monotony. From seaward the coast of the delta was seen to be dotted here and there with native settlements surrounded by casuarina trees and coco-nut palms. Within the peninsulas, practically shut off from civilisation, began that vast expanse where crocodiles were many and the banks abounded in monkeys, elephants, lions and other untamed creatures of the wild. By night large families of the hippopotamus by their bellowing, and buzzing mosquitoes by their stings, contrived to make the white men's burden no easier in war time than in peace.

If, then, it were really a fact that the *Königsberg* was somewhere up one of these Rufiji creeks, the *Chatham* would require to know which, and exactly how far. "We had tried in vain to get natives to go up the Rufiji. They were all in a mortal terror of the Germans." But finally, during the call at Zanzibar on October 29, "we got hold of an Arab *dhow* captain, Ali-bin-Said, a very intelligent man." All natives in German East Africa were compelled to carry a pass or else be shot. The *Chatham* was able to furnish such a pass and the Arab was offered a large reward if he would go up into the Rufiji area and find out a few facts, but the man declined.

However, we took him on board with four men to work a *dhow*, if necessary, together with an interpreter, and sailed that night. Naturally the question of getting someone up the Rufiji to report had been discussed over and over again, and officers had volunteered to go up in a dugout to try their luck, but it was recognised as impossible; for the whole delta was known to be held by German troops.

So, at last a British cruiser was off to follow up the Rufiji trail. Surprise and secrecy were essential to any success, and Mafia Island with its signallers was still in the enemy's occupation. The difficulty was to combine safe navigation with concealment, now that the Simba Uranga mouth had been chosen by Captain Drury-Lowe as the most likely locality, in that it was known to have been used by small steamers. But the off-lying shallows were a great hindrance and source of uncertainty, since a depth of 18 feet was not possible abreast of the Simba Uranga entrance until at least 4 miles from the delta coast: not an attractive region in which to grope about by night.

The approach could be made from the north, or by the Mafia inlet, or from the south through the South Mafia channel. But if the first two were attempted, *Chatham's* presence would undoubtedly be seen and reported by look-outs on the numerous islands. It was therefore decided to use the third, so as to appear off the delta at daybreak, send in armed boats through the shallows, make a short quick raid on the Kiomboni peninsula with the chance of finding the Germans off their guard, seize any natives possible, and then rush back with them to the ship.

> Our friend Ali said he knew the headman of a small village near Kiomboni Point, but untold gold would not induce him to go in the boats ashore. He said the Germans were sure to be on the spot.

So, throughout the night of October 29-30 *Chatham* kept to seaward of the delta coast, steamed through the South Mafia channel by daybreak; at 7 a.m. anchored 5 miles east of the Kiomboni mouth, and lost no time in lowering away her steam-cutter, which took in tow her cutter full of armed men. On the boats sped towards the shore bound for such an adventure as was being made at the Western Front in Europe when a General wished to know what kind of troops were in the opposite trenches and sent a raiding party to bring back a few samples. But this sort of boat-expedition belonged rather to the good old days of Queen Victoria, when bluejackets in wide straw hats chased Chinese pirates. How often as boys most of us loved to devour such incidents so excitingly presented in those large-type, illustrated, volumes of juvenile fiction which came to us on birthdays and Christmas! Which of us has not envied the young officers leading their men forward on such a quest?

Here, then, was fiction turned into fact; imagination into reality. What a glorious chance such as their opposite numbers in the Grand Fleet could never obtain in the North Sea!

The boats traversed the 5 miles without incident and reached the point. The party jumped ashore, rushed to Kiomboni village, found that the German guard were temporarily away for breakfast, collared the headman together with a couple of other natives, got into the boats and steamed back to the *Chatham* before the Germans had time to appreciate what had happened. It was as neat and clean an event as Ballantyne, Henty, or any other novelist could have fashioned from his brain. And it was to have the most fruitful results. For when the police are unable immediately to lay their hands on a suspected culprit, the next best thing is to detain one or two individuals who can throw some light on his movements. Diligent cross-examination is likely to reveal some invaluable intelligence.

And this is precisely what was now happening.

The names of this African trio were respectively Bin Turemi, Athman Bin Santi, and Ali Bin Hassan. The first was the headman, and he soon became known among the British sailors as "Boombi." The *Chatham's* captain says:

> He rejoiced in the possession of the only respectable nightshirt in the village, and though he had left his wife and all his possessions, he seemed extremely happy to be out of it, and never wanted to return.

The amusing and bewildered Africans, standing against the spotless cruiser's decks, were now separately subjected to the following cross-examination:

> First came Bin Turemi.
> *Question.* Have you been to Salale?
> *Answer.* No.
> Q. Have you seen a ship with three funnels and two masts?
> A. I have seen her pass, going in, and coming out.
> Q. How long ago?
> A. The middle of September 3
> Q. Have you been employed by the Germans in digging trenches?
> A. Yes. Putting up huts and digging trenches.

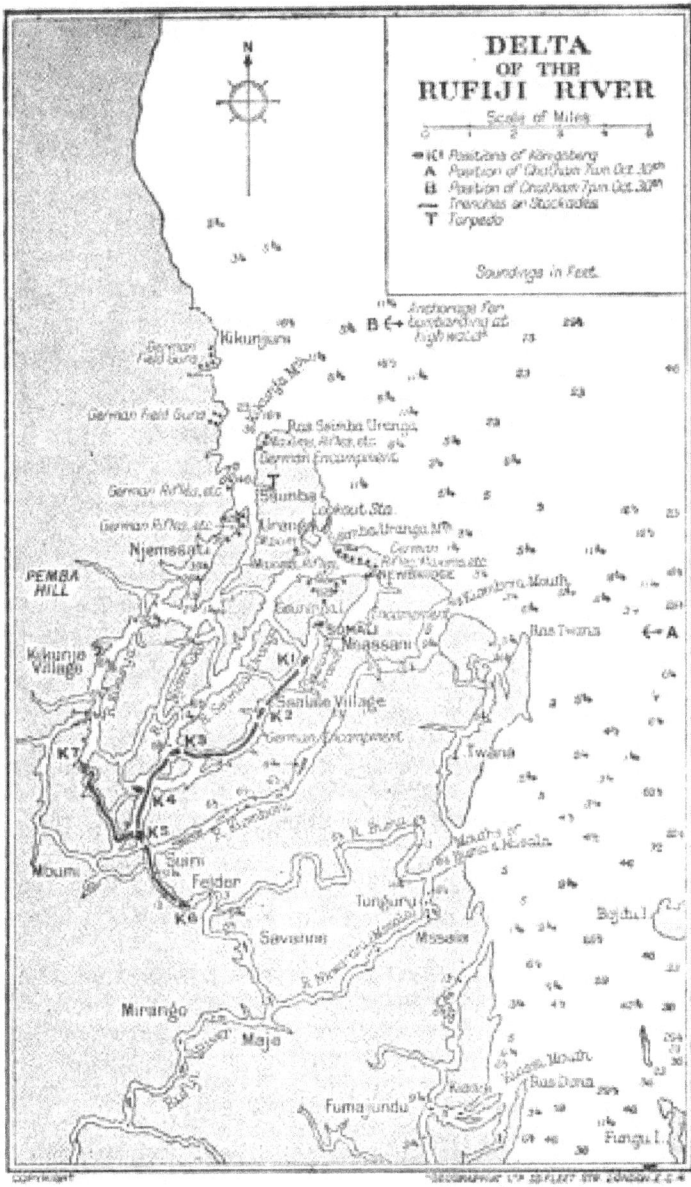

This chart indicates the navigational difficulties of the Rufiji area. Position A shows where H.M.S. *Chatham* anchored off the coast at 7 a.m. on October 30, before making the boat raid on Kiomboni. Position B was her anchorage twelve hours later. The successive positions and track of *Königsberg* until the following July are indicated by K1, etc., and black line.

Q. Where?
A. On the right bank of the entrance, Simba Uranga.
Q. When were you last there?
A. Four days ago, when they stopped work.
Q. What have they got in the trenches?
A. Three Maxims and two 3-pdrs. (The same as shown to him on board.):
Q. Have you seen any German sailors or officers there?
A. Yes. About 25 German bluejackets.

That was all most interesting news, and was the first *definite* information—the initial confirmatory clue —that the *Königsberg* was actually up the river Simba Uranga. And let it be said at once that Bin Turemi, who remained on board *Chatham* from this October 30 until December 2, doing "a lot of work for us," always stuck to the statement that the other branches were impracticable owing to numerous intricate banks in the higher reaches. He was subsequently landed on two occasions, and (so far as it was possible to test them) his affirmations were found always correct. He became popular in the ship, was well treated—as contrasted with the rough handling received from the Germans—and in the end "Boombi" received a handsome reward for his services.

Scarcely less instructive was the evidence derived from Athman Bin Santi, which in some respects strengthened that of the headman, and in others supplemented it.

Q. Have you been to Salale?
A. Yes. Three days ago.
Q. What did you go there for?
A. To buy clothes.
Q. Did you see any ships there?
A. Six ships: *Rovuma, Kingant, Manta, Somali, Königsberg*, and a man-of-war's pinnace.
Q. How many masts and funnels had the man-of-war?
A. Three funnels and two masts. Steamer (*i.e. Somali*) had two masts and one funnel.
Q. Is the man-of-war like this photo?
A. Yes. (He identified the *Königsberg*.)
Q. How long ago did you see her?
A. Three days.

Q. Did you cross over the water to Salale?
A. I went across by a path and then in a canoe, following the bank as closely as possible.
Q. Where was the man-of-war anchored?
A. She was anchored in mid-channel.
Q. Were they doing anything on board the ship?
A. I cannot say.
Q. Have you got a German pass?
A. Only a hut-tax chit.
Q. Have you been doing any work in digging trenches?
A. They came and caught 13 men at Kiomboni to in trenches, and I was one.
Q. They were digging trenches?
A. On both sides of the entrance.
Q. Where did you see the *Somali*?
A. Near Suninga.

From this second native it was of the utmost satisfaction to learn that the *Königsberg*, together with the 2,550-tons Deutsche Ost-Afrika S.S. *Somali*, and three other supply ships, were lying less than half a dozen miles up the river, the enemy cruiser being the furthest inland. And his testimony was corroborated by Ali Bin Hassan.

Q. Have you been to Salale?
A. About a month ago I was employed by the Germans to take a letter to Kikali, and I took the reply back to the *Königsberg*.
Q. Was she at Salale?
A. She was off Salale.
Q. Have you been employed digging trenches?
A. Yes. About four days ago for fourteen or fifteen days.
Q. Where are the trenches?
A. At Simba Uranga, as deep as my chest. Some other people digging trenches at Kiomboni. First put up the tents, and then huts. The trenches were dug outside the trees.
Q. Did you see any guns there?
A. Two guns and three Maxims.
Q. Have you been paid by the Germans for digging trenches?
A. Four *annas* a day. The Germans beat us.
Q. Do you want to go back again?
A. No. Have left everything, and afraid of the Germans.

So that was that. But it was not everything. When measuring the distance on the chart the anchorage of the *Chatham* was seen to be just 9 miles from Salale village in a direct line, and this was as near as she could approach the shore except at top of high-water springs. But the state of tides on October 30 was midway between neaps and springs. Not till November 3 would it be the latter, and it would make considerable difference to the possibilities, for whereas neap tides hereabouts rise only 7¾ feet, the rise at springs is 14¾ feet. The *Chatham* must therefore delay her operations till permitted by that force of nature which waits for no man. At this part of the coast the tide rises for about five hours and takes seven hours to fall.

In the meanwhile, surely—unless these Africans were telling untruths—at 9 miles in such clear atmosphere it ought to be possible to discern some of these enemy ships? Still, no one aboard *Chatham* could see a vestige—even from the masthead. So after the cross-examinations were concluded, and it was now afternoon, the British cruiser weighed anchor and proceeded further north, though the extensive shoals compelled her to keep 6, and up to 9, miles from the shore. It seemed as if every kind of difficulty was in alliance to hinder her: every sort of obstacle thwarting her this way and that.

The blazing sun scorched the steel hull, the engineers sweated at their job, the ship made for herself a slight breeze that ruffled her white ensign. Suddenly from the look-out man at the masthead there was a report: his keen, vigilant eyes had rested on something strange, something wonderful.

CHAPTER 8

Discovered

Hitherto nothing but mangrove trees could be seen rising from the ground at the water's edge everywhere, together with some coconuts and palms, though this barrage was more dense on the south side of Simba Uranga than on the north. And because the *Königsberg* was anchored in a direction sharp round to port, i.e. to the southward, with the Kiomboni peninsula acting like a lofty pier, one might steam past this mouth for ever without suspecting the presence of a ship inside. So valuable to the Germans had been local knowledge.

But now, when the *Chatham* began to open up the coast to the northward, where the growth was neither so high nor so interlaced, the look-out man, through his telescope, had been able with certainty to spot the mastheads of one vessel and then of a second. Great excitement swept through the *Chatham*, when it was learnt that one pair of masts were those of a warship. Presently, even from the fore control position, the masts of *Somali* and then of *Königsberg* above the distant trees could be descried beyond doubt. All hands congratulated themselves that the evasive enemy had been sighted at last: it would not be long now before the *Pegasus* was avenged.

Suddenly there was a second wave of scarcely suppressed emotion.

"*Königsberg* coming out!"

It looked as if the enemy were under way and determined to give battle, so this was good news indeed.

"Action stations!"

And whilst the keen crew ran to their respective posts, the *Chatham*'s engines were rapidly working up to full speed in order that a most favourable situation might be obtained off the mouth wherefrom to engage the emerging enemy. This would have been a most satisfactory occasion, with a speedy ending to all suspense.

But unfortunately, the Germans were still at anchor: there was no movement at all. It was not the first time that a ship going ahead had erroneously supposed another to be doing the same; whereas the mistake arose through the changing angles and cinemalike alteration of the scenery. There was, accordingly, nothing more which could be done today. As there was not water enough for the *Chatham* to get inside, and the entrance was held by German detachments with Maxims and 3-pdrs., possibly strengthened also by mines and torpedoes, this was a clear case for co-operation with the military. An urgent message was therefore sent asking for the assistance of troops. Captain Drury-Lowe's plans was as follows.

Infantry were to land and hold the Kiomboni Point, and the two isolated pieces of territory immediately within the river, namely the island of Suninga and the island of Simba Uranga. Thus, if the soldiers could have seized and occupied both banks, it would then be possible for some light draught steamer to sound her way up, such a ship to be armed with at least one 6-inch gun. Steamboats from the cruisers could then finish off the job with their torpedoes, and *Königsberg* would be wiped off the African map. Now on this self-same evening of October 30 that old-fashioned battleship H.M.S. *Goliath*, which had been launched as far back as the year 1898, a vessel of 12,950 tons, yet had never been known to attain 19 knots in her prime, was just able to limp into Mombasa and then broke down utterly.

But she had arrived escorting the main part of the Indian Expeditionary Force (numbering about 10,000 troops) and the whole attention of the military was occupied for the present with surprise attacks, which were to be made three days later against Tanga and Dar-es-Salaam. Success was considered to be certain, and then the required men would be sent to help the sister service. The poor, incapacitated *Goliath* could be of no assistance: she was out of action with leaky condensers, and at 6 knots had scarcely been able to crawl into Mombasa. Lucky, she had been not to have met *Emden* on the way.

In the meanwhile, over the cables of the Indian Ocean, and across Europe into Whitehall, came the welcome news for the Admiralty that the *Königsberg* had been located up the Rufiji; whilst wireless messages likewise were sent recalling to *Chatham* both *Dartmouth* and *Weymouth*, who could now give up their patrolling and concentrate off the Rufiji. The *Dartmouth* happened to be looking out off Beira when the joyful information reached her, and the *Weymouth* was in the act of coaling at the Comoro Islands.

During the forenoon of October 31, the *Chatham* had a busy time firing 6-inch lyddite into the German signal station on Mafia Island; for the time had come when positively no warning must be allowed to reach Captain Looff of the impending operations. The *Chatham*'s boats were sent off to sound a channel in the approaches to Simba Uranga, a minimum depth of 5 feet being obtained at low water, that is to say barely enough for the lightest of vessels. In the afternoon began the range-finding of *Königsberg*'s and the *Somali*'s masts, and next day a new month began with the first offensive.

Having arrived off the Simba Uranga entrance, boats commenced sounding and buoying, so that at high water in the afternoon the *Chatham* was able to get within 4¼ miles of the mouth. This half-mile to the good was due to the fact that the time was nearer to spring tides' advent, but the distance needed to be lessened still more. According to the range-finder, *Somali*'s masts were 14,500 yards away.

★★★★★★★★★★

According to Captain Looff, the Germans now expected the British cruiser would endeavour to enter the river. The former reckoned that the *Chatham* never approached nearer to the *Königsberg* than 16,250 yards, whereas the range of *Königsberg*'s 4:1's was only 12,760 yards. The Germans made a practice of destroying the buoys off the mouth after nightfall.

★★★★★★★★★★

That was tiresome, for the maximum long range of *Chatham*'s guns was exactly this figure. Although a number of 6-inch lyddite shells were now fired, direction being made from the masthead, the shots fell short of the *Somali*; which was a pity considering that steamer was full of grain and wood for *Königsberg* and would have burnt furiously. The *Somali* had been built at Hamburg a quarter of a century ago, so there would be enough layers of paint to help any conflagration. She was over 320 feet in length and would make a good target if only she could be approached a little nearer.

It was disappointing that shell after shell just failed to reach, and the *Königsberg* who was off Salale, about 1½ miles further up than *Somali*, this afternoon became so uneasy that she shifted her berth about another 1¾ miles still higher. Spotting was extremely difficult at the best of times, and the only definite achievement this day was some shelling of the shore positions at 9,200 yards. The immediate outlook was not too promising, but the enemy must be given no rest. Would Captain Looff make a bold move, turn round, come out, and have a run for it? Could he not have arranged a rendezvous, somewhere in the Indian

Ocean, with the *Emden*?

There might have been a sporting chance of getting out at high water these spring tides, dropping a few well-placed shells over the mangrove curtain just before gaining the entrance, piercing the *Chatham* at her waterline, knocking over a funnel (thereby reducing the British cruiser's speed) and then steaming off during a brief hot running fight. Moreover, the fact that it was high water at Full and Change of the moon when dawn would be breaking (4 a.m.), with a rise of just under 15 feet, could all be reckoned as in the German's favour.

If that intention were being contemplated, it was negatived just a day too soon. For on November 2, after the *Chatham* had again passed the forenoon off Simba Uranga mouth, sending her boats to sound and buoy, then herself bombarding the peninsula, she was joined at midday by the arrival of *Dartmouth* and *Weymouth*. Without wasting even a few minutes, there now began an interesting effort.

The *Dartmouth's* bunkers were nearly empty, and that which ordinarily would have been reckoned a disadvantage was now turned to account, for in her present condition she needed less water in which to float and could therefore stand in to the shallow shore more closely than either of her two sisters. It was high water this afternoon at 3.8 p.m., so at 2.15 p.m. all three weighed, and closed the Simba Uranga mouth. The *Dartmouth* was able to improve on the previous 5 and even 4½ miles, bringing this down to 2 miles, at which distance she signalled she had obtained soundings of "quarter less three," which in lay English means that she was getting three fathoms, less a quarter of a fathom—in other words 16½ feet.

Nearer than that she could not venture, but even at this the high trees prevented her from seeing anything of the *Königsberg*. All three cruisers bombarded both banks of the entrance, and tried to shell the *Somali*. Under cover of these 6-inch guns a steamboat expedition was sent in to examine the river at closer acquaintance, but "Boombi" and his mates were proved to be right: the entrance was too strongly occupied. On the starboard hand there was a lookout station (complete with telephone), and trenches; whilst on the port side there were trenches, Maxims, rifles.

By reason of the thick mangroves, it was quite impossible to indicate precisely where the trenches ran, but it may be mentioned by anticipation that on a later date these were discovered to be of the most modern type, so constructed as to be screened by the trees from all view, and practically secure from all gun fire except for a chance hit.

As they entirely commanded the landing, they could not have been taken by frontal assault; and an attack from the flanks would have required at least 1,000 men, the approach through the mangroves being extremely difficult. The enemy had undoubtedly taken most clever precautions.

At the end of this unproductive day the *Dartmouth* was sent on to Mombasa in order to coal, which of course was inevitable. There was another inconvenience that was peculiar to these shoal waters. For the various mouths, as the strong current rushed out to meet the Indian Ocean, brought down thick mud and deposited it on the bottom. But the cruisers, endeavouring to use the shallowest soundings, stirred up this mud which quickly choked the condensers: in fact, after a fortnight the *Chatham*'s evaporators and pumps gave out, being absolutely choked up, thus requiring the ship to remain idle for 48 hours cleaning with fires out.

We pass now to November 3, an important date, since today was to see the top of spring tides, high water being at 4 p.m. Captain Drury-Lowe these few days had been making plans for a reconnaissance and, if possible, to attack the *Königsberg*. Inasmuch as the *Goliath* was busy repairing her engines, he asked that her steam picket boat might be sent down the coast to this delta as soon as possible, together with dropping gear and 14-inch torpedoes. She was to be towed by a small and ancient cable steamer, *Duplex*, which up till recently had been working off East Africa, but had now been taken over by the British naval authorities.

The *Chatham*'s captain says:

> I had received several offers from adventurous spirits on board for an attempt on the *Königsberg*, such as getting a torpedo up one of the branches with a skiff or dugout, or even Swimming up the river on a flood tide with one. One officer was all ready to go disguised as a native in Boombi's nightshirt and dugout to reconnoitre, proceeding up the Kiomboni mouth. But it would be necessary to have a guide, and Boombi absolutely refused to do anything if anyone landed with him. He said all the branches were watched and patrolled, and the creeks were impossible for those who did not know them. So, before daylight on November 3, we landed Boombi alone in his dugout at Ras Twana, his instructions being to get across and report the exact position of *Königsberg*. He was to be away 24 hours, and departed on this

expedition without the nightshirt and with a mouthful of ship's tobacco.

****

Ras Twana was at the tip of another of these delta peninsulas on the eastern side of a creek some 2 miles south-east of Kiomboni, He could thus paddle his way into the Kiomboni River and then inspect the Suninga.

****

He did his job faithfully, and was fetched back by boat in the early hours of November 4. The position of the German cruiser was confirmed, and it was learned that from *Somali* hawsers had been run out on either side: she was still anchored some distance below the *Königsberg*.

The effort of *Chatham* on November 3 was, if humanly possible, to get within range of the enemy. As the tide rose, she was able this afternoon to reach a spot 2 miles off the entrance, but it will be recollected that two days ago Captain Looff had moved his ship some distance further up the Suninga, so that even with the assistance of high water springs the *Chatham* was not 14,500 but 14,800 yards distant. From aloft the topmast heads of *Königsberg* were just visible—a wretched target indeed—and it looked as if she had housed her topmasts, placing trees at the mastheads for further concealment.

However, the British cruiser was not going to fail for lack of resource, so by taking on a list of five degrees to port and firing with the starboard guns she was able to increase the range to 14,800 yards or thereabouts. More than this she could not do, fire being directed from the masthead, and guns laid by bearing on an invisible foe. But still it was obvious that our shells dropped short of their target, and after half an hour the falling tide made it imperative for the *Chatham* to move into deeper soundings.

Success was not to be yet, and two days later arrived the disappointing tidings that the Tanga expedition had failed disastrously, that the force from India was to be re-embarked, Dar-es-Salaam was not to be attempted, and no troops could be spared for the Rufiji undertaking. Of the regrettable repulse at Tanga it is not necessary to say much. One British, one Ghurka and one Sikh regiment did well: the rest being inferior troops consisting of Bombay natives who had never previously been on active service, had spent three weeks on board transports, becoming weak and dispirited by sea-sickness.

But only the best type of infantry would have sufficed for the delta, which to at least one general "would appear to be one vast mangrove swamp," with land communications "practically non-existent"; and there were difficulties in regard to drinking water as well as suitable camping sites. So, the navy carried on with the job alone, and thus occurred some of the most stirring incidents which happened anywhere afloat throughout the Great War. For resource, coolness, dash, bravery under most trying circumstances they are unforgettable; and no healthy-minded man can consider these brilliant episodes without being deeply envious of those who took part.

Away from all war correspondents and official eyewitnesses, this little band of officers and men in small craft took a gallant gamble with their lives, and added to naval history a golden chapter of brave exploits. It is high time that the world became more acquainted with a series of adventures that at first seem akin to those which were to take place many months later in European waters off Zeebrugge. Not one Victoria Cross was awarded for these Rufiji exploits; possibly it may be because they all happened so far away from home and no imagination could quite appraise what was done: yet, with the limited material at their disposal, one can scarcely conceive of a problem being tackled in a more noble and thorough manner.

CHAPTER 9

Running the Gauntlet

There were only two possible ways of destroying *Königsberg*. The first, as we have seen, was to seize and occupy the land in the delta with troops, and then the light-draught vessels could have advanced. But this, owing to special circumstances, was no more permissible than was to be the capture by the Army of the Dardanelles forts, whose fall would have enabled the navy to have reached Constantinople.

The second plan was to run the gauntlet, force a way through, do all the damage which could be directed against the enemy, his supply ships, his defences; and if the *Königsberg* could not actually be sunk, at least she should be effectually bottled up, sealed in, so that as a fighting unit she could never give any further trouble. But how was this blocking of the river to be done?

The *Chatham's* captain quickly set things humming. A blockship? One of the Admiralty colliers. Which one? The S.S. *Newbridge*, 3,800 tons, lying at Mombasa. She was very flat-bottomed, 350 feet long, beam 509 feet. The wireless got busy. Send the *Newbridge* from Mombasa to Zanzibar; let Zanzibar prepare her for immolation. It was done. Off Mafia Island at daylight of November 6 *Chatham* met the *Goliath's* picket boat being towed by the S.S. *Duplex* which was capable of 7 knots. Two 14-inch torpedoes with dropping gear arrived, and later in the day came *Dartmouth* after her coaling, bringing also two 3-pdr. guns for the *Duplex*. The latter were on extemporised field mountings and belonged to the *Goliath* likewise.

A boat attack was planned for November 7, principally in order to ascertain the enemy's strength up river. Orders were given not to force this attack if the enemy were found to be holding the river banks in strength; for the same essential weakness that we risked at Lindi would be manifest here. When once inside the Simba Uranga mouth, the craft would have to turn sharp round close to the peninsula for the

Suninga river, and thus be henceforth out of the sight and protection of the three cruisers' guns. It was at 5 a.m. that *Goliath's* picket boat with her torpedoes, supported by the armed shallow-draught *Duplex*, and three armed steam-cutters from the three cruisers, came steaming on to the Simba Uranga entrance; but no sooner were they rounding the point than they were received with a heavy fire from the entrenched Germans. Not an enemy could be seen through the mangroves, though the reception which was being given to the boats from rifles, Maxims and 3-pdrs. from both banks was terrific, notwithstanding all the 6-inch shells which the combined cruisers were hurling at the shores.

During this brief but warm encounter one shot hit the port outrigger of the *Goliath* picket boat, thus accidentally releasing a live torpedo. The flotilla were compelled to retire, otherwise they would have been lost, and luckily not one boat was missing. The adventure had not been useless, for exact information had been obtained of the defences in regard to the future, and this was (as we shall soon see) very necessary. But something else had been obtained, which was of no little value and encouragement at that time. For in the cruisers' endeavour to get as close to the shoals as could be risked, the *Chatham* found herself at 13,000 yards from the *Somali*, therefore shelled her and scored at least one hit so that the supply ship started a conflagration which went on burning for nearly two days, finally gutting her, and thus robbing the *Königsberg* of coal, wood, grain and stores.

If the reader will examine the accompanying illustration, he will realise the task of forcing the fortified mouth. This sketch was made on the spot by Staff-Surgeon H. L. Norris, R.N., during the bombardment. To right and left of the opening will be seen our shrapnel bursting over the German trenches, and the thick trees explain themselves. In the centre can be noticed the heavy smoke rising from the burning *Somali*, which was 3 miles up the Suninga. The *Königsberg's* masts are not visible.

The moral effect on the *Königsberg's* people requires no stressing: between now and November 22 she moved up 2 miles further, and whilst this was a confession of impending defeat, it emphasised (what was already fully understood) that Captain Looff's ship was too far up river to allow his rivals any chance of success by means of a boat attack. On the night of November 7 *Chatham* went off to Zanzibar for the purpose of completing the *Newbridge*, leaving *Dartmouth* and *Weymouth* on watch. According to the charts, the narrowest part of the Suninga

THE FAMOUS TUG *ADJUTANT*
Few small vessels have spent such a varied life as this. The illustration is taken from a photograph by a German. Notice the German ensign flying at the masthead.

ENTRANCE TO THE SIMBA URANGA
This interesting sketch was made on November 7, 1914, by Staff-Surgeon H. L. Norris, R.N., during the bombardment. Smoke rising from the burning *Somali* is seen in the distance. Enemy's trenches are cleverly concealed where indicated by arrow.

THE EX-CABLE STEAMER *DUPLEX*
This old vessel is seen in the foreground, with H.M.S. *Goliath* in the background. The *Duplex* was of 874 tons and played a prominent part during the blocking operations.

seemed to be at the first bend about 1 mile from the entrance, sharp round the corner of the Kiomboni peninsula. Although the apparent breadth from bank to bank might be up to 500 yards, yet the channel was not more than half that distance, and the *Newbridge*'s length we saw to be about 117 yards. If she could be sunk athwart this bend, the silt coming down with the tide would doubtless accumulate and complete the job. Natives reported that at this chosen spot the navigable width was very slight, and it was not considered possible that *Königsberg* would find water enough to come out by any other exit.

So, whilst at Zanzibar the *Chatham* was taking in 380 tons of coal from the collier Burbridge, great activities were going on aboard the *Newbridge*. After being dismantled and put in a state for sinking, she was partly loaded with rubble, explosive charges being fitted inside and out. The idea was that as soon as *Newbridge* was placed in the position selected, she was to be anchored bow and stern, the main inlets removed, and the guncotton charges exploded from a boat after the last man had left her. But before that could come to pass, she must get right through the hot defile which the flotilla this morning had failed to penetrate. A conning-tower of steel plating was accordingly built on the fore bridge to afford some protection to the wheel, the helmsman, and the officer. So, too, the anchor party on the fo'c'sle and poop must be defended, for which reason both plating and sandbags were put around.

As to the personnel, the whole of *Newbridge's* crew were put ashore at Zanzibar, with the exception of her master, first officer and chief engineer, who were to remain until the ship arrived off the Rufiji. The volunteer crew consisted of 1 lieutenant, 7 seamen and 9 engine-room ratings, all from H.M.S. *Chatham*. So rapidly had everything been carried out, that by the evening of the 8th *Newbridge* and *Chatham* left Zanzibar, passed through the North Mafia Channel and, having reached a position some 11 miles from the delta, let go anchor next afternoon to complete final details.

The day chosen for the big attempt at blocking up the *Königsberg* was November 10, and two conditions were required. Firstly, in order to make it possible that men and vessels could survive the terrible defile at Simba Uranga mouth, the only hope relied on the element of surprise, which in turn meant employing the cover of darkness. On the other hand, owing to the navigational conditions and the strong tide of a river that not one of these British subjects had ever so much as seen beyond the trees, daylight was indispensable from the moment

THE BLOCKSHIP

The lower illustration shows the ex-collier *Newbridge* after being sunk across the river in an attempt to bottle up the *Konigsberg*. The upper photograph was taken from the air and shows *Newbridge* athwart the deepest part of the channel. Observe the winding character of the Rufiji rivers.

of reaching the Kiomboni peninsula.

It was therefore decided to make the approach of the shore just before daylight, which comes suddenly in those latitudes, and synchronise the time of sunrise with the flotilla's arrival at the river mouth. Secondly, it must be flood tide, with plenty of the same; for the vessels would need every assistance in regard to speed, shoal dodging, and to ensure the blockship swinging across stream when anchored. At the same consideration, if the expedition was ever to make its return—and that would probably be the hardest job—a strong flood tide would seriously delay their craft.

It would be high water on the 10th at 7.53 a.m., and daylight at 5.36. That combination was excellent, allowing the coastal approach to be planned for being made whilst it was yet dark, and for the entrance to be reached just as the sun rose at their backs. Let it be realised that *Newbridge*, though the place for her sinking was only 1 mile up, might prematurely touch the ground and have to wait under the withering fire of the peninsula, and her only friends would be the S.S. *Duplex* with her couple of 3-pdrs., the *Goliath's* picket boat with one 3-pdr. and one Maxim, together with a steam-cutter from both *Chatham* and *Weymouth*, each of these boats being armed with one Maxim. *Dartmouth's* steam-cutter was to enter with the rest but, instead of turning sharp to port up the Suninga, was to carry straight on up the Simba Uranga for the purpose of making a reconnaissance as far as could be done, reporting on the condition of the channel, and depth of water; the object being to make sure that *Königsberg* could not float by this exit.

Every officer and man foresaw (as their brothers later at Zeebrugge likewise perceived) that the most hazardous period would be the abandoning of *Newbridge*, and the retreat past the peninsula (which corresponded indeed to Zeebrugge's Mole). Captain Drury-Lowe felt that it was a forlorn hope to think of *Newbridge's* volunteer crew ever coming back. "I hardly expected to see them again." Every seaman the world over likes the duty of mooring ship to be done quietly and unhurriedly without the attention being distracted. Gear has to be kept from taking charge, and the right thing has to be carried through at the right moment—neither before nor after. But here was an occasion when bow and stern anchors must be let go and cables worked under a deadly fire, the main inlets opened not a moment too soon nor a moment too late; the crew must jump into the steam-cutter leaving the electric firing circuits joined up to the battery, and get far enough away before the explosions burst. Should the charges fail, then the picket boat was to choose a safe distance and discharge a torpedo at *Newbridge*.

All this could not be attempted except by men trained through years of discipline to act quickly but not rashly, to keep their enthusiasm well under control, to be cool-headed when danger seemed warmest. Any individual of the party by one precipitate bit of zeal might ruin the whole show and bring death to his comrades. For instance, there would be a natural human tendency to let go anchor over soon and get away down into the cutter: or the charges through the fumbling of nervous fingers might be fired one second too early, with the loss of valuable lives. For each of these charges comprised 32½ lbs. of guncotton placed in the engine-room bilges and well wedged down, whilst outside the hull and fitted under the ship's bottom by lines were 16½ lbs. more. All steamboats were given a certain amount of protection by iron plating and sandbags in the stern-sheets, and around both boilers and engines.

It is to be mentioned that when volunteers aboard *Chatham* were invited for manning *Newbridge*, every member of the ship's company came forward, so the ratings had to be chosen one by one. The *Newbridge* was put in charge of Commander Raymond Fitzmaurice, R.N., the *Chatham*'s gallant and able second-in-command, of whom mention has already been made. With him went Lieutenant R. F. Maxwell Johnson, R.N., and Lieutenant H. V. Lavington, R.N. The latter had already been under enemy fire, for he was at one time Navigator of the *Pegasus*, but was now one of *Dartmouth's* officers. Four engine-room ratings and seven seamen were also in the *Newbridge* party.

The *Duplex* was entrusted to Lieutenant Reginald S. Triggs, R.N.R., whose experience in merchant steamers would be found invaluable. The *Goliath's* picket boat was in charge of Lieutenant-Commander John C. S. Paterson, R.N., the *Chatham*'s steam-cutter in charge of Sub-Lieutenant J. P. A. Bremridge, R.N.; the *Dartmouth's* steam-cutter was commanded by Sub-Lieutenant J. H. R. Homfray, R.N., whilst two steam-cutters came from *Weymouth*—one under the command of Sub-Lieutenant A. G. Murray, R.N., and the other under Lieutenant-Commander G. H. Lang, R.N.

Thus, here was to be an adventure in which youth could exult and show its pride of existence. What an opportunity for youngsters, not long since out of the Naval College, to be taking their jolly little steam craft into action! What a sudden realisation of all their boyhood days, of dreams inspired by those coloured pictures in story books! What delight to be thought war-worthy, and sent out on a forlorn expedition! Someday, should any of these junior officers survive and reach flag rank, it would be a wonderful privilege to look back—to reflect and compare.

On the afternoon of the 9th Captain Drury-Lowe issued his orders, which may be summarised as follows:

Tonight, the *Dartmouth* was to anchor off the east point of Komo Island for the object of providing *Newbridge* with a leading mark during her night passage on her way to Simba Uranga mouth, the course from *Dartmouth's* position to the centre of the entrance being S. 39° W. and distance 8½ miles. The blockship would therefore have to grope blindly, relying only on dead reckoning to make the peninsula without hitting any of the numerous shoals. This could not fail to be a nerve-trying job for any officer navigating a 3,800-ton steamer out of trim and subjected to uncertain currents in the darkness.

In assembling the squadron ready for morning *Weymouth* and *Newbridge* were anchored 2 miles from *Dartmouth*, with *Duplex* near to the latter, and *Chatham* only 600 yards away. It was arranged that in order to cover *Newbridge* with their fire, both *Chatham* and *Weymouth* should close the river entrance as on the previous occasion, whilst *Duplex* and the little steamboats were to accompany the blockship inside—*Duplex* on the port quarter, *Goliath's* picket boat on the starboard quarter, and the three steamboats astern. This last trio was to assemble off *Dartmouth* in readiness by 4.45 a.m. *Newbridge* was to weigh anchor in time to pass *Dartmouth* not later than 5 a.m. and, allowing for a speed of 6 knots, should be off the entrance by 6.30 a.m. The *Chatham* and *Weymouth* with *Duplex* were to weigh independently so as to close the entrance at 5 a.m. and thus be ready to pour in a deluge of shells at the earliest moment. *Dartmouth* was to remain at anchor, whilst *Chatham* bombarded the right bank, and *Weymouth* the left.

To the *Chatham's* own steamboat was naturally conceded the privilege of standing by *Newbridge* after abandonment, the *Dartmouth's* steamboat remaining within the entrance but in sight of the cruisers. Whilst the *Duplex* and the *Goliath's* picket boat were to cover *Newbridge* by firing at the enemy ashore, and the picket boat was to be in readiness for torpedoing the blockship if required, *Weymouth's* steam-cutter towing a whaler with half a dozen marines was to land and search the left bank immediately after Commander Fitzmaurice's steamer had gained the entrance.

Obviously here was no pleasant picnic, and before the African sun had reached its zenith death must steal some of these adventurers for himself. Captain Drury-Lowe warned them:

> Resistance, may be expected from the left bank of the river as before, and possibly from Suninga Island. It is not expected that the right bank will be occupied, as it is covered by our shell fire.

Besides the guns and quick-firers mentioned, all steamboats' crews were armed with rifles and everyone wore a lifebelt. The steam-cutters all had masts up, and each carried a signalman with hand flags for semaphoring, flashing lamp, and megaphone, Very's pistol and white lights. Special flags could be hoisted to indicate the following important messages:

"Shells are falling close to me."
"Am being fired on by the enemy."
"Am sinking."
"Am disabled. Require assistance."

First-aid for the wounded and one barrico of water were placed in each of these craft.

Such was the detailed scheme for the great undertaking, and it was so perfectly conceived that the well-disciplined naval machine of ships and men moved with the precision of a railway system. There was really only one divergence from the time-table, and that was when the *Newbridge* in her anxiety for self-sacrifice got under way half an hour earlier, so that she actually reached the entrance at 5.20 a.m., which was all to the good, for the dawn was only just breaking. Five minutes later she had turned eight points to port up the winding river of Suninga, and now from the back of Kiomboni peninsula came a fierce banging of 3- to 5-pdrs., punctuated with the *rattle-rattle-rat* of quick-firers, and the clicking of rifles.

Nor did the latter ever ease up for one minute: in truth the shower of machinegun and rifle bullets made a persistent patter against the temporary protective plating on bridge, fo'c'sle and poop throughout the entire operation in which *Newbridge* was engaged. Never was there a moment's respite, for the only variations were the heavy thuds and dull clanging when shells collided with the ship's steel hull or superstructure.

Anxious minutes for any imaginative mind, but tremendous for the commanding officer charged with the duty of bringing her amid all this thunder and excitement to the one and only bend of the river.

The engines were going ahead, the flood tide setting the ship up rapidly, and soon it would be too far round the corner ever to hope for return. And what about the *Königsberg's* guns? Would they not open fire?

"Stop engines!"

It was just 5.50 a.m. The sun had risen in its merciless splendour out of the Indian Ocean.

"Stand by! Leggo!"

Commander Fitzmaurice had put the helm hard over, placed *Newbridge* at right angles to the tide, the heavy cable at the bows went rumbling, splashing into the muddy water at the bows: two stern anchors and wires fell leaping aft.

"Finished with engines," he rang down on the bridge telegraph.

The inlet valves were opened exactly as planned, and at 6 a.m. the whole party had jumped into *Chatham's* steam-cutter after as neat a bit of work as ever was attempted afloat by seamen in any age of sea history. There the blockship lay as intended on the chart, about 50 yards from the left bank at the narrowest part of the bend. At 6.15 came the finale when up blew the guncotton charges, and five minutes later this cutter was speeding down river against the last hour of the flood. One careful glance aft at 6.35 enabled the party to see that their work had been carried through as successfully as it was rapidly: for the ex-collier was settling down by the stern with a heavy list to port, the opened bunker lids on that side taking in water all the time. The *Newbridge* was now a fixture in the Rufiji scenery: a cork in the narrow neck of Suninga.

But there happened thrilling, awkward, awe-begetting incidents which must be considered in detail if we are to complete the picture.

CHAPTER 10

Blocking up the Enemy

In the accompanying photographs the *Newbridge* is seen just as she appeared after this lightning episode, but what the illustrations fail to convey is that her position was more effective than might at first seem likely. The great problem, as we know from naval history, is to leave the blockship accurately placed in the proper depth of water and at the right angle. This sounds and looks moderately easy, but even within the narrow channel leading up to the Zeebrugge lock gates, when at a later date three of our cruisers were one after the other deposited and abandoned, it was impossible to coax them sufficiently athwart the passage, and at such a satisfactory angle as to make a perfect closure. In a very little while German submarines came in and out of the lock, round the three obstructions, and out to sea as before.

But the *Newbridge* had been left where the water was deepest, and thus by her length monopolised all save the shallower portions between the two banks. Before abandonment it had been hoped that soundings might be obtained all round the hull, but the enemy's fire was so deadly that it would have been callous to risk men and boats whilst plumbing ahead and astern with the lead-line. One sounding of 4 fathoms was obtained from amidships (and this only an hour before high water), so there was no chance of the *Königsberg* trying to escape at low tide, and practically little space for her to swing past at high tide.

As soon as the *Newbridge* had let go her bow anchors, the flood swung her rapidly across stream until checked by a stern anchor. Unfortunately, at this juncture, whilst the men on the poop were veering the wire hawser and about to make fast, there came whizzing through the air a projectile which crashed against the heavy protective plating that, in turn, fell down on to the busy men. The result was that just when everything was shaping well, and the vessel was at her assigned angle, the hawser took charge, the end running out into the river.

Such an unforeseen crisis was maddening, and it looked certain that the whole of this morning's complicated endeavours would be set at nought. For the *Newbridge*, secured at one end and free at the other, began swinging so definitely that presently she must become parallel with the banks; a position which would be quite useless.

But Commander Fitzmaurice, cool and skilful in leadership, gallant in example, unruffled by this contretemps, had not lost hope. His bridge was being repeatedly hit, and it is always a fine test of self-control when officer or man endures calmly the enemy's fire without any chance of reply, or without being panicked from the duty in hand. His whole attention was concentrated on the handling and sinking of the steamer, and many a brave adventurer might have been heart-broken by the hawser episode. Swinging, swinging with the tide she continued in this manner until slightly past the right angle which she was to make; and then she suddenly brought up firmly, because her stern became embedded in the shoal. She was drawing 13 feet 5 inches, (an officer who took soundings here at low water, Springs, in 1921 tells me he found 5 fathoms), the angle was not 90° but it was about 50°, and when the main inlet valve allowed the river to pour in, she soon anchored herself beyond all doubt.

That this brave band of brothers should have done so much and got away through all that violent assault of bullets and shells seems wellnigh miraculous; but it is accountable to no small extent by the complete obedience to commands and the entire absence of any impulsive movements. Commander Fitzmaurice stated:

> All hands assembled by order near the port ladder, taking cover as far as possible. Both the ship and *Chatham*'s steam-cutter were under heavy fire at the time. The men did not get down to the boat until ordered, and behaved with the greatest coolness throughout. The electric firing circuit was taken into the steam-cutter, and the charges fired at a distance of about 75 yards from *Newbridge*, the explosion being followed by a large column of water and black objects from the interior of the *Newbridge*. The ship rapidly listed to port. To make certain, I ordered the picket boat to fire a torpedo, but the latter dived, struck the mud, and did not appear again.

The retirement from *Newbridge* in *Chatham*'s steam-cutter was made under the heavy and continuous fire of the enemy's combined rifles, quick-firers, 3-pdrs. and of even more powerful guns. Commander Fitzmaurice informed Captain Drury-Lowe afterwards that the *Newbridge* would never have been able to reach her position unless the supporting craft had so readily exposed themselves, drawing the Germans' fire and thus preventing the latter's heavier guns from concentrating for any length of time on such vital parts of the blockship as the steering wheel, the poop and fo'c'sle. And not one member of the party would have come out of the river, but for the courageous manner in which the steamboats kept the people on the peninsula perpetually sprinkled with shot.

A glance at the rough sketch will readily convey a clear idea of the dangerous gorge which had to be rushed both coming and going. Having this before us let us imagine ourselves with Lieutenant-Commander G. H. Lang, R.N., in his steam-cutter. On the trip inward that morning one or two rifle shots attacked her from point A, which can be visualised by further reference to Staff-Surgeon Norris' picture at the right of where a small arrow is marked.

We were not fired on again till we were opposite point B, when a heavy fire was opened on us with Maxims, 3-pdrs. and rifles between B and B[1]. Shortly after this we altered course to port.

Upriver the *Newbridge* could be descried already with a heavy list to port and a great deal of smoke issuing from her fore-hold, but the enemy was inflicting such a heavy cross fusillade on to the *Weymouth's*

PLAN TO ILLUSTRATE BLOCKING OPERATIONS

steam-cutter that Commander Lang was kept busy enough with his own craft blazing away at his opponents.

It was after he had turned to come out, and was engaging the eastern bank with the intention of keeping the Germans so occupied as to interfere less with the retreating party from the blockship, that on reaching the position C, Commander Lang's coxswain was shot, the wheel rope roller of the steering gear jammed, and the boat swerved off her course heading straight for the shore. Annihilation seemed imminent, the cutter was now only 80 yards from the beach, and in fact several white men in khaki and a sailor in bluejacket rig could be seen dodging between the trees. Luckily, just before it was too late, the helm was righted and this small steamboat by maintaining a rapid shower of bullets all the way out found herself back on the Indian Ocean swell. She had been nearer to destruction than was healthy; for she was punctured at 17 holes. This officer's excellent work was not forgotten by the Lords of the Admiralty, who shortly afterwards gave him promotion in rank.

Brilliantly heroic, too, was the work of young Sub-Lieutenant Bremridge in charge of the *Chatham*'s steam-cutter, which had to perform so many prolonged services of hazard. His own account is so modest and restrained that it needs to be supplemented.

> In approaching the entrance, fire was opened on the *Newbridge*, *Duplex*, picket boat and our steam-cutter. The latter was about 14 cables astern of the *Duplex* who was reached just past the left entrance. Fire from the shore seemed then to be directed from either side at the *Duplex*, and some bullets (probably from rifles) came near the steam-cutter. I decided to go to the starboard side of the *Duplex*, which seemed the lee side from the fire, but on approaching the stern a heavy fire was opened on us by a 3-pdr. and a Maxim from Suninga Island.
>
> On clearing the *Duplex,* we received a heavy Maxim fire from both banks, which we returned. The picket boat (*Goliath's*) was stopped the north side of the *Newbridge*, and I passed her, several 3-pdr. shots pitched near us here from a position up the creek, distance away being 1200 yards. We distributed our fire going up here as necessary, as the different Maxims were brought to bear on us. I then went alongside the *Newbridge's* port side, and brought off the men from her. At this time a Maxim was firing from the shore on the *Newbridge*'s port bow, but this fire on us

was not very heavy.

On receiving the coil of wire, we joined it to our firing battery and, owing to the wire jamming when running out, we fired the charges at about 75 yards distance, then went off on the port quarter of the *Newbridge* and she seemed to settled down on her port side very rapidly. We then made a signal to the picket boat to fire a torpedo, and she approached the *Newbridge* to do so. We stopped to support the picket boat until she was clear. The torpedo did not explode.... All the boats then moved off towards the entrance, under a fire from rifles, with Maxims occasionally coming in.

The fire from the shore on the outward journey was considerably diminished as compared with the journey up, but it was still fairly rapid, and it seemed that no 3-pdrs. fired at us coming down. . ... On reaching the Point again, a Maxim and rifles on the left entrance opened fire on us. There were some heavier guns than Maxims and lighter than 3-pdrs. which seemed to be placed about half-way up on either side. When outside the entrance a 3-pdr. fired one or two shots near us, but I could not locate it. During the whole time we were in the river we kept up a constant fire with the Maxim and rifles, using the puffs of smoke from their guns as points of aim, as no men were visible at all.

The whole of this blocking expedition was carried through with but two killed and nine wounded. The former consisted of two seamen, and the latter included Lieutenant R. S. Triggs, R.N.R., who received a severe wound in the shoulder. Commander Fitzmaurice was convinced that:

> The casualties must have been very much greater if it had not been for the temporary plating, sand and bag protection put up in *Newbridge* and supporting craft; and the coolness displayed by Sub-Lieutenant Bremridge, and the efficient manner in which Petty Officer Chandler worked his Maxim.

For it was really a very narrow escape. The coxswain of this *Chatham* steam-cutter was shot through the head, so Bremridge himself took the wheel and received two bullets through his helmet, one of which grazed his head.

The *Duplex* was an iron steamer owned by the Eastern Telegraph Company, and was already forty-two years old. But she was only 17 feet deep, 214 feet long, and of 874 tons gross, so that she was moderately suited for her new role. Still, she had bad luck. She seemed to be coming along quite well, and her couple of 3-pdrs. doing good work, when suddenly a shell struck her bridge, and it was thus that Lieutenant Triggs got his injury; one signalman and two *lascars* being knocked out at the same time. She became unmanageable and had to make for the exit before—*Newbridge* was sunk.

It was only sometime later that native reports established an interesting fact: a lucky shell from one of the bombarding cruisers had exploded on Kiomboni peninsula and knocked out thirty men just as the *Newbridge* was being sunk. This coincidence was largely responsible for the German firing hereafter becoming very wild; otherwise not many British survivors could ever have reached the open sea again.

The *Dartmouth's* steam-cutter, which during these operations had been sent to make a reconnaissance up the Simba Uranga, got back safely with valuable data indicating that there was no defence of any sort up this river and no navigable channel for a vessel of *Königsberg's* draught. It was thus quite obvious that even at the highest tides Germany's cruiser would by this route find it impracticable to emerge. That was all very pleasing, and still more so because only on the previous day Captain Drury-Lowe's former gun-room mate of the Calliope, now Captain John Glossop of H.M.S. *Sydney*, had put an end to the *Emden's* career at the Cocos Islands in the Indian Ocean.

Thus, was removed within twenty-four hours a dual menace that had caused anxiety to transports and trading steamers on that wide sea. After the *Chatham's* Captain had been able to cable the result of the *Newbridge* obstruction, the Admiralty at once announced to the world that the *Königsberg* was "now imprisoned and unable to do any more harm." The British public, which a few days previously had been cast into gloom by the defeat of Admiral Cradock at Coronel, now felt that there was a brighter aspect.

Nevertheless, whilst the Admiralty were so well satisfied with this blocking of the Rufiji and considered the operation to have been " well-conceived and well executed," and made special note of achievements in the names of Commander Fitzmaurice; Lieutenant Johnsen (who fitted out the *Newbridge* at Zanzibar, brought her round to the Rufiji, and on the fateful day had the important duty of superintending anchors, cables and hawsers); Lieutenant Lavington (who did the navigation of that ship); Lieutenant-Commander Lang, Lieutenant Triggs, Sub-Lieutenant Bremridge and other officers; not one of them received a single decoration for this achievement.

This lack of recognition seems extraordinary, and was much commented upon in the Service; but happily, brave deeds have an historical vitality of their own. Their memory is kept alive through the ages and continues to inspire later generations when confronted with such apparently hopeless crises, for the opportunities of failure and utter disaster outnumbered the probabilities of success. As Captain Drury-Lowe well appreciated:

> The reports of similar blocking operations in previous wars, whether successful or not, did not indicate much chance as far as personnel was concerned.

It is to be added that happily some of the petty officers and men were, however, not forgotten, though it was no easy matter to discriminate when all hands had behaved with such quiet plucky devotion. The efforts of Petty Officer William Chandler, who from a completely exposed position in *Chatham*'s cutter, continued working his Maxim all the while with consummate coolness and efficiency; the endurance of Engine-room Artificer Edgar Wilkinson, who was in charge of this cutter's engines now and during the unsuccessful torpedo attack a few days previously; the pluck of Leading Signalman Frederick Raven aboard *Duplex* who, though wounded, still went on signalling; the calmness of Leading Seaman Walter Wade, who let go and worked the port bower anchor of *Newbridge*, heedless of the fire and his own exposed position—these were not recognised officially. On the other hand, the Distinguished Service Medal was awarded to four of their comrades, who well deserved such honour.

Able Seaman Herbert Dobson, who cleared away under heavy fire the electric circuit for blowing up the blockship; Leading Seaman Frederick Patterson, who had come from the *Goliath* and did splendid execution in the latter's picket boat, serving his 3-pdr. with great gallantry and no cover of any sort; Leading Seaman Alfred Rose, who acted as helmsman on the perilous upper bridge of the blockship, and was afterwards promoted to Petty Officer; Petty Officer Walter Harmer, who was in charge of the scuttling arrangements and had been a volunteer in *Goliath's* picket boat when under fire a few days previously—these rightly received the D.S.M.

The wounded were put aboard the *Duplex* and sent back the same night for Zanzibar, and this led to an incident which would have been amusing but for the thought of suffering men. Lieutenant Triggs being one of the latter, *Duplex* was now restored to the care of her own skipper, who was regarded as "a good seaman but fond of the bottle," and as a result of an unduly prolonged celebration after the *Königsberg*'s metaphorical bottling-up, this skipper ran the old cable ship on to the Dira Reef. It was 9 p.m., pitch darkness, and now he sprinkled the black sky by immediately letting off all his rockets. Away went the *Chatham* to find out what on earth was happening, stood by till day returned, towed her off at high water in the morning, and despatched her again. But the patients with injured faces, jaw shot away, and other painful wounds, had a thoroughly pitiful time, being too ill to be transferred aboard another ship.

Chapter 11

The Enemy at Bay

The situation now simplified itself in one sentence: the *Königsberg* was believed to have been locked in, and now she must be destroyed. But how? By what vessels?

It was quite evident that valuable modern cruisers, such as *Chatham* and her two sisters, could not be thrown away by sending them to follow in the *Königsberg's* track. They would certainly get aground (maximum draught of *Chatham* was 18 feet)—for it was considered that the German was afloat only at high tide—and it would be a difficult matter keeping them provisioned when every British supply ship would have to run the same perilous gauntlet which had only just failed to wipe out the flotilla this morning. Moreover, there was a dearth of light cruisers. They were needed on every ocean—Indian, Atlantic, Pacific—for the protection of trade routes. Raiders were bringing about serious results on the two latter, whilst on the former there might still be one of *Emden's* armed auxiliaries.

For Africa there was, too, a grave suspense following the Coronel disaster and preceding the Battle of the Falklands. Whither was von Spee bringing his victorious squadron? Was it not to South Africa? That would most certainly expose the British expeditionary army which was to be landed at Walfisch Bay against German South-West Africa: indeed Admiral King-Hall had declined to guarantee the safety of the necessary sea communications until von Spee was located and accounted for. The Cape squadron consisted solely of *Hyacinth* and *Astraea*, which the German admiral would have sent to the bottom with no more difficulty than he had disposed of *Good Hope* and *Monmouth*.

The difficulty of the Cape was overcome by sending Admiral King-Hall the two armoured cruisers *Minotaur* and *Defence*, and also the two light cruisers *Dartmouth* and *Weymouth*, and by this combined strength von Spee's force would have been well matched. Now the whole of the *Newbridge* episode of November 10 had worked with such clock-work precision that at 8 a.m. it was all over and the boats were back alongside their respective mother ships. So that same afternoon *Dartmouth* was already on her way south to the Cape, the *Weymouth* (after temporarily remaining as a watch off the Rufiji whilst the *Chatham* went up to Mombasa for coal) following on November 14 to join Admiral King-Hall likewise.

Then by what means was Captain Looff's ship to be wiped out? Long ago had Captain Drury-Lowe foreseen that the undertaking would require: (1) airplanes, and (2) very light-draught men-of-war, but able to carry 6-inch guns. In the meanwhile, the Rufiji delta must be blockaded both in order to prevent the *Königsberg* from coming out, and any vessels from bringing in stores that were so much needed now that the *Somali* had been burnt to a charred wreck. Airplanes seemed never to have been more desirable, for they would surely be able to reveal those secrets which the high trees effectually hid. The exact position of *Königsberg* could be located, the details of dark central Africa more adequately revealed than was manifest from the charts; and there would be little risk from the German forces at the river mouth.

The advance in aerial science and art during the last seventeen years (at time of writing), has been so vast and revolutionary, that one finds it scarcely easy to place oneself in those primitive days of the year 1914. Even during the first few weeks of the Great War some of the best experts expressed doubts as to the hostile value of airplanes, which were still as unreliable as the early motorcars, and as yet had to convince the incredulous. When, therefore, the *Chatham*'s captain asked the authorities for some assistance from the sky, it was a request which was as startling as it was original: the Royal Navy was only just accustoming itself to this new arm, and it was by no means universally approved among officers of the old school. Furthermore, not one of the seaplanes could be spared from Europe.

Now it so happened that, just before the war started, some commercial pioneer work was already under way in South Africa. A single-engined hydroplane of the Curtiss type, in charge of a Mr. Cutler, was engaged at Durban giving exhibition flights to a wondering public. Admiral King-Hall during his visit to that port in July discovered this young airman, and presently got him to bring his machine down to the Cape (Simon's Bay). The next thing, after purchasing this not very up-to-date seaplane, was to give Cutler a commission as a temporary officer in the Royal Navy, overhaul the machine in the best practicable manner, and put her aboard a liner which had been taken over as an Armed Merchant Cruiser.

The latter was the Union-Castle S.S. *Kinfauns Castle*, which in August had captured the German barque *Werner Vinnen* with 4,000 tons of coal. The liner, so familiar to South African passengers from England, had for a time been acting as guardship at Walfisch Bay until relieved by a battleship, but could now be spared for the East Coast. So it was, then, that on November 5—several days before the *Newbridge* affair—Captain Drury-Lowe was made happy by the receipt of Admiral King-Hall's telegram that the Curtiss seaplane might be expected on November 15.

Lieutenant Cutler, both then and today, deserved and won the highest admiration on the part of naval officers no less than aviators. Here was one who was both technically able and brilliantly fearless, but cursed by a machine whose chief characteristic was its erratic and unreliable nature. Add to this that the departure was very hurried, there were no spares of any sort available, and he had no mechanics. Fortunately, at a date when the flying enthusiasts in Britain and the colonies scarcely exceeded the number of swallows in an English winter, there happened among the junior officers of the *Kinfauns Castle* to be a midshipman of the Royal Naval Reserve named Gallehawk, who became a great ally of Cutler, and the two worked manfully in the hope of making the seaplane of real use.

Whilst the tug *Adjutant* and the big steam-launch *Helmuth* (both of which were taken from the enemy, though at different occasions) were now being armed at Zanzibar as blockade patrols off the Rufiji, it was hoped that *Duplex* might serve as the shallow craft that must give to *Königsberg* a series of knock-out blows. But here was to be disappointment. The bows of this old cable ship were found too weak for sustaining one of the lame *Goliath's* 6-inch guns, and a rather unfortunate dilemma arose. There was no other light vessel available off East Africa, so Durban was asked to produce one fit to carry such armament. Durban replied that she was unable, and thus the plain fact had to be faced: the enclosed German cruiser could not possibly be sunk until protected shallow steamers could be sent all the way out from England.

That must inevitably necessitate several months of delay; for, firstly, there might not be convenient craft as yet available; possibly they were being employed in other spheres (as for example along the North Sea littoral in expectation of a German landing); more than likely they had yet to be built. But in any case, such small vessels would need considerable time for the long passage out down the Bay of Biscay, through the Mediterranean and Red Seas, down the African coast to the Rufiji delta. In the meanwhile, it was much to be hoped that Lieutenant Cutler's seaplane would have good results. On November 14 the *Chatham*, once more coaled, was able to leave Mombasa, and next day met the *Kinfauns Castle* off Mafia Island. (The official history (*Naval Operations*, Vol. 1) errs in giving this date as November 6. Had that date been correct, the seaplane could have been used for the *Newbridge* operations of November 10.)

Welcome indeed was the sight of that converted liner! And still more warmly received was Cutler's seaplane, of which so much was expected. The next few days were busy ones, for whilst Cutler and Gallehawk were engaged doing some repairs, tuning up the engine, and getting the outfit into an airworthy condition, *Chatham* landed an armed boat's crew to examine the possibilities of Nioro002 Island (just north of Mafia) with a view to future use; chased and captured a dhow carrying interesting papers; and maintained the watch off the delta.

On November 19 all was ready for the long-expected ascent: the seaplane was to make a much-desired reconnaissance over the delta. But it may be explained from the first that not even a plucky, resourceful and eager young aviator can perform miracles with an impossible and already antiquated "bus." Admiral King-Hall has referred to Cutler as an officer of "the greatest gallantry and ability." To this day the Royal Air Force regards this warrior's feats as "brilliant." Captain Drury-Lowe's opinion of him was, "an entire novice at observation work, but a good Pilot and absolutely without fear." Nor has the world yet appreciated the hopeless task which was about to be attempted, with a seaplane that was satisfactory in scarcely one item. The *Chatham*'s captain summed up:

> She was old, the boat was very fragile, and the radiator leaked like a sieve, so that her time of flight was limited to about fifty minutes.

Fifty minutes? That would not allow her much margin, since she would have to start from Nioroor Island, cross the intervening sea to the mainland before going over the rivers, and then come all the way back again. This island had been selected as the base for *Kinfauns Castle* since it provided the seaplane with the best lee. That was an important consideration, for the machine refused to rise if there was the slightest lop, or if there was more than one person in her.

No Observer being possible, Cutler took the air single-handed, and this first trip was thoroughly thrilling. In order to give him a mark, the *Chatham* had anchored off the Simba Uranga mouth, and at 7.15 a.m. Cutler was seen coming over from Niororo at a height of about 4,000 feet. Thence he was swallowed up in some very thick clouds. Naked eyes, binoculars, telescopes, look-out men, saw no more of him. The fifty minutes sped by, and still not a sign. Perhaps he had crashed into the sea? Perhaps into the river? Was he a prisoner of the enemy? Or victim of a crocodile? Who could tell?

Both *Chatham* and *Kinfauns Castle* steamed about, searching here, there, the back of this island, the front of another. On everyone's lips was the unspoken sentence: "Cutler's gone! Bad luck!" In those early days of flying none but the brave and potentially heroic ever soared aloft: there were too many chances of disaster to tempt the average man. But Cutler had just the right temperament for not being hampered with thought of self-preservation as a primary principle. The hours ticked by, noon passed, one o'clock arrived: even the optimists began to doubt.

But just six hours after he had taken off from Niororo, he was discovered on Okusa Island, some 34 miles to the south of Niororo, and 18 miles to the southward of Mafia's most southern point. Was he dead? No: very much alive. Was he agitated? Quite the reverse. They found him, says Captain Lowe, "placidly bathing, under the impression that it was the same place he had started from." He had lost his bearings in the clouds, come down, and the machine was not destroyed. That day had the "Darkest Africa" of Livingstone and Stanley, the primeval forests and savage scenery, first become acquainted with a form of navigation which was within a few years to make the Cairo-Capetown voyage a mere pleasure trip. But Cutler had been more fortunate than chance usually permits. His radiator was incredibly incapable, and must be scrapped forthwith. Yes, but where could another be obtained at short notice in East Africa? Was there one city, town, or village in the whole continent which stocked spare airplane parts?

Certainly, no country could seem less encouraging, until someone thought of a Ford car running about at Mombasa. So, they wired to Mombasa, the Ford radiator was taken off and sent down to Niororo by H.M.S. *Fox*. This was fitted, and the seaplane once more got ready after the boat-hull had been rebuilt by willing hands. In the meantime, the *Chatham*'s evaporators had broken down through being choked with mud, and she had to lay off for two days at Zanzibar; but the *Adjutant* and *Helmuth*, each armed with one 3-pdr. and a couple of Maxims, together with minesweeping gear, arrived for patrolling and swept the channel to within 1½ miles of the river entrance. Then the weather became unsuitable for flying, but on November 22 Cutler made his second trip across the sky.

The Ford radiator worked satisfactorily, he was able to get right up the Suninga, make a fine reconnaissance and to locate the *Königsberg*. There she lay, a couple of miles beyond where she had been sighted three weeks ago, and we have no doubt as to the effect which this aerial visit had on the enemy, who must rely solely on concealment if she were to avert the fate which seemed to be awaiting her. Thus, far from unsuited as the seaplane was for the job assigned, it had proved already that with the help of aviation and the provision of shallow warships the task of wiping out *Königsberg* was a quite reasonable proposition. Unfortunately, this day indicated likewise the tenderness and frailty of this new arm; for on returning to his base Cutler's machine got smashed up so badly that the hull was beyond repair.

There happened by now to be another seaplane at Durban, so a telegram was sent to have it got ready, and in the morning *Kinfauns Castle* steamed off to fetch a new hull together with bombs. Those were the days when, happily, no wave of economy had swept over men's energies, and money was unlimited. Today it would seem strange that a great liner was despatched for so trifling an object: yet that object had immense possibilities, and no other vessel of such speed could be spared.

The *Chatham* was a hive of activity, one day arriving off Dar-es-Salaam and sending in Commander Fitzmaurice to inspect harbour and shipping once more; next day landing those trusted native spies at Ras Twana as before, and bringing them safely off two mornings later, in the meanwhile visiting one of those signal islands where an armed party found the German flag flying and destroyed the signal mast. The *Somali*: was shelled again, Komo Island received another search, three *dhows* were captured, of which one provided information concerning *Königsberg* and the other two were found full of foodstuffs.

Other *dhows* laden with goods intended for the blockaded enemy cruiser fell like ripe pears into the *Chatham's* lap, Kiomboni was once more treated to a bombardment, and now the collier *Assouan* was being prepared at Zanzibar by the same Lieutenant Johnson who had performed a similar duty in regard to *Newbridge*: for, if the Suninga needed this second blockship, it should be in readiness, and a special crew from *Chatham* was on board her. So passed the active interval.

If it were true (as some opined) that there was a passage between the *Newbridge* wreck and the western shore, sufficient to allow the enemy to squeeze through, then this could be remedied by another daring little expedition.

And now it was December 3. At 8 a.m. the *Kinfauns Castle* got back from Durban to Niororo. An hour later her commanding officer, Captain Denis Crampton, R.N., accompanied the seaplane as Observer, this being the first time that officer had ever been in the air. The *Königsberg* was clearly sighted, but she had evidently moved yet further up river. Next day Cutler took Commander Fitzmaurice up as Observer, further flights being made on the 7th, 8th and 9th, the seaplane working with every success.

But next happened such an incident as cast dull, heavy, gloom over all in the blockading force, sending a feeling of sharp pain and bitter disappointment through every ship's company.

CHAPTER 12

Within the Blockade

The flight of December 4 in company of the *Chatham*'s Commander had shown to a remarkable degree how readily it was now possible to be kept informed of the *Königsberg*'s movements: but simultaneously, it revealed how real these movements had become. It was essential that her progress must be watched from day to day.

She had apparently pushed her way further than ever, and round the corner, so that she was in one of the small cross channels which united the Simba Uranga with the Suninga. Indeed, if after all there should have been enough water, she had only to turn her bows a little eastward and she would be heading down the Simba Uranga seawards. This fresh development obviously demanded attention. Commander Fitzmaurice had noted that she was lying with her head approximately NNW., but into such a maze of creeks was the delta here cut up that it was hard to say exactly which she occupied, accurate fixing during one flight being not easy. Still, there she lay beneath the two aviators, with all awnings spread against the fierce sun, and very much alive. An interesting fact discernible was that all her *small* guns had been dismounted and placed along the river banks. The *Königsberg* was going to make a glorious fight till the very end.

By this tenth of December—just a month since *Newbridge* had been sunk—the seaplane had suffered deterioration and was incapable of carrying more than one at a time; so today Cutler rose up alone without an observer. Something went wrong, the engine gave trouble when in the vicinity of *Königsberg*, and it was seen with horror to come down—not off the Simba Uranga—but apparently further to the north off the Kikunja entrance. The *Helmuth* steam-launch, together with a motor-boat, proceeded to the rescue, and the latter with an armed party under Midshipman Gallehawk made a brave dash into the river. That young officer, ever so loyal and valuable a friend to the pilot, succeeded himself in making fast a line to the seaplane which had been beached. Regardless of the heavy fire from a party of Germans on the bank, Gallehawk carried through his work till the job was complete and the motor-boat went slowly ahead.

There was, alas! no sign of Cutler. He had cheated peril too often, and now the chapter was ended. Subsequently it was learnt that this brave officer had not been drowned, but had swum ashore and been taken prisoner. The seaplane was damaged by enemy fire till she was beyond repair, but Gallehawk did not fail to bring it back to the *Kinfauns Castle*, where it was packed up for transport. Such a machine and such a war pioneer, which had in spite of its natural deficiency performed novel and valuable work, could not be forgotten hurriedly: it had passed into the realm of proud historical relics. So, it was brought down to Durban, unpacked, and given an honoured resting-place in the local museum.

The British naval forces were now considerably handicapped, and kept on the alert without being able to know what the *Königsberg* was intending. Lucky it was that the *Emden* had been destroyed at the ripe opportunity: otherwise, her arrival with well-timed surprise might have wiped out all the small patrol craft and done sufficient damage to the *Chatham* as to weaken the watch that was being maintained. There was, too, always the possibility that one of Germany's raiders, disguised as a merchant vessel, but armed with torpedoes and guns, might suddenly swoop down out of a clear ocean and dominate the Rufiji entrance what time the *Chatham* was away at Mombasa coaling.

The next few weeks, in the absence of suitable shallow river craft, and reliable airplanes, must be spent marking time, carrying out the essential yet monotonous routine of blockade duties with only slight variations. The intense heat, the lack of fresh provisions, the absence of cold drinks, the difficulties of moving about in shoal waters at night, were decidedly trying though inevitably part of the campaign. The present predicament was not dissimilar to that when an armed culprit has barricaded himself within a house and the police await him impatiently outside. But sooner or later the house must be broken in, and the attackers with their lives in their hands must make a rush through the defences.

For the present every effort should be made to keep *Königsberg* isolated, (*a*) from news, (*b*) from food, fuel, or any other stores. With regard to the first, of course, she still possessed her wireless, but we could render the off-lying signal stations definitely useless; and, in respect of the second, it was possible by active vigilance to round up every dhow at sea, since the fine race of Arab seamen whose ancestors had sailed the ocean long before Englishmen made any progress in the marine arts, were still busy trying to make contact. It was, indeed, a pretty contest between sailing craft (whose rig remained much the same as it had for centuries) dodging about with confidence in tricky but familiar waters—and a modern turbine-driven cruiser relying on indifferent charts.

In these subsidiary efforts to starve out the enemy, much useful work could be accomplished by the smaller steamers, but their numbers were few and must be supplemented. One thing was quite certain: the *Königsberg*, after all these weeks of seclusion, must be reaching a state when the supply problem was approaching crisis. And the effect of immuration up a lonely mosquito-pestered African river must be as baneful for the German crew's spirit as it was for their physical health.

On the second day after Cutler's debacle, the *Duplex* was able to work off some revenge against the Kikunja detachment of Germans who had (some Opinions maintained) shot the aviator down to sea. On the northern Kikunja shore were enemy field guns, whilst on the south were Maxims; the stockades being on either bank. The *Duplex*, after shelling both these, announced that the stockades had been destroyed, but not a man was visible nor could a gun be discerned: so cleverly did the enemy ensconce himself. But that same night from 6 to 6.30 p.m. there was some extraordinary signalling noticeable. At the Simba Uranga entrance two pale green lights were burned, which were answered on Mafia Island by a blaze. Now and again would be shown from Simba Uranga a red light, and there would be fires everywhere on the island. Three nights later occasional lights were observed at all three delta entrances of Kikunja, Simba Uranga, and Kiomboni.

Helmuth was sent to inspect Komo Island (where, it will be remembered, the German signal officer had been captured weeks ago), but every house was found to be shut up, the place deserted, the hens and cows being the sole evidence of life. So, this signal station had ceased to function. Kwale Island (just to the north of Komo) was similarly discovered to have been deserted; so, the *Chatham* partially demolished the Customs House where a signal mast had been fitted on the roof facing the African shore. It seemed not improbable that the Germans would again attempt to use Komo, for it was conveniently adjacent to the Rufiji mouths; so, an armed party of a dozen men was sent to occupy this island and prevent leading marks being erected at night as aids for some dhow or other vessel trying to enter Kikunja. In charge of the twelve men was Sub-Lieutenant Bremridge who had acquitted himself so splendidly on the day of *Newbridge's* sinking.

The Kikunja now, in truth, becomes of greater importance during our story, and a reference to the chart immediately indicates the reason: for if we regard the rivers Kikunja and Simba Uranga as two sides of a triangle with their base on the Indian Ocean, then the apex was that very spot inland where the *Königsberg* had been sighted by Cutler's seaplane. A new phase seemed imminent, and perhaps the imprisoned enemy might after all attempt escape down the Kikunja. So now soundings were made at the approaches during low water to compare them with the figures on the German chart, and three dummy mines were laid two miles off the entrance, whilst another three were deposited off the Simba entrance. Tidings of these precautions would soon reach Captain Looff and cause him to hesitate, should he really be contemplating a dash into the open.

Not long was the interval before the Simba Uranga encampment began communicating; for between 7 and 8 p.m. on the same night (December 18) the *Königsberg's* searchlights were busy from aloft making signals, either to that post or at any rate to Mafia Island. A weird glare this was, proceeding from 9 or 10 miles inland, through the black African night and over the still forest tops, suggestive of some impending coup, a token that the ship's company, sealed up within sweating steel sides, were restless and getting desperate.

Every one of the outlying islands now seemed to have added potentialities, and some of the other delta mouths to demand greater attention. Thus, the *Adjutant* was sent to examine Boydu Island, whilst *Chatham* inspected the Msala mouth which opens just opposite. At Christmas-time, then, the Rufiji blockade consisted of H.M.S. *Fox*, the armed merchant cruiser *Kinfauns Castle* (after her return from Durban), the S.S. *Duplex*, the tug *Adjutant*, and the steam-launch *Helmuth*; the *Chatham* being away at Mombasa for coaling and defects. Nor did the *Fox's* people on Christmas Day forget to remind the enemy of the inconvenience that was being caused this festal time. A poem of greeting was sent that began thus:

'Köny,' we wish you the best of good cheer,
But blame you for stopping our Xmas beer."

To this greeting the *Königsberg* replied as follows:

'Thanks. The same to you. If you want to see me, I am always at home. Looff. *Königsberg.*

But there could have been little enough "cheer" for either the men in the German cruiser, or those detachments entrenched at the harbour mouths kept perpetually expectant. In the meanwhile, *dhows* continued to be shadowed and captured, the terrific sun made the lives of all combatants unenviable, but for the blockaders there was this one satisfaction: just as the Grand Fleet in the North Sea was producing that pressure which would eventually after several years starve the German nation into weakness of will and body, so the miscellaneous squadron off the Rufiji had effectually set up its barrier against any more supplies entering by sea.

This being so, the time had come when the *Chatham* could be better employed elsewhere, and on January 2 she left Mombasa for Aden. Now that the Falklands Battle had long since abolished von Spee's threat to South Africa, the *Weymouth*, on December 29, had been able to arrive back off the Rufiji and take charge, but it was already obvious that the thin squadron must be strengthened by other units capable of patrolling shoal waters. For this reason, Admiral King-Hall got together a number of steam-trawlers as well as whalers, armed them, fitted them for minesweeping, and sent them up from South Africa.

In many respects these, by their moderate draught, good sea-keeping qualities, and stoutness of hull, were just the types for remaining closer to the shore than such valuable units as the cruiser and liner. For some time past the whaling industry off the South African coast had been developing a singularly wholesome little steamer, which under the command of a lieutenant R.N.R. now began to relieve the original patrol organisation. Than a whaler or a steam-trawler there is no abler vessel—size for size—the whole world over. By this date every area of the British Isles was relying very considerably on such craft; so, when the *Fly, Pickle, Childers, Salamander* and *Echo* undertook the watch on the Rufiji, with well-trained crews, they were to uphold the same excellent standard that had been set by the improvised navy in European waters.

During the last weeks of 1914 those three previously mentioned steam-craft, *Duplex* (commanded by Lieutenant Bryan Gordon of the Royal Indian Marine), *Adjutant* (commanded by Acting Sub-Lieutenant W. Price, R.N.R.), and *Helmuth* (commanded by Acting Sub-Lieutenant C. J. Charlewood, R.N.R.), had been hard at it. Captain Drury-Lowe recorded:

These three officers had shown great zeal and ability in carrying out their duties, which necessitated their almost constant employment during day and night in waters difficult for navigation, and had shown coolness and courage under fire in action.

But the ships' companies consisted of scratch crews from the *Chatham*, *Fox*, *Goliath*, *Kinfauns Castle* and the sunken *Pegasus*, the trio of Captains being lent respectively from the *Fox*, *Goliath* and the *Pegasus*. Whereas we have seen that such a cruiser as the *Chatham* drew about 18 feet, and had to keep her distance from the river mouths at low water; the *Duplex* with her 13 feet, the *Adjutant* drawing only 11 feet, and the *Helmuth* but 8 feet, could stand well in. The trawlers and whalers—some of them were fitted with wireless—whilst needing more water than the steam-launch would be able, among other duties, to keep a look-out during an airplane reconnaissance and if necessary, steam to the assistance of such flying craft as the enemy's guns should wing.

Such, then, was the reconstituted system which was to ensure that in the New Year the enemy should not under any circumstances escape without such an act being immediately made known. The light patrol steamers, being allocated close up to the respective mouths, would be able to give warning of any such attempt. It was realised that the *Königsberg* with her 4.1-inch guns would have no difficulty in sinking the patrols and then steaming away to sea. But at the ocean end of these narrow channels there would be a cruiser ready to settle the matter once and for all time.

It was fitting at the beginning of January to take stock of the situation, review the position, and consider it afresh from the enemy's mind. It did not seem unlikely that the smart *Königsberg*, which at one occasion had escorted the *Kaiser*, when the latter visited England in the *Hohenzollern*, would at her selected date make a bold effort to break through this encirclement of miscellaneous vessels. For over three months more than 300 German officers and men, sweltering in the terrible heat, had been compelled to endure their ship's inactivity. Some, indeed, though a mere handful, were being employed on the river banks, and she could afford to sacrifice them, together with her eight 2.1 inch as well as four machine-guns, for purely defensive land purposes. The ten 4.1-inch guns, if not both torpedo-tubes, were likely to suffice when she sallied forth. And was it not conceivable that

Captain Looff's hand might be forced? That his people might even persuade him against his will to take a big risk and get away?

This immediately brought into prominence two fundamental questions which required meticulous examination before satisfactory answers could be given:

1. Was it possible for *Königsberg* to emerge by all, or any, of the delta rivers?
2. If such a possibility were conceded, was she *capable* of coming out?

With regard to (1) the whole sum of evidence, and of opinion, derived from three only sources: (*a*) the charts and sailing directions British and German, but especially the latter; (*b*) the reports of well-tested, and apparently reliable, natives; (*c*) the seaplane reconnaissances, consisting of the two flights made respectively by Captain Crampton and Commander Fitzmaurice. Now it boiled down to this: Which of the five rivers, Suninga, Simba Uranga, Kikunja, Kiomboni, and Msala could be navigated by *Königsberg*?

There was complete unanimity on the part of *(a)*, *(b)* and *(c)* that the Suninga certainly was navigable. Both (*a*) and (*b*) agreed that there was not water enough in the Simba Uranga, though (*c*) conveyed the idea that it was practicable as a channel. Similarly, was the testimony concerning the Kikunja, though the practicability seemed more doubtful. As to the Kiomboni river all three sources ruled it out as impossible. Similarly in respect of the Msala river, but with this proviso: whilst according to (*a*) there was insufficient depth over the bar at the entrance, there was adequate water within, though on the authority of (*c*) the river was too narrow and winding for a ship so long as *Königsberg*.

"Boombi" and his two brother Africans were insistent that a ship which had proceeded so far up the Suninga as *Königsberg* could return by no other way than that by which she had advanced. There were too many intricate shoals in the higher reaches of the other rivers. And certainly, no warship had ever used any branch other than the Suninga. On the other hand, the seaplane observations had been made from a height of 3,000 feet when it was low water springs, though one must not forget that it was scarcely easy to tell exactly where the mud banks ended.

The *Newbridge* had been sunk in the centre of the Suninga channel with bows to the northern bank and stern aground to the southern;

and whilst the officers who sank her did not consider it possible for a ship to pass between the northern bank and the *Newbridge's* bows, yet the seaplane observers thought otherwise.

On the whole, then, it was no rash assumption that the *Königsberg*, under the most favoured conditions, could not emerge from her imprisonment except by the way she had entered, and this was barely practicable.

Then as to (2), Was she in a condition suitable for such an attempt? The only available information was from the three above-mentioned natives, who were unanimous that *Königsberg* had used up all her coal and was now burning wood. Fast cruisers such as this 23-knotter are notoriously greedy of fuel and need frequent replenishing. That which she had received from the *Präsident* would not last long at fast steaming, and her maximum coal bunker capacity being 850 tons, she would not be able to get far over the Indian Ocean if the same space were filled with the less serviceable wood.

Even if she still had quite a modicum of coal, the inference continued that the *Königsberg* was for some reason not fit to try a dash into the open and there hope to rely on capturing a casual merchantman; for, otherwise, it was difficult to explain why from the date (September 20) when she sank the *Pegasus*, until the day (October 30) when she was located by the *Chatham*, she deliberately remained inactive. Had she been in all respects ready for further fighting, why had she taken such steps to conceal herself?

The motives of this mystery ship were becoming manifest now that the mosaic of known facts was so nicely being pieced together. She had coaled from the *Präsident's* lighters on September 15; she had, after sinking the *Pegasus* at dawn, scurried back at once to enter the Rufiji by the Suninga; she wanted to be sure of getting in without risk of grounding, and therefore needed high water springs. Now in September 20 the tides were at springs, and it was high water off the Rufiji about 4 p.m.; therefore, she had time enough to reach the delta after her Zanzibar trip, and water enough to reach her anchorage 3 miles upriver. It was fortunate for the enemy that the *Pegasus* had chosen her boiler-cleaning dates to allow all this to be possible.

Having regard to the highly efficient, widespread intelligence and signalling system along the coast and between the islands, the German cruiser must have known that the *Chatham* did not arrive on the scene till over a week later. Captain Looff must likewise have learned when Captain Drury-Lowe was away to the south, leaving the rest of the

East African area unprotected as to its shipping. Why did not *Königsberg* make a sortie across the trade routes and sink one of the French liners? Why not treat Mombasa to a spectacular bombardment?

The answer still seemed to be found in the statement that she lacked coal. And there was other evidence that could make it look as if she was about to come out: the landing of all her smaller guns on the river banks might or might not indicate the intention to prolong her stay, but if one day these guns were suddenly removed, then this could be taken as a true warning. There were only two methods of finding out such a hint. Aerial investigation would be the surest: but that just now was impossible. The other way was to keep sending the smaller patrol craft within reasonable distance of the entrance, make occasional attacks, and so draw the enemy's fire. If the Germans made no reply, then something might be impending at the next spring tides.

It was for this reason that two days before Christmas our armed tugs carried out such an assault, and ascertained the permanence of defences. No imminent departure was probable.

There remained the primary duty of completing the *Königsberg's* isolation by cutting off the last and largest of these islands. This was Mafia, which in spite of the reefs and islets that extended between it and the mainland was in close touch with Captain Looff and a valuable outpost. The difficult navigation through uncharted coral patches gave to Mafia Island a certain amount of natural security; but, as we have perceived, it was within searchlight signalling distance of the *Königsberg*, and this could not be tolerated.

Mafia was altogether too adjacent, it was too conveniently placed off the Rufiji mouths for us to feel happy as long as it remained in German hands: it must be captured and occupied, but such was a soldier's rather than a sailor's task, and 400 troops would be requisite. However, these were forthcoming, and on January 10, 1915, Mafia was taken; work at once was started to prepare a suitable ground whereon airplanes could land. There was also found to be a good anchorage off the island at Tirene Bay where the reefs made a sheltered enclosure.

Whilst it was evident that the *Königsberg* could not yet be prevented from obtaining supplies from the mainland—and that must continue until the British Army in East Africa had obtained the upper control— these were of minor importance compared with the other results. Never was there a better illustration of what sea-power can mean in war. For whilst ashore Germany was in a military sense far superior to our strength, yet we possessed superiority afloat, which in turn permitted transports to be moved at will and kept the enemy's colonies in perpetual suspense lest an expeditionary force would descend upon them. Command of the sea enabled the military to pass in safety to Mafia, and thus transform an enemy outpost into an excellent base for flying, much nearer to the scene of operations than the original Niororo, a splendidly protected against all the prevailing winds.

With the departure of *Chatham* from the Rufiji ended the first great phase in the *Königsberg* campaign; but all these separate steps which we have so closely followed cannot convey the full extent of the vast picture. The danger of uncertainty and partial knowledge is that it tends to create false inferences, wrong theories. But *Chatham*'s Captain by working logically, gathering every fact and rumour, sifting the probable from the improbable, raking through the potentialities until only one remained to be tested for final veracity, solved the mystery with the minimum of naval forces and in the most convincing manner. As an example of intellectual achievement, this initial part of our story by its neatness and promptness, its steady approach towards a definite end through a maze of side issues, is in itself of compelling interest.

But it was really only the first act of the drama, wherein we become well acquainted with most of the players, the dominant problem, the setting, the tempo, till the curtain suddenly descends and leaves us curious to know the complications leading up to the crisis. The pace now quickens, mystery has given way to intensive action, novelty has added a keener zest to the struggle.

CHAPTER 13

The Sky Service

When at length, the *Chatham* had dispensed with the services of those three Kiomboni natives, it was indicative of the change which had come over the problem: the old must give way to the new, the primitive methods to the most up-to-date. "Boombi" was landed for the last time. He was secure and happy, there was no longer a chance of getting his throat cut by the Germans, or even of being beaten. On the contrary he had been able to avenge the ill-treatment, to obtain sound and helpful information against the common enemy; and by several plucky secret trips along the Rufiji delta at great risk of his life, to provide valuable intelligence.

So now he was revelling in his personal liberty, enjoying the freedom of the Indian Ocean: for he received the handsome reward of Rs. 600, and this made of him a rich man. Captain Drury-Lowe remarked:

> I last saw him in Zanzibar, dressed in all the colours of the rainbow, the possessor of a fine *dhow* and a new wife.'

And before we finally quit this subject of espionage, which was so assiduously practised by the Germans not less than by ourselves, it is interesting to find that our late enemies were impressed by what they regarded as a "highly efficient system of espionage" along the whole coast and directed from Zanzibar. This is a post-war statement and made by a German naval officer. It shows that in a period when we were disappointed with our own intelligence service and were brought face to face with the efficiency of all those signalling stations, we were unduly pessimistic.

One of the most attractive features in this *Königsberg* conundrum is the valour of both combatants. The uncertainty of the last act, the surprises that each side was continually springing: these were indeed most significant. But outstanding were the persistent patience, the refusal to admit that any circumstances could overcome stout hearts; and with all this there was a daring cleverness which arouses our admiration. As an instance of varying fortune—of that sudden twist which makes drama so fascinating—consider the 250-ton tug *Adjutant*. This German steamer, as we have watched, had been made a prize by H.M.S. *Dartmouth*, who found her in the Mozambique channel and towed her up to Mombasa.

Thereafter very excellent was the work which was performed under the White Ensign, and we can well understand how galling it must have been for the German detachments holding the Rufiji entrances daily to see this steamer so near to them yet too far away. How the gunners, many a time, must have set their sights on the tall thin funnel and blazed away in the hope of disabling her, and ending this insult!

The *Adjutant* led a charmed life, and all was well until the beginning of February in this year 1915; but now she tempted fate unduly. She was making one of her reconnaissances and nosing her way in too closely, when the shore shelled her with such violence and accuracy that her steam pipe was severed and she was put out of action. Finished! She could go neither ahead nor astern. All energy had been taken away from her, and there was no alternative for the crew but to surrender: so, the British patrol was weakened by one unit, and the Germans were able to place this armed vessel inside the Simba Uranga mouth though not far from the entrance. She would be perfectly placed for dealing death to any more of those expeditions coming round the Kiomboni corner with a blockship.

We must here leave the *Adjutant*, though in a later chapter we shall not fail to see the brilliant adventures which were to mark the remainder of her war career. In the photograph (which was taken by a German officer) where she is proudly flying her national flag at the masthead, she looks not very different from any other ocean tug, except for the improvised t'gallant bridge. But, whilst in other naval wars the same vessel can be found being captured and then recaptured, this *Adjutant* not merely changed over from a mercantile to a war ship, but she changed her locale from salt water to fresh, making a great leap of several hundred miles— not by river, but by land. It is just such an ingenious achievement that we shall presently find so admirable.

In the meanwhile, there was a choice bit of feverish activity going on within a London building: one of those incidents which the cinema can convey to the mind with just a few feet of film as a flash-back, but an historian needs far more words in narration. Captain Drury-

Lowe had been pressing the Admiralty to send out new airplanes, and the loss of Cutler had been more than that of a gallant pilot: it was a robbing of the East African Navy's eyesight just at the least convenient moment. No other means of seeing over the mangrove-tops was possible; and even the most conservative, critical, imaginations had suddenly become convinced that aerial reconnaissances were invaluable, that flying-machines could do something besides crashing. They had proved, beyond all manner of doubt, that they were the squadron's eyes, its elongated telescopes too. But in those days, there were still so few airplanes and aviators, and they were badly needed in Europe. The great traditions of the Sky Service had not yet been made, and in any case was not this Rufiji affair just another of those side shows?

But so long as the *Königsberg* remained afloat, even up the swampy river, she was too serious a threat, and her sister *Emden* had left behind unforgettable impressions of the danger to our trade routes. Moreover, the more protracted was *Königsberg's* survival, the less did it increase British naval prestige. The public and press wished for results, and something more than the steady silent pressure of blockades whether in the North Sea or off the African coast. Something must be done. The sudden stoppage of aerial activity must be remedied.

So, in December 1914 the Admiralty and Air Department decided to send out a small squadron of seaplanes, whilst Flight-Lieutenant J. T. Cull, R.N., was selected to proceed in command. This choice could not have been better. Today he is one of the most distinguished officers in the Royal Air Force, but in those early times he was a pioneer, whose foresight and vital energy allied with an utter ignoring of personal peril to form a connection between the old Navy and the new Air arm. The nearest analogy is to be found in that earlier enterprise which had already been performed by naval officers specialising in submarines.

Cull received his orders in the first week of January 1915, and with him were sent Flight-Lieutenant H. E. Watkins, R.N., together with a party of eighteen men, one of whom joined up at 48-hours' notice straight from Messrs. Sopwiths' works, and another was actually a director of a well-known firm, his expert knowledge of propellers being a most desirable acquisition when so little was known of the problems connected with tropical flying. Expressive of that undeveloped age is the fact that though officially here was the Royal Naval Air Service's Expeditionary Squadron No. 4, it consisted of exactly two seaplanes, with 100-h.p. engines, and a certain amount of stores (including 2000

THE AVIATOR WHO SPOTTED FROM THE SKY
Flight-Lieutenant (now Group-Captain) J. T. Cull, whose gallantry in the air was largely responsible for the destruction of the *Königsberg*. A pioneer of naval flying, this officer had some remarkable escapes from death in the Rufiji district.

gallons of petrol) hurriedly collected, before the whole outfit sailed from Tilbury Docks on January 16 aboard the S.S. *Persia*. On February 8 the expedition reached Bombay, where the *Kinfauns Castle* had arrived, and thus Midshipman Gallehawk was again to employ his enthusiasm with the best advantage.

The two machines were unpacked at one of the jetties of Bombay dockyard, erected, flown and tested within a couple of days, notwithstanding the heat. Unaccustomed to tropical climate, the scratch party toiled day and night; unloading, assembling, towing out of the basin, till finally flying. Quick work!

Thence, leaving Bombay in the *Kinfauns Castle* for Africa, the expedition arrived at Niororo Island on February 20, and the difficulties forthwith began. Young aviators of today scarcely can realise the temper-breaking obstacles which in the early days of flying confronted a zealous officer at every step. This expedition had been despatched with the intention not merely to observe the *Königsberg*, but to destroy her by bombs weighing from 16 lbs. to 50 lbs. It should be added that the two Sopwiths were new productions, whose characteristics were practically unknown.

Everything had to be learned, and that meant a great deal: but the first discovery was something of a shock. When at Niororo the first machine with pilot, observer, petrol, two 16-lb. and two 50-lb. bombs started to take off, she determinedly declined to leave the water. After four days of experimenting, trying this combination and that, she certainly rose into the air with the pilot and enough petrol for one hour; yet even under these disappointing conditions the maximum height to which she could be persuaded was only 1,500 feet. As against this there had been the breaking of propellers and other mishaps, and within the first week of reaching this island station the second seaplane had suffered a hopeless crash.

The outlook was none too bright, and to each mind it seemed pretty definite that the *Königsberg* would never be bombed. In the whole of Africa no other machines existed, it would be months before replacements could come out from home, and the same catena of worries which Cutler had experienced now had to be repeated. But such hindrances are the opportunities for men's resource and renewed efforts. The surviving seaplane must be experimented with, nursed, maintained as nearly towards efficiency as possible, and above all the mishaps must not be permanent; all of which tried the tempers of the party not less than the sun taxed their bodies. They had, indeed, come

THE BLOCKADE-RUNNER

The S.S. *Kronborg* (ex-*Rubens*) got into Mansa Bay through H.M.S. *Hyacinth's* engines giving out. The photograph shows the excellent effect of the *Hyacinth's* shooting over trees from outside. A 6-inch shell has wrecked the blockade-runner's funnel.

out to carry on war with weapons whose technique still remained to be learnt.

For example, the engines were of the "*Monosoupape*" type, which depended for air supply on the opening of the exhaust valve and the passage through a nose-piece. That might function satisfactorily in Europe, but it was unsuitable off Africa where the atmosphere is of thinner quality. This led to a series of experiments which in peace time would have been of entertaining duration, but every failure meant another day's grace to the German cruiser. Petrols of different densities were tried after being fetched from such stocks as Zanzibar could supply, and mixed in varying proportions with the aviation spirit; changes were made in the engine's timing so as to leave the exhaust valve open for a longer period; a funnel was fitted to induce more air through the nose-piece; compressed air (and likewise oxygen) were even attempted, but the results remained uncertain and discouraging. The only appreciable bit of discovery was that on days when the air was unusually humid the machine climbed less badly than on other occasions.

But amid all these tantalising preliminaries there was quite a humorous aspect, which cannot be better described than in the following words which Flight-Lieutenant (now Group-Captain) Cull has been good enough to give me, he writes:

> The usual method of getting machines out from the ship, was to hoist them out by the main derrick in a folded condition, a line being rove through a small block on the tail float, which a whaler would secure before the machine touched the water. On arrival in the water alongside the ship, pilot and passenger would unfold the wings, while the whaler would stand by to tow the machine clear. When clear of the ship's side, the passenger would start up the engine from his seat, and since passengers were usually at a discount, the passenger, as soon as he had started up the engine would take a header over the side and swim to the boat, which by this time had allowed the line to reeve through the block thereby releasing the machine.
>
> For some reason or other, although it was known that the waters we were working in were infested with sharks, no signs of these were seen until about the end of April, which coincided with a change in the monsoon, and apparently brought the sharks round from the other side of the island.... The last occa-

sion on which the passenger jumped overboard was when, having left the machine, the pilot observed two large and ominous-looking fins between the boat and the machine. Luckily the attention of the passenger was called to the danger as soon as he broke surface, and he managed to clamber back on to the floats.

Early in March there arrived off the Rufiji delta H.M.S. *Goliath*, now flying the flag of Admiral King-Hall, who was free to take charge of operations, seeing that the South African anxieties had passed. Before the month was out, he shifted his flag to the *Hyacinth*, and the *Goliath* was sent off to the Dardanelles where in the month of May she was sunk by enemy torpedoes. It was about the middle of March that in an endeavour to solve the seaplane engine trouble, Admiral King-Hall summoned a committee of local "experts" from Zanzibar. Lieutenant Cull remarked:

> We were rather perplexed, as to whom the committee could consist of, as we knew everyone in Zanzibar and none of them had ever professed any expert knowledge of internal combustion engines; while Gnome engines were an unknown factor before our arrival. However, the admiral, attended by staff and committee, duly arrived, were received with great ceremony and escorted down below to our workshops, an attempt being made on our part to appear as though we did not recognise in the committee old friends of ours of the Club, whom we certainly never had suspected of being experts up to that day. On our arrival down below, where everything was nicely laid out, one of the committee rather spoilt the effect by jeering at another member who had accused a Gnome engine of possessing rotating cylinders; but everyone kept a straight face.

So, whilst nothing practical directly happened from this amusing incident, it had indirect results. The admiral and his staff could not fail to be struck by the fact that in those trying conditions of sticky heat neither the engine nor structure of the seaplane could be relied upon. Seeing how long-suffering and forbearing were the flying officers and mechanics created, indeed, a sympathetic interest which was to express itself by the Admiral cabling to England for more machines and further supplies of spare parts. Nor was that all. He had appointed as his Flag-Commander one whom he had reason to regard as "a most gallant and valuable officer." This was commander the Hon. Richard Bridgeman, whose heroism and pathetic end we shall witness in a later chapter. From the first the flag-commander became a good friend to the Air Squadron amid all their troubles: he "took the keenest practical interest in flying," says Cull, "and was everything to us."

As illustrative of the unforeseen problems which the aviators had to wrestle with—quite apart from the engines themselves—let us mention the seaplane floats. Frequently the bottom of each would peel off, thus causing the machine to heel over and sink, consequently creating additional work of salvage and long hours of refitting. Of course, the excessive heat was responsible for these defects, and every effort was used to make such modifications as would cure the trouble. With no little ingenuity the floats were now given exhaust pipes to let out the hot air; the float bottoms were covered with plates fashioned from beaten-out petrol tins, and the floats were kept filled with water when the seaplane was hoisted inboard. For even whilst resting on the *Kinfauns Castle's* deck, the air within the floats would rise to an alarming temperature.

Salving the machine even from shallow water, with all hands on the tow rope hauling through the mud, was not always one jolly frolic splashing about in the sea. Sometimes half a dozen men would be laid up in bed for the next three days with severe sunburn, swathed in picric acid bandages. But such inconveniences were forgotten when it was learnt that, as a result of the cabling to England, the Air Department had decided the present seaplane could not be usefully employed, but three others of a type more suited for tropical conditions were being sent out as early as possible.

By the middle of April, then, we can imagine with what happiness the R.N.A.S. officers and men arrived down the coast at Durban where they met H.M.S. *Laconia*, which had just brought the heavy packing cases. This fine steamer was none other than one of the latest Cunard liners, now commissioned as an armed merchant cruiser carrying eight 6-inch guns. She brought not merely the packing-cases, but a capital motor-boat (together with a crew of three) for the Royal Naval Air Service's use.

Splendid! Most considerate! The boat would become exceedingly useful.

But it was decided to open the great white packing-cases, and to erect the machines on one of the Durban jetties where cranes were convenient. The fastenings were undone, the contents revealed themselves, and now came the shock. Here was yet another disappointment: here was a most distressing surprise. This second batch of machines were not new marvels, but old, old friends of the type which the R.N.A.S. had been using last year off the Medway at the Isle of Grain station. Not only that, but the engines were found to be in a bad condition, necessitating a great deal of overhaul before flying could be attempted.

On the voyage back to Niororo Island the hours aboard *Laconia* were thus fully occupied. These seaplanes were of the Short type, and they had barely reached Niororo on April 23 than trial flights demonstrated that if the machines were old they certainly appeared an improvement on the two Sopwiths. What was more, it seemed beyond the realm of doubt that at last the *Königsberg* reconnaissances, which had been unattempted during the last four months, could now be resumed and Cutler's work continued where it had been left off.

So much, then, for the new development already begun, of which important effects might accrue quite soon. Wireless and ocean cables, liners and harbour organisations, had co-operated to supply the Rufiji blockaders with three fresh pairs of eyes. Distance of a few thousand miles had meant nothing, expense was not considered, safety of transit was negligible thanks to that other blockade which the Grand Fleet and its Northern Patrol of armed merchant cruisers off the Scottish coast was imposing. Command of the sea, once established, had made it possible to move packages of airplanes in war time with scarcely more difficulty than in days of peace. Thus far, so good.

But even the most stringent enclosure by sea is not wholly inviolable, and for the right kind of men with the right kind of ship there is a wonderful fascination in blockade running. In the past this sort of adventure has provided some of the biggest thrills of history and fiction alike, for the reason that the chances of disaster heavily outnumber the possibilities of success. So now events of previous wars were to repeat themselves, and the German Admiralty, at the very time that the British Admiralty was completing these aerial details against Kongsberg, was launching a most enterprising task which aimed to relieve the German cruiser of her long-endured agony and suspense.

And before we pass on to watch Lieutenant Cull soar into the air, we must needs grasp the details of the enemy's astute counterstroke. Once more the pace was quickened, once more the approach of spring tides brought along increased anxiety for the Rufiji squadron. Of unsubstantiated reports concerning the German cruiser and her friends there had not been any lack. The problem from the first, as we have seen, was to determine which were false bits of hearsay and which were genuine clues. But now there reached Admiral King-Hall a certain piece of intelligence, a specified warning, which could not possibly be ignored, even if it should prove as unfounded as the other tales.

CHAPTER 14

The Relief Ship Comes

Those of us who paid attentions to the opinions uttered by German naval experts before the war will recollect the prediction that whenever hostilities should break out between their country and Britain, the latter would base its main strategy on a powerful blockade. This forecast was not inaccurate, and our enemy was not slow to perceive that the only way of bursting through the patrol cruisers would be to make every possible use of darkness, moonless nights, short days, thick weather; keep a smart look-out for any masts or funnels, and even go right up to the latitude of Iceland before passing into the Atlantic.

On August 4, 1914, the North German Lloyd S.S. *Kaiser Wilhelm der Grosse*, which was the first of the blockade runners to leave home, passed by the coasts of Norway and Iceland, got safely down to the north-west of Africa and after a brief success came to a sudden end. In the following October the *Berlin*, another big steamer of the same line, started out from the Jade, passed between the Faroes and Iceland, eventually reaching her assigned area off the North Irish coast, but on the return journey was compelled to intern herself in a Norwegian port. But the interesting fact had been established that in spite of the Grand Fleet, and all the detailed arrangements to deny egress from the North Sea, it was not wholly impossible for a vessel to succeed.

This point requires no further stressing beyond calling attention to the truth that subsequent attempts usually occurred not earlier than the month of November in any year and not later than March, whether for departing or returning. Short days of more or less bad weather in those northern latitudes could generally be relied upon during such a period. (Readers who care to pursue the subject will find the exploits of the *Maewe, Seeadler, Greif, Wolf* and *Leopard*, with details of how they rushed our blockade, narrated in my *The Sea-Raiders*.)

Encouraged by the evasion of these two somewhat unsuitable liners—for they were far too big and conspicuous—the German Admiralty resolved to send out a steamer which was not likely to attract immediate attention on the horizon, but was of a kind that might be seen any day of the week round the British Isles trading between Denmark or Scandinavia and England or Scotland. This vessel was to go round the west of Ireland, down the North and South Atlantic, past South Africa and up the Indian Ocean to German East Africa, where she was to carry out the dual task of bringing war supplies for the German troops and effecting a rendezvous with the *Königsberg*.

One can afford at this date to admire the daring conception of such a plan no less than the pluck of those who were keen to attempt its execution. For, be it understood, this was the most ambitious voyage hitherto attempted by Germany's mystery ships. It paved the way for such able adventurers as Count Nikolaus zu Dohna-Schlodien, Count Felix von Lückner and Captain Nerger whose achievements will never be forgotten; it showed that nothing at sea is impossible when courage is united with determination. For, on the face of it, the scheme seemed suicidal. Even if the black nights, the rain storms and the gales of wind, permitted the steamer to bluff the Northern blockade, she would still have to run the gauntlet of British cruisers patrolling in the neighbourhood of the Canaries and Cape Verdes, to say nothing of a chance meeting with some man-of-war in the Bay of Biscay.

If she gave the South of Africa a wide berth, she must close the land again and make a very risky attempt to penetrate the second blockade that included the Rufiji mouths. Indeed, the entire trip from Germany to her destination must be one prolonged suspense, and the nearer she approached the journey's end the more likely would be her sudden demise. Could she have the slightest hope of dodging those vigilant cruisers, whalers, trawlers and others so intent on their job? Certainly, on paper the relief steamer seemed to have one chance in a million.

It was the month of February, 1915, the Northern blockade was daily becoming more stringent, but the days were still short and the nights long. Admiral Jellicoe wrote, (*The Grand Fleet*):

> The activities of the 10th Cruiser Squadron, were daily increasing, and the number of ships passing the blockade line unexamined was becoming very small. During one week in February

sixty-seven vessels were intercepted, and eighteen of them sent in with prize crews on board. . . . There was a good deal of mist and fog in the early part of the month, and a considerable amount of snow towards the end.'

And this was the period chosen for the departure of the very ordinary-looking steamer bound for the tropics.

Her real name was the *Rubens*, but she was a British ship accustomed to trade with Germany and at the opening of hostilities had the misfortune to be in Hamburg, where she was presently arrested. Of 3,600 tons, she was quite the ideal vessel for the trade routes, being representative of a familiar type. Not even the most critical patrols would suspect her appearance, and (in accordance with the practice of German mystery ships) she was disguised as a foreigner. In this case the *Rubens* pretended to be the Danish S.S. *Kronberg*, but other blockade runners usually obtained faked ship's papers purporting to come from Norway or Sweden. The most notable part of her cargo consisted of 1,600 tons of coal, which was chiefly meant for the *Königsberg*, but there were also fifteen hundred rifles and ammunition for the German land forces.

Notwithstanding the considerable risk and probable failure, there was a psychological reason for this venture. Matters on the high seas were not going too well just now with Germany. The whole of von Spee's squadron had been sent to the bottom with the exception of the *Dresden* and she, like *Königsberg*, was in hiding from her pursuers. The *Emden* had concluded her meteoric career, and the *Blucher* had been sunk at the Dogger Bank action; whilst out in the Atlantic both the *Prinz Ettel Friedrich* and the *Kronprinz Wilhelm* raiders were approaching the end of their endurance before interning themselves at an American port.

Now was the time to do something which would prove to the world that Germany disputed the claim of Britain to exercise command over the ocean; here was the grand opportunity to extricate *Königsberg* from the swamps of Central Africa, and in so doing to win eternal fame.

During the third week of February the *Kronberg* set forth; on the 19th she made her departure up the North Sea from the Skaw; two days later, instead of choosing the longer but safer route adjacent to Iceland, she took a great gamble and steamed during the prolonged darkness between the Orkneys and Shetlands. This was a most dangerous decision, but it was rewarded with that good fortune which not unusually accompanies boldness. She was not held up, but kept straight on into the Atlantic, was never intercepted by French or British cruisers off North-West Africa, gave the Cape of Good Hope a wide berth, passed up the Mozambique channel and was off Aldabra Island (less than 500 miles short of the Rufiji) by April 8.

So far, the voyage had been uneventful, and the arrival was well timed for the spring tides which were just about to make. But here, again, was that old trouble in regard to communications: here was that self-same wireless problem which had just sent *Dresden* to her doom in the Pacific. It was essential for *Kronberg* to establish contact with *Königsberg*, but as the former steamed through the Mozambique channel her signals were picked up by the French wireless stations of Madagascar no less than by the British. The alarm was spread, though it was impossible to say exactly where she now was.

After delaying a couple of days at Aldabra she was steaming north again, for the spring tides were ripe for a rendezvous and once more German wireless was intercepted. But the *Königsberg* was too closely hemmed in, and the latter had not moved from that remote up-river position. Admiral King-Hall says:

> We had many rumours of attempts to escape, some on very good authority, and at spring tides especially, when the height of the water gave greater facilities for a dash, our vigilance was redoubled, but, as a matter of fact, no effort was made.'

The inference therefore was that the stranger was heading for some spot in the neighbourhood of Tanga, though it might possibly be Manza Bay where good and sheltered anchorage could be relied upon.

As it was impossible to send off the *Weymouth* from the Rufiji, as she was the only craft capable of catching the *Königsberg* if the latter broke out, I went in my flagship, the *Hyacinth*, to capture her. It was impossible to simply go and lie off the entrance to Manza Bay, or even to approach the coast during daylight, for signals by wireless would have been made to the storeship, who would simply have diverted her course to another harbour.

So, we arranged to stand in from sea at such a time that at daybreak we should make the entrance to the channel which, running behind a line of reefs some miles in length parallel to the coast, led to the entrance of Manza.

Thus passed the night of April 13-14.

Everything worked out according to plan, and, as the darkness of night began to disperse, we were steaming slowly into the land past the north end of the long reef.... As dawn approached, we made out a dark shape inshore of us, and at once realised it was our quarry.

It was a tense moment for both ships. Here was the *Kronberg* at the very completion of her two months' voyage, through thousands of miles and two blockades, safely arrived at the German colonial coast with her cargo intact. But here, too, was the British Admiral himself ready to finish off the runner. Full speed, then, and get the duty done!

But at this precise minute, this critical situation, the *Hyacinth* suddenly became the frailest of flowers, and her strength seemed to fade away sadly.

The captain had just ordered an increase of speed, when *crash* went the starboard engine, which instantly stopped. Up came the chief engineer to report that the connection between the piston and connecting-rod had collapsed, and that only by wonderful good fortune we had not had a bad accident, both to the ship and the men in the engine-room. So, with the port engine only we limped along like a wounded animal after our prize, who rapidly increased her distance from us.

Under the fire of our bow guns she got away and through the narrow entrance into Manza Bay, where, on our arrival some quarter of an hour or so later, we found her run on shore, anchors down, sea cocks open, and her holds ablaze with burning timber.... As the *Hyacinth* came in, the crew of the blockade-runner scuttled ashore in their boats, and a party from the *Hyacinth* went off to see what could be done towards putting out the fire and floating the ship. Fire was opened on our boats from the shore, but no harm done, and a few shrapnel from the ship soon cleared the surrounding woods.

It was soon reported that nothing could be done, so the *Hyacinth* opened fire with shell on the stranded vessel, with the result that three or four immense explosions took place, and I felt that, though no doubt guns and rifles might be saved, there would be little or no ammunition for them. Meanwhile the engine-room department were hard at work replacing our damaged connecting-rod with the spare one, and at last, at the end of some hours, having effected our repairs, and done all that was possible to destroy the storeship, we left Manza Bay on our return to the se blockade, where I found things as I had left them.

It was, of course, impossible to do anything towards preventing the enemy from salving the arms as soon as the fire was extinguished, for, short of an occupying force of troops to hold the surrounding district, it was out of the question for a man-of-war to remain in an enemy's harbour day and night for weeks, even had a ship been available. Shortly after this occurrence I proposed returning to Manza Bay to disturb any operations of salvage that might be in the making, but on hearing of my intention the Admiralty prohibited the proceeding, on the grounds that the approaches to the bay were mined.

And sure enough mines were subsequently discovered in the narrow entrance.

The lesson to be learned from this incident is that the retention of an obsolete warship on the active list may be the falsest economy. During over fourteen years the *Hyacinth* had become so outworn that when a sudden spurt was demanded, she collapsed. But for this accident the *Kronberg* would have been sunk with no delay, and the accompanying photograph indicates the effect of a 6-inch shell which the *Hyacinth* fired from outside over the trees. The storeship's funnel has been completely wrecked at its base, and there could be no possible hope of her steaming down to the Rufiji neighbourhood. So, the *Königsberg* never received her much-needed coal, and the utmost result to the Germans was the arrival of some rifles and ammunition in a more or less damaged condition.

One can afford to admit that fortune had been not too kind for the plucky *Kronberg*, and it was rather hard luck on her skipper that he should have steamed so many thousands of miles through patrol areas of danger only to be pounced upon immediately at his arrival. But here, again, just as the *Dresden* met her death through being compelled to call up her colliers, so the act of *Königsberg's* collier in broadcasting through the ether was the indirect cause of the blockade-runner's destruction. Once more was wireless proved to be a curse at sea.

The Rufiji problem was towards the end of April in pretty much the same condition as when Cutler crashed in the previous December. On the other hand, the German Admiralty was being kept informed of the East African proceedings; was aware that *Kronberg* had failed by such a narrow margin, and that the blockade off Scotland could be penetrated. Having regard to the consideration that *Königsberg* was the only German cruiser which now remained beyond the North Sea intact—still with hull, armament and ammunition ready to fight—it was worth while making a further relief attempt. Indeed, a report did reach the British naval authorities that another storeship was coming along; and whilst such a steamer actually did not immediately materialise, the feeling of suspense was increased, and the watchers off the Rufiji were unable to ease the heavy strain imposed.

More than ever must efforts be made to demolish the *Königsberg* before a second *Kronberg* should arrive and complicate matters. Lucky it was that the seaplanes which the *Laconia* had brought to Niororo Island on April 23 had been so quickly tuned up; and two days later Lieutenant Cull was ready to try a first reconnaissance with one of the Short machines.

CHAPTER 15

Over the Delta

It was Sunday, April 25, and at 9.30 a.m., taking with him Air Mechanic Boggis as his observer, Lieutenant Cull taxied away from the *Laconia*, rose into the brassy sky and after reaching 1,200 feet made off towards the delta.

It was disappointing to find this machine climbed so badly and that any more height was out of the question, so no further time was wasted and he steered due west for the African coast. He resolved to make the latter at the southern end of the delta near the Msala mouth but on crossing over that entrance a downward bump occurred due to descending air currents and the seaplane dropped to 800 feet. It was evident that the enemy were still very much on the alert, for the seaplane was now greeted by rifle fire which continued all the way as he flew over the channel leading inland.

Above the dense growth of mangroves, the machine zoomed, whilst below was an amazing network of dark trees and silvery rivers. On he sped still westward, but the *Königsberg* was not visible in this southern area, so the seaplane turned north as soon as it reached the head of the delta. Having arrived at the spot where the channel branched N.W. and S.E., he discovered the German cruiser lying just about where she had been reported in the first week of December, that is to say in practically the most western of the many channels.

It was possible to see quite definitely that during this period, at any rate, Captain Looff had not camouflaged his vessel by tree-branches. Moreover, it was not less clear that the enemy was far from regarding the situation as hopeless; for there she was quite smart and warlike with bows pointing to the northward. This flying officer says:

She looked as though she had been newly painted. Her sidescreens and awnings were spread, smoke was issuing from her

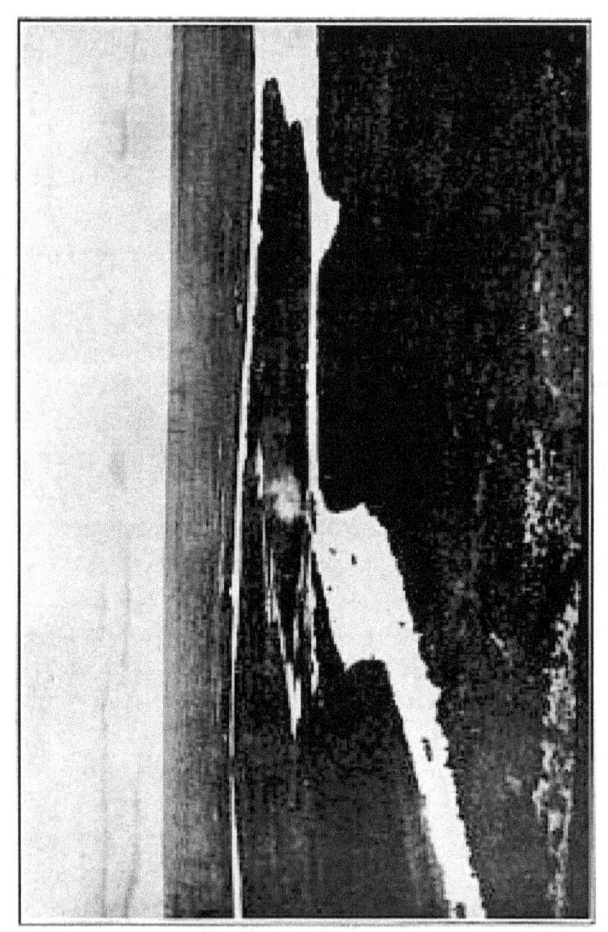

S.M.S. KÖNIGSBERG IN HIDING

This unique photograph was taken on April 25, 1915, by Flight-Lieutenant J. T. Cull, D.S.A.S., from a height of 700 feet. The German cruiser is seen at low state of conditions. The smoke is that of the wood fuel she was compelled to burn. Astern of her are attendant small craft. It was even the hero by this sight that the limits of the community pounded at a deluge of death.

funnels and in general she was looking very spick-and-span."

Having had a good observation of her starboard side and seen all that could be noticed, notwithstanding that the guns were hidden by the canvas, Cull turned eastward when only half a mile from her, for the machine was not flying too well, and now headed seawards. But the *Königsberg* had spotted the visitors and opened fire with shrapnel.

'My observer distinctly heard the bullets, and for a first attempt she made some very pretty shooting, shells bursting just astern of the machine which, however, was soon out of her range.'

Returning down river towards the mouth, "we saw the *Somali* and *Newbridge* in their old position," and the machine was speeded up, followed by a heavy volley of rifle fire where sea joined land at the entrance. German officers and *Askaris* were easily distinguished from a height of 600 feet "firing for all they were worth and in no way disconcerted by pistol and Very's pistol fire from the machine."

Those were exciting moments, and the wonder is that either Lieutenant Cull or his companion ever came out alive; for it was only by the merest fluke that the sea was gained.

From now onwards the engine started failing gradually, and packed up altogether within some six or seven miles of the anchorage where the ships were lying. On landing, it was found that a rifle bullet of about ½-inch bore had entered between the observer and the engine, at a very flat trajectory, tearing away the air intakes and succeeding in practically closing the main oil pipe. This latter was naturally the cause of the engine failing, and several blued cylinders resulted.

Five other holes were discovered in the plane.

In spite of this narrow escape from death, the flight had been a success. No such thing as a proper airplane camera existed at that time in Africa, but Cull had taken up with him one of a commoner type by which he was able to obtain the first photographs ever made of this primitive scene, and he has been good enough to let me reproduce the accompanying picture. Here will be seen the narrow river, with *Königsberg* in the middle distance making considerable smoke (apparently from wood fuel). The smaller craft seemed to consist of a whaler, a fairly large steamer, and a couple of big dhows. Taken from a height of 700 feet, this was one of the most remarkable aerial photographs which so far had come out of the Great War, and it definitely estab-

IN COMMAND OF THE MONITORS

Captain (now Admiral) Eric J. A. Fullerton photographed aboard his monitor *Severn*. This distinguished son of an Admiral married the daughter of that famous Admiral of the Fleet, Lord Fisher.

THE MONITORS LEAVE MALTA

H.M.S. *Severn* and *Mersey* are here seen on April 28, 1915, starting out on their long voyage to the Rufiji. Each was towed by a couple of tugs, and the cables are being made fast. Notice the 6-inch for'ard gun and extremely low freeboard of each monitor. The journey was accomplished only with the greatest difficulties.

lished in naval minds the enormous utility which seaplanes possessed for obtaining and bringing back home accurate information.

A new era had been begun, not merely in regard to marine warfare, but as pertaining to the dark continent. No longer were those waterways and forests to be hidden from the eyes of civilisation, and development must follow on knowledge when hostilities should give way to peace. In the meanwhile, the *Königsberg* conundrum was slightly eased, for the position already marked on the chart was confirmed and more readily visualised. Further air reconnaissances were carried out, in which Commander Bridgeman of *Hyacinth* usually went as Observer, and of this brave officer, Lieutenant Cull refers to "his interest and keenness in our flying operations being a great incentive to make the best out of what was available."

But these intrepid aviators were contending with great difficulties. As the machines were such bad climbers it was too risky to send them into the delta frequently: disaster would certainly have been inevitable. So, usually, they flew within easy reach of the sea but just far enough to keep an eye on the *Königsberg* in case she should contemplate moving. During one of these coastal reconnaissances the machine which Flight-Lieutenant Watkins took up received a shot from the enemy which hit the rudder, causing a crash landing on the water to the complete wreckage of the seaplane. It was a critical situation just off the enemy's shores, and perhaps the captured *Adjutant* would come steaming out to finish off the job.

Up in the air went Lieutenant Cull with his Mechanic Boggis to search, who after a while luckily spotted the wreckage but not a minute too soon. The Indian Ocean today was in a lively mood, a nasty sea was beating against what remained of the airplane, but clinging to one of the floats could be seen Watkins and his passenger. It so happened that no patrol ships were in sight, but there were sharks, and even if they were kept off it could not be long before some enemy craft emerged. With splendid airmanship Cull brought his machine safely down on to the rough sea, snatched Watkins and mate out of their peril, taxied along for mile after mile head on to the waves, and found a patrolling whaler at last. The next duty was to call up a second whaler, to which the rescued pilot and passenger were transferred, whilst the first whaler turned back to try and salve the seaplane's engine.

Now the accident had occurred about 3 miles from the Simba Uranga entrance; the whalers (*Fly* and *Childers*) had been hampered by haze: otherwise, they would have seen Watkins hit the water. It was the afternoon of May 5, the light was failing rapidly, and the sea rising ominously. Strenuous efforts were made to contend with this combination, but at last a line was made fast to the engine and it was buoyed. That was all which could be done at present, and the whaler stood by for the night. Now on April 20, H.M.S. *Chatham* had come back to East Africa, after the *Kronberg* incident, as a necessary addition to the *Hyacinth's* unreliable strength. So, at daylight on May 6 the *Chatham* approached the seaplane wreck, alongside which the whaler *Childers* was sighted.

There now followed another of those interesting but difficult bits of seamanship which were always cropping up in this campaign. How much water was there at the wreck? Could the *Chatham* get in so close? The *Childers* signalled that she herself was in 3½ fathom (21 feet), that the machine had sunk and she was unable to raise it. The *Chatham* cautiously sounded her way in, but at this time she was drawing 17 feet 10 inches, and at times the soundings dropped to 3 fathoms (18 feet), which left exactly two inches of water under her bottom. Not every commanding officer would care to risk his 5,200-ton ship by such a margin, though fortunately the tide had another three hours to rise before high water. But airplane engines were scarce, and the task had to be attempted.

Necessarily this approach must be made at slow speed through the shallows, and the strong wind made it extremely awkward to keep the big vessel under control. However, the spot was reached and regardless of sharks the *Chatham* tried to lift the engine, the machine being quite invisible, having sunk with its head in the mud. Then another complication ensued, for the hawser which was secured to the machine's tail fouled one of the *Chatham's* propellers. Divers were sent down to clear this, who were much impeded by the short choppy sea; but they were prevented by the extremely thick mud from getting at the wreckage. The machine's tail had carried away, it was now just on midday—three hours after high water—and the *Chatham* would soon be aground; so, the salvage efforts were called off and she returned to Tirene Bay. Ten days later she was ordered to the Dardanelles.

The *Königsberg* was therefore causing a chain of trouble, which seemed unending; and what with the demands of the Grand Fleet, the Dardanelles, the Trade Routes, the interned German steamers whose possible egress from so many Atlantic ports had to be watched, there was more work for the cruisers than could be carried on. Off the Rufiji Admiral King-Hall's squadron had only one unit—the *Wey-*

mouth—with speed enough to chase *Königsberg* if the latter in her new grey paint should come out. And even the *Weymouth* must at times go away for coaling, boiler cleaning, overhaul. As to the airplanes, they had shown both their great possibilities and their inherent unreliability. So long as everything worked efficiently, they were beyond all praise; but the practicability of bombing was a theory no longer tenable, and reconnaissance as a part of steady routine was equally ruled out.

The following cable, which was sent early that May to the Air Department in London, well summed up the deadlock:

> Machines not climbing well. Average speed attained 60 m.p.h. Engines giving 1,140 revs. Climbing best when humidity great. Consider great deal of slip present. Glue not holding on any propellers. Wood only for one more propeller. Has india-rubber tubing been sent? As all ours perished. No fabric and few spares left.

And whilst this was being considered at home, and the necessary steps taken to make yet another attempt to satisfy the Rufiji requirements, a desperate scheme was being evolved by the Royal Naval Air Service officers at the delta. They had been repeatedly thwarted at every end and turn by the combination of atmospheric effects and seaplane deficiencies, to a degree that was unendurable for men with stout courage and vital energy. It was past all passive patience that for month after month the *Königsberg* should be defying their efforts. Could not some original measure be devised for settling the matter at one blow?

Yes, it could. But it was just that kind which only such plucky personalities as Lieutenants Cull and Watkins, Midshipman Gallehawk, Commander Bridgeman, and a very few others, would ever think of; and even then, as a last resort. We mentioned on an earlier page a motor-boat which had arrived from England for the R.N.A.S. About the middle of May the plan had so far ripened that a special silencer had been made out of a 6-inch cartridge case and fitted to this boat, for the idea was that one dark night she was to motor noiselessly up the river and get within range of *Königsberg*.

Not shells but a torpedo should be used, and the dropping gear came into the scheme as previously. With any luck at all perhaps the enemy cruiser might be maimed for life, yet the reader can well perceive that when once the *Königsberg* 's searchlights should suddenly illumine the darkness of the placid river, and the rain of shells begin to pour on the discovered motor-boat, it would be certain death for all.

But even if, by the fortune of war, the motor-boat had entered the river untouched, could she hope to get past the mouth on her return journey? The crew had weighed all this, and were determined to go through with their expedition. There was enormous and unanimous enthusiasm, the party to consist of Commander Bridgeman, the R.N.A.S. officers, together with an Engineer Petty Officer. The boat was quickly fitted, and a most satisfactory trial trip was carried out in the presence of the Admiral who watched and listened from his stern walk; everything, in fact, was just about ready for the night of nights when the Admiralty at home vetoed the whole gallant proceeding.

A bitter blow! A terrible disappointment to a brave band of potential heroes! But there was good reason for this denial. A much more comprehensive plan was on the eve of maturing; scarcely less original in conception, and much more likely to succeed. It was to be one of the War's surprises, yet a most logical conclusion which had been merely delayed in fulfilment till circumstances would permit. That which was now about to happen consisted of a return to first principles. Ever since the *Königsberg* had been located, essential need for knocking her out had never been lost sight of. Local light-draught craft had been considered, but found unable to carry 6-inch guns.

Then the idea of bombing from the air had come and gone; next the torpedo-boat had returned into popularity. But now, at length, the wheel of change had turned a full circle, and come back to the point where the shallow ship with 6-inch armament must advance to fight out a duel against the German cruiser's 4.1-inch guns. And the fitting opportunity was now just arriving, the month of June had just opened. The setting of the stage was practically complete.

CHAPTER 16

The Monitors Arrive

One of the most intriguing characteristics in the study of human progress is that of repetition as in a pattern; of reversion to type; of one generation doing the same acts as its grandfathers performed, yet under circumstances entirely dissimilar.

During the Great War it was not once, but many times, that old ideas were resuscitated; but with regard to the navy there was quite a surprising revival of a certain ship class which no one had ever expected to see flying the White Ensign alongside twentieth-century men-of-war. Still less expected was the necessity for this particular species as the sole kind of vessel suited for the special need. By way of introduction, we must cast our minds back to the American Civil War of 1860, and remind ourselves of that historic 60-gun frigate *Merrimac*, which was cut down to her waterline and armoured with two thicknesses of plating that were pierced for the guns.

But, to outrival this Confederate ship, the famous Captain Ericsson designed a 614-tons ship of iron, protected with 4½-inch armour, the hull having such low freeboard that only a couple of feet showed above the waterline. In the centre of the deck was erected a turret, circular in shape, revolving on a spindle, and containing a couple of smooth-bore guns. Here, then, was a low-lying warship intended primarily for coast defence, so that speed and fuel capacity could be sacrificed in favour of a steady gun platform, whilst inconspicuousness was more desirable than sea-going qualities. Now that vessel was named the *Monitor*, and set an entirely new fashion afloat.

In the British Navy a number of ships afterwards adopted this revolutionary design when the *Royal Sovereign* was cut down from being a tall three-decker to having only six feet of freeboard; and a further stage was reached with the *Monarch*. We need not pursue the subject beyond stating that the building of monitors was based on a well-remembered naval heresy, which was summed up in the phrase "coast defence." Later on, when enlightened minds proved that *offence* was the most powerful form of defence; that a mobile fleet of battleships was far more strategically sound, as a principle, than that of scattered monitors employed as local units close to the shore, waiting till the enemy should choose to arrive on the scene; the *Royal Sovereign*s and *Monarchs* passed into oblivion though the word monitor—as indicating a class—was not forgotten.

There was at least one navy in the second decade of the twentieth century which still actively believed in monitors, and that was the Brazilian, which had given Messrs. Vickers an order to build three. By August 1914 they were so nearly ready for service that the British Admiralty stepped in, took them over and commissioned them, naming these monitors respectively *Severn*, *Mersey* and *Humber*. The first two of these now concern us closely and, for reasons that will quickly become apparent, it is worthwhile to note their details: the *Humber* we can omit.

The *Mersey* had been launched in 1913, and the *Severn* in 1914. Each was of 1,260 tons displacement, measuring not quite 267 feet in length, and exactly 49 feet in beam. The draught when loaded was 4 feet 9 inches, which is to say they could float in almost the shallowest channel; and their speed was 12 knots for a short radius only; the fuel being limited to 187 tons of coal and go tons of oil. Their armament consisted of two 6-inch guns and one 4.7 inch-howitzer.

Like the original Ericsson prototype, this "River"-class was of low freeboard, but unarmoured. In appearance they were neither stately nor beautiful; but flat, squat, and altogether different from existing European vessels with the exception of perhaps those funny little antiquated naval "flat-irons" occasionally to be met with in the Dutch canals and on the Danube. At a distance the *Mersey* or *Severn* resembled nothing so much as a steam-ferry, with a square-shaped structure raised box-like amidships and a funnel coming up through the centre. They were lightly built—and this requires emphasising—but their general appearance still further suggested to the sailor mind that here was a quaint freak rather than a genuine sea-going man-of-war. Surely these ships would be hopeless in bad weather?

However, on August 8, 1914, they were actually commissioned at Barrow, and two months later we find them at Sheerness. On October 10 the *Severn* was there in a condition of temporary disablement cleaning boilers, when her captain (Commander Eric J. A. Fullerton) received sudden orders to raise steam immediately and leave at the earliest moment. Within a couple of hours, he had collected his liberty men, and was steaming out through the boom defence to sea. In the Downs *Severn* met the *Mersey* with *Humber*, and they set off for Ostend, but on the way *Severn's* engines gave out, fires had to be drawn, and the *Humber* took *Severn* in tow. Speed 4 knots!

It was a curious manner of going to war, but more than once did monitors' machinery try their engineering staffs severely; and it was lucky on this occasion that no German submarines sighted her. Before the monitors could reach Ostend, the latter had been evacuated, but the *Mersey* was able to escort some transports from Dunkirk to Grisnez, and the other two monitors returned to Dover, *Severn* being attacked by a submarine in the meanwhile. The Dunkirk forts, never having seen such a strange apparition as a monitor, took the *Mersey* for a German and shelled her.

From this initial cruise several disappointing facts had become manifest: the monitors could not get their maximum speed, and 10 knots was the utmost rate of travel. They were not particularly seaworthy, and in heavy weather extremely difficult to handle, especially when the wind was on the beam. A few days later, however, owing to an urgent request from the Belgians, the French, and the British Army, the three monitors left Dover to bombard the German right wing along the coast. They did excellent work in assisting to check the enemy's onrush, and continued to shell the German batteries. Presently our allies were able to inundate the country surrounding Nieuport, and the enemy was held; so that it was now possible to withdraw the bombarding ships from the risks of submarines and shore batteries. The *Mersey* had been damaged by the enemy's shell-fire, and the *Severn* was already leaking, through the combined effect of her own guns and rough seas. There was no question as to her lightness of build.

We next find Commander Fullerton with his monitors up the Wash, near to Boston; and those of us who were serving off that coast during the first winter, 1914-1915, well remember that their presence was quite a puzzle for some weeks. Today we know that there was much expectation of a German invasion along the East Coast being made during the early spring, and it was thought that the monitors would be useful for going into shoal water where no other warships could float. Thus, by a curious cycle of events did the old "coast defence" theory come to life again. However, spring arrived and passed, there was no attempted landing, so the monitors were available for other duties.

Ever since the *Königsberg* had been located, the Admiralty had been pressed to send out shallow draught vessels, and now at length with the present trend of the European situation it was possible to despatch the *Severn* and *Mersey*, whose features seemed exactly fitted for work up the Rufiji rivers. It should be mentioned that at this date the armament of each monitor was one 6-inch gun for'ard, one 6-inch gun and one 4.7 inch aft in addition to 3-pounders and machine-guns from either side. But the difficulty was how to get these short-radius, and not too seaworthy, vessels out to Africa. And how would officers or men be able to endure the Red Sea heat in such?

We can shorten our story by imagining that Malta has been left astern, the Suez Canal and Red Sea passed, and the Indian Ocean just entered. Both *Severn* and *Mersey* had been battened down and made as watertight as was possible with such low-lying ships. The crews had been put aboard H.M.S. *Trent,* which was one of the many merchant steamers the Admiralty had taken up. She was commanded by Commander Richard Hayes, R.N.R., with a personnel all likewise from the Royal Naval Reserve. Two tugs were assigned to tow each monitor, and a collier accompanied them also. It was thus a curious flotilla of eight which fought its way through terrible heat and trying seas, till Mafia Island was reached on June 2 after a slow passage.

The next proceeding was to make the monitors more war-worthy by the addition of steel protective plates such as on deck, as well as around the wheel and bridge. The rudders were lengthened for quicker steering in confined areas, all the empty store-rooms of each monitor were filled with several thousands of empty petrol tins tightly packed to preserve the ship's buoyancy in case the hull should be penetrated. All this was done at Tirene Bay and occupied a month of strenuous labour. But on June 18 there arrived yet another armed liner—H.M.S. *Laurentic*—who brought not merely three more flying officers, together with Petty Officers and Mechanics, but two Henry Farman and two Caudron airplanes. Here, then, was a reply to the desperate request cabled to London a few weeks ago. In the meanwhile, after Mafia Island had been captured from the Germans, a great deal of activity had been expended to provide an aerodrome thereon. The only suitable site consisted of a small piece of ground that was overgrown with short trees and scrub, but had a swamp at one end.

The Military Governor, Colonel McKye (mentioned in an earlier chapter), had commandeered most of the natives on Mafia for clearing

UNPACKING A CAUDRON
This illustrates the difficulties under which an airplane had to be carried from ship to shore athwart a couple of the steamer's lifeboats, and then bodily lifted by the natives up to the beach.

OFF MAFIA ISLAND
Ready for the attack on the *Königsberg*. H.M.S. *Severn* is seen lying in the foreground, with H.M.S. *Hyacinth* (flying Admiral King-Hall's flag) in the middle distance. This photograph clearly shows the monitor's guns, and slight freeboard in comparison with the *Hyacinth's* seaworthiness.

the ground, burning and uprooting the trees. The R.N.A.S., with the assistance of Seedie boys from the *Laconia*, essayed to drain the swamp, until the task proved impossible. A wood and corrugated iron hangar was manufactured in Zanzibar, sent down in sections, and erected on Mafia two days after the *Laurentic's* arrival. This smart piece of work was carried out by the original R.N.A.S. party, who within 36 hours of the *Laurentic's* arrival had disembarked, transported to the aerodrome and assembled, the two Henry Farmans in readiness for flying.

In an accompanying photograph will be seen the manner of landing the Caudrons under the primitive conditions which prevailed. Each case weighed 2 tons and had to be taken ashore from the ship in, or rather athwart, a couple of *Laurentic's* lifeboats until the latter grounded in the shallows. Then any number from fifty to a hundred dark-skinned "boys" appeared wading out, who with much shouting swarmed all over the case, and those who could not get underneath encouraged others from the top. The machine was then unpacked and carried for 1½ miles over a rough path which had just been widened through the jungle to the aerodrome. Again, no time was wasted, for a reconnaissance was immediately carried out over *Königsberg* and several others followed, Commander Bridgeman usually being the observer. The nett result of these flights was to confirm the position of Captain Looff's cruiser as located on April 25.

Mafia Island, together with Tirene Bay, had thus become a busy naval hive, where (though it was the African winter) anyone off duty was glad to wear nothing more than a hat and a towel. How Mafia appeared from the sea will be realised from the next illustration which shows H.M.S. *Severn* in the foreground, trimmed for action, with H.M.S. *Hyacinth* in the middle distance flying the Admiral's flag at the fore. Every requisite had now been assembled, the aerodrome was ready, and the geographical proximity of Mafia was a great improvement over Niororo. A not inconsiderable organisation of shipping and aerial craft, with a large personnel, now waited for a brief period at the delta's gates. If the new airplanes were far from perfect, they certainly were such a great improvement that whereas the seaplanes only rarely and with pain attained 1,000 feet, the latest additions climbed to 4,000 feet readily.

On the other hand, this African climate still was utterly without mercy, and after the first few days more than half the number of spare propellers had become warped into uselessness. One Caudron was wrecked on its trial flight, and a Henry Farman crashed beyond repair

STRIPPED FOR THE FRAY

The monitor *Severn* lying alongside the Cunarder *Laconia* ready for the attack on *Königsberg*. Observe that the monitor has housed her topmast. She has camouflaged her fighting-top, fore 6-inch gun, and protective plating. All superfluous gear has been removed.

TAKEN DURING ACTION

This photograph was taken from aloft during the action of July 6, 1915, and shows the *Severn's* boat deck with the 3-pounders, the ammunition boxes, the hammocks and protective plating. The hose pipe will be seen ready to deal with conflagrations.

through engine failure. Such accidents, whilst pathetic in their annoyance, could not be helped, and the hope existed that when the "day of days" should arrive there would at least be one airplane able to function. Everyone of both branches was feverishly busy in preparation for the great attack in combination against *Königsberg*. The monitors were completing their improvements and practising indirect firing over a small island at a *dhow* anchored out of sight, the range being 8,000 yards, which was the presumed distance at which the enemy would be shelled. Similarly, the airmen were spending long periods in flight, making dummy attacks with the monitors doing wireless tests, dropping bombs and so forth.

Numerous consultations between Captain Fullerton of the *Severn*, Commander R. A. Wilson of the *Mersey*, gunnery experts from all H.M. ships present, and the aviators who were to do the spotting, resulted in a simple "clock" code wherein letters took the place of numbers. All this was rehearsed again and again until proficiency was beyond any possibility of doubt. Tuesday, July 6, had been selected for the big attack, a date that was convenient by reason of the tides and the break in the monsoon. Confidential books were deposited by the monitors aboard the flagship for safety, and everyone was energetically adding the last touches of preparation for the fateful day that was at long last to arrive. Behind the steel plating, bolted on to the monitors, hammocks were packed as further protection; and these two strange warships, stripped of all superfluous gear, became just bare mobile gun-platforms peopled by men in khaki—or, where that fabric gave out, in whites duly stained by permanganate of potash.

Monday was a period of disciplined excitement, of suppressed suspense, of optimistic uncertainty. As everyone went about his particular duties there was a quiet brooding and wonder. Would these lightly-built monitors get inside the Rufiji before being knocked to pieces? Would they succeed in reaching a spot some 4 or 5 miles upriver, where no man-of-war had hitherto steamed? Even then, would their indirect fire over the trees at the unseen *Königsberg* end efficaciously? And the airplanes? Could they be relied upon for communicating the essential information as to how the monitors' shells were dropping on the target?

Officers and all hands had been kept so fully occupied during these four weeks that there was little enough time for letter-writing, but now there was a hurried chance to scribble a few lines which for some might be the last ever to be sent. And here came the medical officer grave of face supervising a few items "in case of"—well, certain eventualities. There is a silence among brave men that is more eloquent than fiery speeches; and a benevolent cheeriness (restrained yet buoyant) communicates itself from one to another on such occasions as this. For tomorrow these crews were due to go "over the top," and it was impossible to say what would be the outcome of this long sweltering voyage all the way from Europe.

But the hours ticked by, and Monday afternoon passed into night. By this time tomorrow it would all be over. An extraordinary feeling of confident content, of courageous happiness, seemed to seize both ships' companies, but on everyone's tongue was the unspoken prophecy:

"We're in for a pretty hot time."

CHAPTER 17

The First Attack

It is to be noted that on this occasion there was not intended an incursion *via* the Simba Uranga mouth and past the Kiomboni peninsula; but a totally different route was selected which was practicable for shallow craft, so that the sunken *Newbridge* need not affect the operations. In other words, the plan was to approach the *Königsberg* by a northern and not a southern waterway. That was done for the express purpose of enabling our 6-inch guns to be moved up to a position whence the range was not too great. Nor will the reader need to be reminded that these monitors, in spite of their temporary plating, were scarcely better than thin steel tanks.

It is true that between them the *Severn* and *Mersey* numbered four 6-inch guns against the *Königsberg*'s ten 4.1 inch; but in a straight fight even at anchor the German could have sent either or both of these light ships to the bottom. As the British Navy learned to its loss in the Battle of the Coronel, the range and effectiveness of German 4.1-inch armament compared very favourably indeed with our 6-inch. Obviously, then, an open combat such as is normally fought at sea would have been decided against the monitors within a very few minutes.

The idea accordingly was to enter by the Kikunja mouth, steam up till they were under the lee of an island covered with high trees and, with this protective barrier, to shoot over the tree-tops at the enemy moored on the up-river side of this island. Of course, this forest island (about 4 miles long by 1½ miles wide) would be just as much a cover for the *Königsberg* against the monitors' gunners. On the other hand, Captain Looff had his spotting stations linked up with his ship for signalling the fall of his own shells. One such station seemed to be on Pemba Hill to the west, and roughly abreast, of the position where the monitors were to arrive. But a suspected spotting station was on a tiny island which remained between the high tree island and the monitors.

Moreover, it was conceivable that information might also be sent from detachments on the river banks. But where the enemy remained at a grave disadvantage was in regard to aerial possibilities: and if only our airplanes should not fail, it ought to be possible so to direct the monitors' firing that the target should be found within a limited time. Here was a new phase in naval warfare, and theory does not always work out accurately in execution. For reconnaissance we have seen how valuable sea planes and land planes could acquit themselves; but whether they would be able to keep in the sky, observe the fall of our shells, wireless back to the bombarders accurate information as to how the attack progressed, was at present doubtful. Of the aviators much was expected, and more was hoped: they had it within their efforts either to make the whole operation a dismal failure, or to create an historic precedent of enormous success. And the weakness which existed was only what is always inevitable when operations are combined rather than independent.

For the monitors the problem divided itself into, (*a*) the approach, (*b*) the attack. It was by no means certain that the first would be permitted on the enemy's part, who would thus ward off the second. Exactly what his strength might be at the mouth and on the banks further up it was impossible to say. Certainly, the actual mouth was a little wider than that of the Simba Uranga, but outside there were similar restricting shoals which made it possible for the German defences to concentrate on the one funnel-like channel. Whatever ambushes might exist further up in the narrows, it was quite within probability that torpedoes might be waiting to be fired from either side of the exit, and the slow-moving monitors would be perfect targets—except for one possible saving feature. That was their shallow draught.

Having regard to all these initial difficulties and snags, the approach must be made under the screen of darkness, yet so well timed as to have the aid of daylight when in the river itself. Thus, we get a fair analogy of the soldiers in France with every detail working according to the clock, and every part of the plan timed to the minute. But there the similarity ends, for such factors as tides and unseen shoals and ships' leeway have to be taken into account, and the least diversion from determined course might upset the whole attack. Picture, then, that memorable eve of the great effort.

By 6 p.m. a last look round was made aboard each monitor to ensure that nothing was lacking and everything was in its assigned place. Ammunition was piled up near the guns, and rations for tomorrow issued, water bottles filled for quenching tropical thirst, and cans full of water placed everywhere. Imagine the ship's company being summoned aft to the quarter deck where the captain makes a short address, reads out a telegram of good wishes from the admiral, thanks them for having toiled so hard and cheerfully this last month, and ends up with an expression of good fortune for the morrow. At 6.45 p.m. the monitors, without any dramatic farewells or fuss, shove off from alongside the steamship *Trent,* which is to remain anchored in a safe position as a hospital ship.

It is now stygian darkness, and the Admiral has already despatched the Armed Merchant Cruiser *Laurentic* to make a demonstration off Dar-es-Salaam lest the enemy should have got wind of what was impending, and be sending troops or guns down to the delta. Admiral King-Hall himself has transferred from *Hyacinth* to *Weymouth,* because the latter drew less water, and thus was able to get in fairly close to the shore and bombard not merely the enemy's guns at the entrance but one of his observation posts well inland. Having got within a convenient distance away from Mafia, the monitors anchor for a few hours' sleep, but under the present conditions neither monitor is a luxurious home. For the officers, dinner consists of a scratch meal in a bare wardroom minus any table, the cabins being so stripped that not an article of combustibility remains, so even the captain sleeps with his mattress on the damp deck.

Soon after 3 a.m. the quartermaster's voice is calling "All hands, turn out," but it is still dark and the shapes of men moving quietly to their tasks about the decks occasionally collide without recognition. By 4 a.m. the monitors are under way, with a motorboat towing at each side amidships; for perhaps there may be need for these. Off Komo Island two whalers, each burning a light, act as light vessels and enable the monitors to set a course S.W. for the Ras Simba Uranga peninsula, which separates the Kikunja mouth from the Simba Uranga entrance.

It is not easy navigation and *Severn,* being senior ship, is leading the way. In the accompanying photograph of this vessel alongside the *Laconia* will be seen the fighting top at the stunted mast, and herein Captain Fullerton, together with his Gunnery Lieutenant, a signalman, and the rangefinder have taken up their stations. Steaming cautiously, and sounding all the way through the tricky shallows, the *Severn* begins to discern the indefinite outline of sand, and the keen eyes of the signalman see the Kikunja mouth forming itself. The outlying bank off Ras Simba Uranga is avoided and at 5.20 a.m. the entrance of Kikunja is being approached, but it is still dark though the light will burst all of a sudden very shortly.

Boom! Boom! Boom!

The enemy's look-outs have sighted the monitors, three blank charges from a field-gun on the northern shore at the widest part of Kikunja mouth are giving the alarm to *Königsberg* and all the delta defences. It is cold up in the monitor's top whence the ship's guns will be controlled, but all sleepiness, all wonder, are now dismissed as simultaneously at 5.40 the dawn brings back visibility to the African continent, the two ships begin entering the river, a shot is fired from a field-gun to starboard, and then two more—all directed at *Severn*. *Mersey*, just astern, comes in for a similar reception, together with some attention from a pom-pom. Some sniping is also being made by rifles on the southern bank, but they are hidden by trees and rushes, nor is the light quite good enough for them yet to be discriminated.

The monitors return the fire with their 3-pdrs. on either side, and the sun has risen to illuminate the river so clearly that speed is increased to 7½ knots. The first suspense has ended satisfactorily, the Maxims' fire on the south side has been rather feeble, and the enemy's attack has been soon silenced by the monitors' batteries. But it might have ended differently had not the monitors' advent been a complete surprise; for shortly after passing Ras Simba the *Severn* sighted a torpedo alongside a log or dugout under overhanging trees, and two or three men were standing by in these trees. One of *Severn*'s heavy guns was brought to bear, and promptly destroyed the danger.

The time of entry was dead low water neaps, so the monitors would be able to take the young flood up river, and if they remained for only a few hours after midday they would be able to come out with the ebb. For the moment there was reason for feeling happy that the first stage of today's work had been reached according to schedule and without mishap; though it was somewhat of a relief to find the entrance not more strongly fortified. But when Captain Looff chose to withdraw into the Rufiji, he had by that act put a great strain on his defences. Instead of daring to be immune at one single impregnable mouth, he was compelled to scatter his slender forces at four or five exits, for the initiative was in British hands, and the German was kept in a condition of doubt.

An entirely new departure had been taken today by the Kikunja choice, but to make him still more embarrassed, H.M.S. *Weymouth*,

Hyacinth, Pyramus, Pioneer—the two latter being fourteen-year-old cruisers recently added to the station and somewhat similar to the sunken *Pegasus*—together with the whalers and tugs, were demonstrating off the Simba Uranga and other mouths. Dawn on July 6 revealed to the Germans an impressive, formidable blockade.

Kikunja had beheld never so strange a sight as this morning; nor since the world's creation had there been such human or mechanical energy afloat. Here was another of those lonely rivers, about 700 yards wide, its banks green with trees down to the edge, and everywhere flat land until on the starboard or northern side the Pemba Hill rose up. To the German outposts, the natives in their huts, or even the crocodiles lying motionless in the sun, this bold entry of two quaint flat naval steamers with upper works and guns all dazzle-painted must have seemed hardly credible. It was like waking up after a long Rip van Winkle somnolence.

Muddy creeks, that would be covered at high water, opened out on either side, three *dhows* and a boat showed themselves but had to be sunk. This combined noise of the monitors' 6-inch, 4.7's, 3-pdrs., machineguns; and the distant deep booming of the vessels outside the mouths; shook East Africa as it had never been roused in all its history. No risks could be taken, for at any possible position the enemy might have some trap, some entrenchment, encampment, signalling or torpedo station.

At 6.23 a.m., having reached the appointed spot to the east of Gengeni Island, the *Severn* proceeded to anchor bow and stern, estimating her distance, (the chart, however, was very inaccurate), from the *Königsberg* as 10,800 yards, *Mersey* taking up a position 400 yards astern and to the W.N.W. Owing to the flood tide which was now coming up somewhat strongly, the *Severn's* stern was swung round in such a manner as to obscure the bow gun. Thus a few minutes' delay ensued, the stern anchor had to be hove in, but at 6.48 a.m. she opened fire across the trees, followed by the *Mersey* soon afterwards.

For the interest of those who like to watch other people handle ships it may be explained that the *Severn* had come up the middle of the stream, eased down, swung slowly to port, let go the stern anchor, veered out 70 fathoms of wire, let go her bow anchor, then went astern and tautened in on both cables. She was thus a fixed gun platform. But on referring to the chart and the position of *Königsberg* thereon marked, it had been found that there was a curious sweep of tide past the island, so that the for'ard 6-inch gun would not bear.

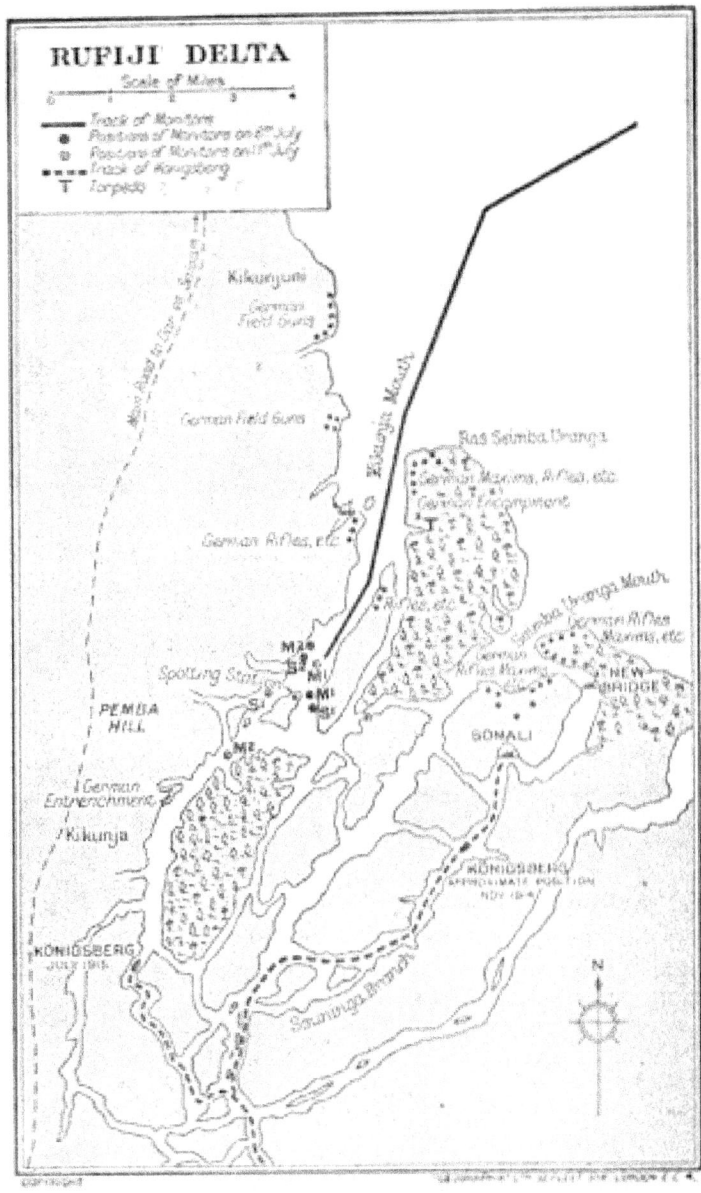

THE MONITORS' OPERATIONS

This illustrates the attacks on the *Königsberg* by the *Severn* and *Mersey* on July 6 and 11, 1915. The various positions of the *Königsberg*, as she withdrew further and further up river, are indicated until her final resting-place. M1 shows the first position of the *Mersey*; M2 her second position. S1 and S2 refer to the *Severn*. The respective dates are distinguished by the small circles.

There was nothing for it but to weigh and get properly square towards the invisible foe.

Up till now the *Severn* had been barely hit. Her plating was scratched by a few bullets which had struck the sides when running the entrance, and some of the hammocks had been penetrated, though not a man had been touched. But the *Königsberg's* spotters had wasted no time, and five minutes before *Severn* was ready for action, the enemy cruiser opened fire, though the first two shots fell on the intervening island. Very quickly, however, she began to straddle the *Severn*, and the river around the monitor was alive with bursting shells throwing up masses of dead fish. A curious spectacle, yet an ominous sight for any man who had never been previously under fire.

How much longer could this be endured without being hit and destroyed? That was the question in everyone's mind, and it was the unanimous opinion that the arrangements which Captain Looff had made for spotting could not have been bettered: the enemy rapidly found the range and never lost it. It was a further proof of that lesson which our navy had learned at Coronel, and was to discover again at Jutland. The German gunnery was excellent.

Let us go back for a moment to Mafia Island to watch the co-operation which the Royal Naval Air Service were to afford today. Soon after 5 a.m. one machine, piloted by Lieutenant Watkins and carrying bombs, left the aerodrome bound for the Rufiji entrance in order to distract the enemy's attention whilst the monitors were coming in. The distance from aerodrome to delta was between 30 and 40 miles, and at 5.35 a.m. Flight-Commander J.T. Cull, who had made the valuable reconnaissance of April 25, took the air in a Henry Farman machine, his Observer being Flight Sub-Lieutenant F. S. L. Arnold. Their passage over the sea was so rapid that they sighted the monitors moving up river, firing (as Commander Cull described it) "heartily" at the banks, and. at 6.17 a.m. this airplane started signalling the monitors that he was ready to begin spotting. When at length the *Severn* was moored and able to fire, the airplane reported her first shot as 200 yards short and too far to the left.

The first two salvoes from *Königsberg* had been for ranging purposes, the last shot falling about 500 yards short, but she was firing only two guns. When presently she was straddling the monitors, she was seen to increase the guns to five, that is to say the whole of her starboard battery, for the port side (as will be seen in the photograph earlier) was next to the western bank and would not bear. No one was in so perfect a position to witness the German cruiser's gunnery as Commander Cull, he says:

> Her firing, which was obviously shore controlled, was magnificent, and the monitors were continually straddled, it appearing from the air that they had been hit many times, as the splash of the salvoes often hid the two ships from observation.

On the other hand, the monitors' fire about 7.25 was very wild, and so frequently fell on to the land, that at first the airplane found some difficulty in spotting.

Fifteen minutes later the *Mersey* was hit twice, the first shell knocking out her for'ard 6-inch gun, killing the whole gun's crew of four and wounding four others, including the quartermaster in the conning-tower. A part of the gun-shield was blown away, and the ship herself had a miraculous escape from being blown up; for the flash set fire to a charge that was being placed into the gun, and this in turn ignited a charge which was being passed up, severely burning the chief petty officer in the magazine. Fortunately, the flaming charge was put out at a crisis when split seconds separated the ship's life from complete disaster. The second shell hit the motor-boat that was alongside *Mersey*, burst, sank the boat, but was thus prevented from sinking the monitor, though at the time everybody was convinced that the *Mersey* was holed.

The *Mersey's* captain now signalled *Severn* to say he was retiring, and again she had the most wonderful good fortune. The first shell in addition to killing some and rendering others insensible, had splintered, so that one piece went through the for'ard bulkhead and wounded an unfortunate man in the sick bay. Two more men literally felt the touch of death pass them by; for they happened to survive solely because they had just gone forward to weigh anchor. But now, she had barely cleared out of her anchorage and got under way, than the airplane saw a complete salvo of five shells fall exactly on the beginning of the propeller's wake—not twenty yards from the *Mersey's* stern. It flooded the whole quarter-deck, but once more this monitor came through: she had moved off barely in time.

In the meanwhile, *Severn* carried on, about 7.55 scored her first hit, and it had struck splendidly, for it seemed to knock out the *Königsberg*'s foremost gun, so that her salvoes now dropped from five to four. During the next quarter of an hour five or six more shells were seen by the airplane to hit the German, and most of the rest fell just over her, covering her with showers of Rufiji mud. None the less, Captain Looff's gunners still maintained their magnificent shooting, "and from the air it certainly seemed that the German luck was out in not scoring more hits." It was only after several corrections by Sub-Lieutenant Arnold that the *Severn* had finally found the target, the wireless messages being received on board from the observer in the air and then passed to the gunnery lieutenant, who after making the necessary deductions informed the guns.

It was with no small pleasure that pilot and observer looked down to behold the vanquisher of *Pegasus* now receiving her punishment. When that first hit occurred under the fore-bridge, there was a large burst of brownish smoke. The next two hits were seen respectively to be amidships and on the port quarter, the *Severn*'s shooting being beyond all praise: but by 8.15, and for no apparent reason, she seemed to get completely off the target. In fact, there was only one chance shot which arrived before 8.30.

But several incidents had just been happening. At 8.10 the *Mersey* reappeared, and came to anchor about 500 yards downstream yet on the north side, and began again—this time with her after-gun. About five minutes later the tide had swung the *Severn* round again so that her for'ard gun would no longer bear. Now at 8.10 Commander Cull's airplane was due to leave the scene and be relieved by a Caudron machine; but the latter was delayed in arriving, so the former remained until 8.40 by which time shortage of fuel made it impossible to spot any longer. On landing safely at Mafia aerodrome by 9.10 and examining his machine, Commander Cull found scarcely any petrol in his tank, but a bullet hole through the port centre upper plane; for during that hectic morning his machine had been under constant fire from both the *Königsberg* and Pemba Hill.

About nine o'clock Captain Fullerton also was compelled to make a move, he reported:

> The enemy salvoes continued straddling *Severn*, and it only seemed a matter of time before she was hit; and this in conjunction with the fact that the aeroplane had gone home, and *Severn* had swung round again so that her fore gun would not bear, decided me to shift billet and open range.'

Now this decision had two fortunate results, which happened with strange immediacy. The *Severn* had barely weighed anchors and begun to move downstream than some vigilant eyes in the monitor suddenly caught sight of four men up a tree on the small island. There seemed to be a platform with a khaki figure not quite hidden by the mangroves less than half a mile away from Captain Fullerton's ship.

So this explained, in part, the excellent shooting by *Königsberg* ? At once the spot was shelled by a 3-pdr.:

> .... and as we swung round I fired three 6-inch lyddite into the position. This was undoubtedly a prearranged spotting position, and shows that the enemy must have somehow got hold of the very day of the attack, and of the exact anchorage.'

From now onwards *Königsberg* 's fire lessened, and for the rest of the day became less accurate. It was quite obvious that there was still the alternative spotting station on Pemba Hill, but its distance was most of 3 miles away from the monitors' first anchorage. We have here in this episode a notable example of how thorough was the German intelligence system; for it must have been some motive other than pure chance which enabled the enemy to know which of all these rivers was to be the monitors' sphere; which was to be their anchorage; which was to be the day of attack. The Germans had in fact designed an interesting triangle, whose apex was the *Königsberg*, one side of the triangle extending from the latter to the Pemba station and the second side from *Königsberg* to the island station. An imaginary line drawn between Pemba and the island formed the base, and exact information could have been passed back to Captain Looff from the very first salvoes.

But the second result was this. The *Severn* had only just moved from her position than *Königsberg* dropped a salvo from several guns, all beautifully together, at the very spot just vacated by this monitor. She had barely gathered way than the shells fell ten yards clear of her stern, flooding the quarter-deck and giving the men who were securing the stern anchor a thorough wetting. So it was that this morning each of the two monitors escaped being blown up, with only the smallest margin available. During the 2½ hours in which the *Severn* had been under fire her captain insisted:

> In my opinion it was sheer good luck that kept the ship from being sunk, as shells were continually falling ten yards short or over.

By 9.45 a.m. the *Severn* had moved down river 500 yards to the other shore and anchored near the *Mersey*, opening fire at 11,300 yards. During the next thirty-five minutes the attack continued without an airplane to spot, and this was not satisfactory even though from the new position it was possible to see the tops of *Königsberg's* masts. It was essential to have some means of ascertaining how the monitors' shells were falling, but the difficulty of flying had repeated itself just at an awkward development. Commander Cull's engine was in a bad humour, and it was not till 11.50 a.m. that he could take off from Mafia again.

We got away as quickly as possible, arrived over the coast at 3,000 feet, but found ourselves in the middle of severe bumps, both cloud and land, and in consequence I had great difficulty in keeping my height for the first two hours, only managing to keep at about 2,500 feet. We shaped course the same as in our last flight, and again received the attentions of the *Königsberg* and Pemba, which probably accounted for most of the bumps: two very loud reports were heard as we arrived on the port side of the *Königsberg*, and my observer saw the flashes of the two guns, and the smoke of the burst beneath us.

But whilst at last this airplane managed to reach 4,000 feet, and to wireless the corrections, not more than a couple of good shots seemed to find their target; those from *Severn* for the most part being over and those from *Mersey* a long way short. The *Königsberg's* were wild and short likewise, though falling at times near the monitors. Captain Looff, either of necessity or economy, was now firing with only two guns, but at times with one. Clearly the loss of her island spotters was being keenly felt. On the other hand, both *Severn* and *Mersey* were being hampered by the wireless confusion, which made accurate gunnery out of the question.

It was disappointing to keep receiving the same signal "600 short," in spite of the sights being altered. "Up 1,000," came the order, but still no hit was seen. Then the guns were gradually given extreme elevation, and the wireless once more complained, till finally *Severn* got under way and made for her original position off Gengeni Island. Unfortunately, in so doing she got aground at the bows, but it was only a temporary delay and at the original range of 10,800 yards she resumed indirect firing over the trees.

No good results seemed to accrue, and the wireless spotting was confusion itself. Regrettable such a deadlock certainly was, yet there was every excuse. In the first place, these were the very early days of communication between ship and aircraft, and the latter was under heavy fire all the time. But secondly, the problem was complicated by the presence of two ships instead of one. For whom was this message intended? Was the *Severn* firing short? Or was it the *Mersey*? And, thirdly, could it be that the *Königsberg* was cleverly butting in with her wireless to throw our gunners off the mark.

At any rate no good purpose could be achieved by remaining any longer. It was now 3.45 p.m., the ebb tide was running down swiftly, the wireless communications had broken down, so it was time to "pack up" and go home. Even a second airplane had made matters more difficult, since spotting directions came from two sources which differed widely. It had been an expensive day, and on the whole discouraging. Apart from the sad loss of lives and injuries to her people, the *Mersey* had received serious injuries. No fewer than 635 shells had been fired by the *Severn* and *Mersey*, and only 78 corrections received from the air. The guns had become very hot, and this again did not make for accurate shooting. Keyed up with enthusiasm and toiling mightily, the ships' companies had already been on duty for exactly twelve trying hours: they were now physically, as well as nervously, tired out.

The two airplanes between them had kept up aloft for a total of fifteen hours under the riskiest conditions, with every rifle and light gun directed that the *Königsberg* still possessed. So much for the debit side. On the credit side of the account, it could be claimed that the moral effect against the enemy was severe, his seclusion had been violated, and his very existence severely menaced. It was the opinion of Captain Fullerton at this time that, "I do not consider the enemy fit for sea without considerable dockyard refit." That is to say, she would be less likely than ever to attempt running the blockade and resuming an offensive at sea. Against this theory of the damage inflicted we have Captain Looff's affirmation of a later date that the British naval attack of July 6 did not impair the *Königsberg* 's fighting capacity. She had been injured, though not vitally; five men being killed and eleven severely wounded.

The two monitors recovered their anchors and proceeded downstream. As they sluiced along with the tide, there was not a powerful opposition, and both sides were swept by the ships' guns; but when they reached the river mouth a hot reception awaited them, just as some months previously the *Newbridge* party, returning from their operations, had an exciting departure through the Simba Uranga narrows. Two field guns on the north side of the Kikunja entrance at short range made determined and good shooting, the shells falling extremely close. One of these just missed the *Severn's* top, a second burst fifteen feet over, a third exploded within fifty feet of the *Mersey*, whilst a fourth actually struck the latter.

It was now getting dark, so that every moment of daylight had been spent within this river. At full speed the monitors—scarred but still able to carry on—hurried past the one-fathom line into the three-fathom soundings and at 4.45 were beyond the danger zone. The rest of the blockading squadron was awaiting them near Komo Island and welcomed them back with cheers. To the *Mersey* there fell the sad duty of committing her dead to the Indian Ocean, but her wounded were received aboard the *Trent* alongside which the monitors secured. Every officer and man was worn out with fatigue—"done to a turn"—and a meal was followed immediately by an attempt to sleep. Unfortunately, the wind was not in a consoling mood tonight, and the sea got up. Tugs, monitors and *Trent* maintained a noisy bumping contest, and it was little rest that anyone was afforded.

Next day the admiral paid a visit to the wounded, whilst another airplane reconnaissance (this time with Squadron-Commander Robert Gordon as pilot, and Commander Bridgeman as Observer) was sent out to investigate the amount of damage sustained by *Königsberg*. The information seemed to be that whilst the *Königsberg*'s foremost gun had been knocked overboard, and that she was otherwise damaged—on the quarter-deck, amidships and between the funnels—she was very far from being destroyed. It was therefore quite manifest that a second expedition must be made by the monitors, and the same risks must be endured again: but the same mistakes could not be repeated.

To this aim the intended date was kept a secret until late in the preceding day. By such means alone that essential condition of success—the element of surprise—could be ensured. But in the meanwhile, the monitors were falling to pieces with the strain of the first day. Firing at extreme elevation had wrecked cabins and damaged bulkheads, and the work wrought by German shells needed attention. So, for most of a week there was plenty to occupy hands and minds in making hulls fit to bear another bombardment; taking in fresh ammunition; formulating new plans.

And among the latter was a method for avoidance of any more wireless confusion. The monitors were to fire singly, and not together. There should be no doubt as to whom the airplane was addressing.

So, we come to the night of Saturday, July 10, when sudden orders for tomorrow's attempt sent another thrill of expectation vibrating. The last sandbags were in their protective positions, the last chair was removed, a few officers and men from the *Hyacinth* came aboard as reinforcements, and now Sunday dawned but not as a day of rest. For the engine-room department there would be sweating toil with the temperature registering 135°, whilst on deck or in the top no doubt the enemy's shells would make life quite hot enough. The one great question which exercised sailor and aviator alike could be answered by neither. Was this to be the final and decisive effort at destroying the enemy; or would she continue to remain a menace till long after the monitors had worn out their guns, shaken their structure into scrap; and the last airplane had collapsed into wreckage?

CHAPTER 18

The Second Attack

The arrangements for July 11 were in many respects similar to those of July 6, but in details a few alterations were made. As tides wait for no man, and it was not possible for man to wait till dead low water coincided with the dawn again, the only possible compromise remained to take advantage of the flood tide into the Kikunja River and ignore the cover of night. It was further planned that the *Mersey* should offer herself as a target for the *Königsberg's* concentrated attention and thus allow the *Severn* a free offensive hand to shell the enemy without interruption.

In setting forth on this second expedition there was frankly nothing of the same natural enthusiasm which characterised the first. Neither officer nor man, who had been through the prolonged ordeal of Tuesday, could look forward with any pleasure to a repetition. On the physical side must be reckoned the effect of tropical sun on crews cooped up within steel decks, the disinclination to eat, and the ceaseless toil before overstrung nerves had opportunity to settle back to normal.

But there was also the sense of having failed in the first instance, and the fear that even now the task would be beyond their capabilities. It is in retreat that an army's discipline and good training best show themselves, and by just these same qualities can crews gird themselves to go back and try again. An unpleasant, thankless, dispiriting job had to be tackled, but the motive force was massed obedience and respect for tradition, rather than a cheery light optimism. The advance towards *Königsberg's* river was with that stolid resignation of a man, about to undergo a major surgical operation, entering the theatre.

It was decided to puzzle the enemy by the sight of tugs, though any cloak of uncertainty would last but the shortest while, and the main object was to get the *Severn's* guns pumping shells on to the cruiser without wasting more minutes than were required for anchoring. At 8 a.m. the tugs *Blackcock* and *Revenger* took *Severn* and *Mersey* in tow from Tirene Bay; at 10.40 the tow ropes were cast off, the crews were sent to general quarters, and the monitors steered towards Kikunja mouth. Twenty minutes later in broadest daylight the bar was passed, and at 11.35 the ships were now alone steaming through the gauntlet with the same field guns booming indignation as before.

There was for the monitors' people an unpleasant familiarity in everything that could affect the senses of sight and sound. The very noise and positions of those German guns were identically the same as on the two previous occasions of passing, and the expression of hate would last neither longer nor shorter than hitherto. Altogether there was unrelieved monotony, which to tired nerves brought merely an increase of irritation. The whistle and scream of German shells, the dull thuds, and the vibrating din of the monitors' guns banging in reply, were too reminiscent of a recent event.

Not less uncomfortably recurring was the *Mersey's* ill luck, for again she had to suffer. Two shells plomped on board, one striking the captain's cabin, then bursting and wounding a couple of men, knocking down the officer in charge of the after 6-inch gun together with some of his crew; whilst the second fortunately burst among the sandbags round the after capstan and thus did little damage only. Still, it was such a prelude that could not be conducive to confidence for better success further up the river.

By 11.40 this brief spasm was over and the river expanse lay clear ahead, but already the enemy appeared to be despatching messages in a hurry; for when 7,000 yards from the north end of Kikunja Island a boat was seen "pulling furiously" (as Captain Fullerton describe it) "for dear life" (as another eye-witness saw it) across the river from east to west. Fire was opened with the *Severn's* for'ard 6-inch till the occupants beat a hasty retreat into the nearest bank and, leaping ashore, disappeared.

The same machine-guns and rifles on the port side of Kikunja entrance had crackled and spat their bullets, and in turn been quickly silenced. It was all so precisely what had been expected, and as the progress continued up stream, revealing one creek after another, the monitors' fire would be directed on objects which only a few days before had aroused suspicions immediately. Each bend of the shore, indeed almost the trees themselves, had now become so familiar as to inspire unutterable contempt for the whole pestilential river. How many more trips would have to be made through this fever-breeding area?

And when it was past noon, the *Mersey* was left to remain in the vicinity of the very spot which had been her second anchorage last Tuesday after she had come back from licking her wounds. Her duty today was to keep moving and draw the *Königsberg's* fire, whilst the *Severn* was able to moor a little higher up than on the previous date. Whereas at the occasion of the first expedition Captain Fullerton originally brought up just to the east of the small island containing the German spotting station; on this Sunday the *Severn* chose the western side, being thus within a slightly shorter range of the cruiser.

But events did not quite work out according to plan, for the enemy's fire refused to restrict itself to the moving *Mersey*, however tempting a target she offered herself. Having treated the latter to a couple of salvoes, the *Königsberg* concentrated on the *Severn* both now and for the rest of the day's episode. It was at 12.12 p.m. that the engagement was opened by *Königsberg*, whose first salvo went over the *Mersey*, and the second dropped short though dangerously near. Five minutes later the German was firing rapid salvoes of four guns, one salvo falling about 50 yards ahead of the *Severn*, which was extremely inconvenient since the latter was permitted no peace during the act of anchoring.

Rarely has British naval discipline been put to a severer test, and the trial was far worse than that which had to be borne when the *Newbridge* was being moored. One has to take into consideration the force of the tide, the river's width, the way left on the ship, the exact spot marked on the chart, the length of cable to be veered at each end, so that when finally squared up the monitor should be in the assigned position for her guns to bear. All this demands careful and unflurried seamanship, perfect self-control and unquestioning obedience: the whole evolution could be ruined if the men lost their presence of mind and let cable or wire take control. Consider, for example, the parlous peril in which the helpless vessel would find herself if through lack of seamanlike skill, the stern anchor's wire got wrapped round a propeller!

But these perspiring men remained steady at their mooring duty in spite of the terrible accuracy with which *Königsberg's* gunners were trying to knock them out. Over and over again the deadly shells fell so close as to flood the *Severn's* decks without hitting her, and meanwhile the anchor parties carried on as if it were a peace-time practice.

Without any bungling or mishap bow and stern were secured, guns were laid and fire was opened seven minutes after the second anchor was down; and by 12.30 the monitor was beginning her first salvoes whilst the first airplane was aloft ready to do the spotting.

This again had for its pilot the intrepid Flight-Commander Cull, with whom as observer came Flight Sub-Lieutenant Arnold once more. They had left Mafia aerodrome at 11.50, found the sky very cloudy and therefore bumpy. They had crossed the sea at 3,200 feet, but came down to pass just beneath the heavy cloud banks hanging over the delta. The fleet of ships had been seen intentionally making a great show of proceeding apparently to Zanzibar, but of suddenly turning back to the Rufiji when the two monitors entered. Then H.M.S. *Weymouth* and *Pyramus* had come within the Kikunja approaches, bombarding fiercely, whilst the remainder of the fleet by reason of their draught were compelled to remain outside. Certainly, all this display was an impressive sight and symbolised a tremendous effort.

"Before the delta on this day" recorded Captain Looff, commanding officer of S.M.S. *Königsberg* in his report of July 20, were the *Cumberland*, *Weymouth*, *Hyacinth*, *Astraea*, *Pyramus*, two gunboats, three auxiliary cruisers, six armed whalers, the Duplex and two other large steamers. Although this German officer is not strictly accurate, and includes a number of units which happened to be elsewhere, it is interesting to have his assertion that all ships opened fire on the *Königsberg* and very soon found the range. It is always valuable to have a second witness whenever possible, and Commander Cull's evidence from aloft is unique because he could see both sides of the game in much the same manner as a spectator perched high on a grand stand views an athletic contest.

As his airplane crossed the mainland, he noticed the monitors "well inside the entrance delivering a terrific strafing to the surrounding country," whilst all the other ships outside were attending to the supposed spotting station at Pemba Hill. Cull next kept flying at about 2,000 feet between the enemy and the monitors, with heavy black clouds covering the sky above. It was noticeable that the *Königsberg* was shooting with her customary accuracy and some important results would be seen before long.

But a secondary theme now demanded part of the airman's attention, so that there was a kind of anxious undertone which inspired no great happiness. Up to the time when the Severn began firing, the flying machine's engine had been running with moderate satisfaction, but now it began to fail at the most awkward period, with the resulting loss of height. However, this Henry Farman had caused no delay, but was ready the moment *Severn* went into action, which we have remarked to have been 12.30.

Her first two salvoes were unobserved by the airplane, and evidently pitched wide in the mangrove forests or in the sandy mud of the banks; so, a correction of "400 yards down" was wirelessed to the monitor. This was not enough, and the next three salvoes were still unobservable. Again, from the sky came the signal "400 yards down and 20 yards left," which caused the sixth salvo to be visible in the forests beyond the *Königsberg*: an improvement, yet not perfection. All the same it was thrilling work to sit up there below the clouds with the finest view of rivers, channels, monitors, cruisers, smoke and splashes; to watch each rival barrage drawing closer, ever closer, till it seemed as if the finale would be one simultaneous holocaust of German and British.

From the air came a third signal: "100 yards down, and 20 yards left." The effect was quickly visible, for the seventh salvo was now accurate for range but too far to the left. One more correction, then!

So, the eighth salvo was a direct hit. There could be no question at all, and a couple of shells clearly landed on the enemy's fo'c'sle. It was now 12.42, the target had been found, hits continued to be made repeatedly and very few corrections were needed. This, indeed, was the day's crisis. On Tuesday one of *Königsberg's* five starboard guns had been knocked out, so that today she began with four. After 12.42 she could use only three; after 12.44 only two, and after 12.53 only one. A terrible explosion was heard at 12.49, which indicated something ominous aboard the *Königsberg*; but simultaneously, the *Severn*'s wireless took in the following brief poignant message from Cull's airplane: "We are hit. Send boat for us."

It would be impossible without the aid of moving photographs to convey the full import of this announcement, which came as the climax to separate contestants. Thrill after thrill, suspense following suspense, excitement overtaking excitement, had followed with the speed of flashing thought, and every tick of the watch meant another change. It had been only just when the *Königsberg* had got the *Severn's* range, and the monitor's destruction seemed to the aviators "very imminent,' that the latter succeeded in getting the monitor on to the target, throwing up a large column of dense smoke. But now, at what might have been the culmination of the enemy's troubles, the danger-point shifted from river to sky. Commander Cull stated:

> For the last eight or ten minutes, the machine had been losing height rapidly; though I was flying her at a speed and angle she should climb very rapidly at, something was obviously wrong with the engine, and I put it down to a small injury from rifle fire. We had also observed puffs of smoke in the air beneath us. When at 2,400 feet, about 12.45, a shell must have burst beneath us, as I experienced the most violent bump I have ever felt, and the machine was out of control for several seconds. This was on our journey towards the *Königsberg*, and I turned shortly afterwards, as the engine could now be heard running very badly, and the machine was losing height more rapidly.

A few moments later the engine stopped dead: one of the cylinders had been blown right off. Now the amazing coincidence remains that this injury chanced to be the work by one of the last two shrapnel shells which the *Königsberg* fired. She was at her final gasp, enduring the ultimate stages of her agony, when she delivered a knock-out blow to the Henry Farman. But this news was not vouchsafed to the monitors, robbed of their aerial eyes; and there is something immensely moving when we think that only an island of dense trees curtained off the grim, awful drama that was ending aboard Captain Looff's vessel. Rarely had a battle been so persistently uncertain, so wave-like in its phases as the destiny rose and fell.

Those in the airplane were now in real peril. Momentarily poised between two barrages of shell, its loss of control spelled certain fatality. Like a wounded bird, it was flopping now helplessly. Would the *Königsberg* be able to claim it as a prize? Or could it last out until well within the monitor's reach? Perhaps death would come with tragic celerity when a machine struck the tree-tops and smashed human skulls.

The episode is one worthy of remembrance because it shows the brave calm, the unexcited pluck, of two men careering through space yet thinking of their duty first and their loyalty to comrades in priority to personal safety. Flight-Commander Cull narrates:

> I started to glide towards the *Mersey*, as, though the *Severn* was nearest, I did not want to interfere with her fire.... On our way down my observer, with great coolness, gave a correction by wireless to the *Severn*, bringing her hits from forward on the

THE RESCUE ON JULY 11

H.M.S. *Mersey* is seen up the Kikunja river. She has just rescued from drowning, and attack by crocodiles, the two aviators, Cull and Arnold, after the latter have effectually directed the *Severn's* guns on to *Königsberg*. The *Mersey* is now passing the *Severn* to continue firing on the enemy.

TOWARDS THE ENEMY

This is the view of the Kikunja river as seen from the *Severn* on July 11, 1915. The *Königsberg* is right ahead, made invisible by the high trees on the left. Owing to the height from which the picture was taken, these dense trees do not appear as tall as in reality.

Königsberg to amidships."

A small correction was applied, and the last view of the *Königsberg* from the machine, before she was hidden by the trees, was the satisfactory sight of hits being registered amidships, one funnel having already been knocked over and the ship in general appearing to be on fire."

By prolonging the glide as much as possible, Cull made a tremendous effort to cheat the enemy of two prisoners and one aircraft. It was a close shave, but whilst Arnold was wirelessing the letters "H.T." (signifying that the monitor was registering a hit) and now wound in his aerial with methodical resignation, having to the end done all that could be expected, Cull managed to make what Captain Fullerton considered "a magnificent landing"—not among the mangroves but—on the water, and within 150 yards of the *Mersey*.

Cull says:

Our landing on the water was very slow but the machine, on touching, at once turned a somersault. My observer was shot over my head well clear. I, however, had foolishly forgotten to unstrap my belt, and I went down with the machine. My feet also were entangled, and I had the greatest difficulty in freeing myself, tearing off my boots and legs of my trousers in so doing. When I came to surface, my observer was hunting in the wreckage for me, and we both then started swimming for the *Mersey* whose motor-boat picked us up.

Now the *Mersey* at that moment had happened to be the least busily engaged of the two monitors, which was fortunate; and the practical utility of having a motorboat ready to shove off at once, without even the smallest delay, was readily demonstrated. None the less for both pilot and observer there passed an interval which was one of those occasions when the clammy hand of death can almost be sensed. Both officers had been jolted badly, yet continued sufficiently conscious to begin inflating their lifebelts and start swimming; but simultaneously each mind wondered how soon a sniper's bullet would pierce them, or how quickly would be felt the cruel bite from a crocodile.

The suspense was real and profound, though it lasted not more than minutes. Luckily no snipers were within reach, and the din of battle had scared all crocodiles away, so both officers were hauled into the motor-boat and brought back safely to the *Mersey*. Fortunately, someone chanced to be standing by with a camera amid all this thrill-

THE STRICKEN *KÖNIGSBERG*
The German cruiser is seen lying with a heavy list to starboard, after being shelled by the monitors during the final attack of July 11.

THE FINAL INSPECTION
This interesting aerial photograph shows the terrible effect of the monitors' shells. The *Königsberg* is lying a complete wreck, with central funnel gone and hull partly submerged at high water. Observe the sharply defined road across the sand used by the German survivors.

ing adventure, and the accompanying photograph shows the *Mersey*, after having picked up the survivors, closing in past the *Severn* to resume firing.

As there was no chance of salving the doomed machine, the motor-boat returned and blew up the Henry Farman with a ¼-lb. tin of gun-cotton lashed to the engine. No one reading this chapter can fail to agree with Captain Fullerton's summing up of the aviators' conduct as "extremely gallant," and they had kept up communication to the last second, he added:

> The twenty minutes they were spotting, were the most critical time of all, and the fact that they had the pluck to remain in the air with a failing engine over enemy's country, and still manage to get *Severn's* shots into the target, is in my opinion worthy of the very highest praise and reward.

So now they had the interesting experience of witnessing the fight from afloat: of completing the most perfect picture which has ever been permitted of a naval engagement. A large explosion, followed by thick clouds of smoke, indicated how terrible a drama was proceeding aboard the *Königsberg*. Despite the absence of an airplane for spotting, the *Severn* during the next hour fired 42 salvoes of two guns, using the same range as before but with greater deflection to the left so as to bring the shots farther aft from the *Königsberg's* fo'c'sle. Eight more explosions were heard, and again rose large clouds heavy with yellow-black smoke drifting away to leeward.

All this time the *Mersey* had been, as we have noted, not anchored but under way. She had opened fire at 12.15, but in order to prevent confusion, Cull's airplane had not spotted for her. It was now 1.40, so Captain Fullerton ordered her to advance up river beyond the enemy's old island spotting station, and to a point only 7,000 yards from where *Königsberg* lay.

This, of course, was the nearest approach to the enemy hitherto attempted by water, and there now arrived a second airplane with Flight-Lieutenant Watkins as Pilot and Lieutenant Bishop as Observer, who spotted for *Mersey* so ably that she belched forth 28 salvoes, and began hitting with the third. Every officer and man had been told on the quarter-deck the previous night that today the enemy must definitely be destroyed, and if necessary, the monitors would have gone still further upriver; for the contest must end one way or the other. Sunset could not come before either the monitors or the cruiser were vanquished.

Every time the terrific explosions came from Captain Looff's vessel there rose great cheering from the monitors, and when the *Mersey* steamed up past the *Severn* (whose guns had become too hot for further accurate shooting) there was again loud enthusiasm from the former. The *Severn* had gone into action with topmast housed (as seen in one of the accompanying photographs), but now she raised it so as to afford a better view. Captain Fullerton remarked:

> I personally went to the topmast head and saw the enemy on fire fore and aft... and a stream of smoke coming out of the top of her mainmast. It is estimated that she must have been struck with from some fifty to seventy 6-inch lyddite.

She presented a pathetic sight minus her middle funnel, one mast leaning over, the other broken at the maintop, and a lyddite pall stretching from bow to stern punctuated by flames.

But one small incident will show the risks awaiting even such shallow-draught vessels as these river gunboats. The *Mersey* had not proceeded more than 1,000 yards up river than she got stuck on one of the numerous bars which are formed by the twisting island-dotted channels of the Rufiji. Twice she essayed to find a crossing, there were only eight feet on the bar, and the tide was falling: there was thus a great risk that she might have to remain immobile for several hours a fair target to the enemy.

The situation scarcely bears contemplation, and if only the *Königsberg* still had guns available with other forces entrenched (as indeed they were) on the northern bank a little further up, the duration of at least one monitor's life would have been exceedingly brief. Actually, however, she got off, anchored as requested, and carried out her firing. At last came the momentous signal from Watkins' airplane: "Target destroyed." Nothing now remained but to be thankful and depart. Captain Fullerton recorded:

> At 2.20, I had come to the conclusion that a further expenditure of ammunition was a waste, and decided to proceed up and have a look at her.'

Ten minutes later, however, was received through the ether a signal ordering both monitors to retire, so the downward trip with the ebb tide began.

It was, in the words of Flight-Commander Cull, "a somewhat noisy passage" to the Kikunja mouth, both banks being well shelled by the British gun-layers who were saying farewells to a pestilential river that they hoped would never have to be revisited. At the entrance, as usual, the German field guns sent in a hot fire which was as determinedly answered, with no advantage to either side, though fragments of shells were afterwards picked up on the *Severn's* deck. Then out into the open sea, where safety lay, beyond the range of all enemy guns, the monitors found the two tugs waiting by the bar to tow the conquerors back to Tirene Bay. Along came the *Weymouth* steaming fast, her forefoot sending up a fountain of fine spray, the white-figured admiral on his bridge calling upon his officers and men to hail the monitors with three rousing cheers.

A memorable evening indeed, a marvellous lull after the storm of shells and raucous sounds, to be sitting peacefully alive amid the sandbags smoking a cigarette and scarcely realising that months of work had suddenly ended; that the *Königsberg* riddle of the Rufiji had been solved, that the cruiser could never come forth from her tangle of bent steel, but must remain for all time cemented to the Rufiji mud. The Royal Navy had avenged itself for the sinking of *Pegasus*: yet the expense had not been inconsiderable, about 1,000 shells and 3,000 rounds of small-arms ammunition being used on those two July days.

These Rufiji operations are unrivalled in naval history, not merely because they show how much attention can be diverted from other spheres of activity by a cruiser who likes to take every advantage of natural facilities for temporary immunity; but for a strange combination of the old and the new. No one could have foreseen that monitors would come back to the navy, still less that they would be indispensable, or that they would work in conjunction with that youthful Air branch of the Service. Hitherto river expeditions had suggested such minor motives as the suppression of pirates and slave running, whilst in truth the monitors in their advance from the sea were really protecting the ocean routes against a deep-water raider. Conversely, the *Königsberg*, if she had met her two assailants anywhere outside the river, could have chosen her own distance and wiped out *Severn* with *Mersey* in a few minutes.

Thus, the intricate channels, the intervening island of trees, and all the other physical defences of inner Africa placed the German cruiser at a disadvantage; and from the moment that she had been compelled to discard her mobility, changing her character from an ocean vessel to that of a ditch-crawler, she threw away her essential superiority. Once again, then, is manifested the weakness of a fast warship. For great speed means large expenditure of fuel, which in turn connotes either a convenient and protected base whither she can dash for coal or oil; or, at any rate, the organisation of supply vessels so perfect that it will never fail when the cruiser's bunkers are empty. But where there is a superior naval power contending, which has in its grasp the command of sea and trade routes, the coaling system for enemy cruisers can be rendered of no avail: neither collier nor oiler can dare to attempt a rendezvous except at grave risk. Thus, the *Königsberg's* fate was determined even from the very first, and her offensiveness could only be a short-lived gamble. When once such opponents as the British "Town"-class cruisers, with their well-filled colliers and bases at Mombasa and Zanzibar always in readiness, came on the scene it was possible to perceive that the German would never get her fuel. She had, in effect, interned herself; the command of the ocean belonged to her rivals, so that succour was out of the question.

Strictly speaking, the *Königsberg* was first starved of supplies, then driven into a navigational dilemma, and finally maimed rather than utterly destroyed. A man-of-war is a mobile hull carrying artillery and crew, but so long as her guns and personnel survive and only her mobility is lost, the victory over her is far from complete.

Here, then, was another curious situation which this Rufiji undertaking supplied. If all those British shells, which found the target, had struck her in a sea engagement, she would have gone down below the surface with the loss of all her guns and most of her crew. In other words, there would have been a definitive conclusion. But the *Königsberg* had dragged herself so far up a shallow waterway that it was impossible for her to founder under any circumstances: she merely sank deeper into the African mud, became more immobile than ever, whilst such guns and men that survived were now available for other hostilities.

When, therefore, Captain Looff on July 20 wrote his report of this action, and concluded with the affirmation that "S.M.S. *Königsberg* is destroyed but not conquered," there was something more than rhetoric or empty theatrical bombast. He was stating a plain fact whilst making a true prophecy. Under him still remained a well-trained body of disciplined fighters, whose endurance had been tested by ten months of secluded monotony varied only by sudden onslaughts; and there could be no more determining trial of a crew's will to win than such an experience, up such a dull river, in such a deadly climate. That amid all this discouragement, uncertainty and isolation from the civilised world, Captain Looff managed to keep up a wonderful standard of fighting efficiency is a brave lesson for all of us. Compelled to look out daily, for nearly a year, on to those fever-laden swamps and snake-shaped mangroves, must have been a heartbreaking trial, but the final artillery duel proved that there had been no moral deterioration, and that the German gunnery had maintained a remarkable standard to the bitter end.

We have it on his authority that the monitors' shells fairly deluged his ship on this eleventh of July, causing at first especially heavy losses on his fo'c'sle, which is exactly in accord with the airplane evidence. In his official report Captain Looff adds that the gun crews and ammunition parties in the fore part of *Königsberg* were all killed, whilst he himself was badly wounded. Then came corresponding disaster at the after end of the ship where a fierce hell flamed, and there was the awful thunder of ammunition exploding, during which further considerable casualties occurred. These detonations had not failed to impress the crews of the monitors.

Such was the climax reached aboard the *Königsberg* that the upper deck was in a state of devastation and all the gun-crews had perished, so further continuance of reply to the monitors became impossible, the last two shrapnel shells (as we have seen) bringing down Flight-Commander Cull. The task of *Königsberg's* crew now became transformed from that of firing the guns to putting out the fierce conflagration which threatened to consume every German in one terrible holocaust, and the magazines had to be flooded.

The engagement had been fought out fully so far as our enemies were concerned, though the monitors were still carrying on across the intervening forest belt which for the most part concealed the target, and at 1.30 p.m. Captain Looff, who had again been badly wounded, ordered his First Lieutenant to blow up the *Königsberg*. It was a painful yet inevitable decision, and in the meanwhile the ship which had been their home for so many months now was being abandoned. Under our heavy fire the survivors landed quietly in the ship's boats, fell in with perfect discipline ashore, having brought the wounded with them.

At 2 p.m. the *Königsberg* was blown up by exploding the head of a torpedo, which tore the ship apart under the fore-bridge. She developed a heavy list and sank to the level of her upper deck, there to remain till the last piece of steel shell should corrode through long

African ages, a symbol of man's inhumanity to man, an ironical lesson in civilisation from Europe to the savage primitives of the Rufiji.

At sunset her riddled flag and pennant were ceremoniously hauled down, whilst three cheers were raised for their Emperor. The wounded were presently taken to the field hospital at Neustrieten, whilst the rest began a totally different phase of warfare under the Governor of German East Africa.

Such was the contrast existing to landward and seaward, respectively, of the delta at the close of a day which had been so replete with uncertainties that both monitors had just as likely a chance of being demolished as they had of demolishing. But by the fortune of war these two British gunboats had escaped death with the narrowest margin, and no more causalities than a few men slightly wounded; so that there arrived at Mafia Island an entire muster for the great dinner which awaited them, though by 10 p.m. sleep could no longer be denied by tired bodies and worn-out nerves. It was the end of a perfect day and the completion of a river campaign, yet behold how slender a reliance was aviation in those experimental days. Of two airplanes sent up, the Henry Farman was now lying a wreck for the Kikunja crocodiles to sport with; whilst the Caudron machine, which had arrived afterwards and taken over, Flight-Commander Cull humorously records:

> . . . was so delighted with what she saw that on her return to Mafia Island, she landed in the swamp and capsized, the pilot being thrown out without damage. He promptly forgot his Observer, in the excitement of giving the glad news to the interested crowd, and left the last-mentioned officer upside down, struggling to undo his belt with his head in the swamp. His feeble cries, however, soon attracted attention and he was hauled out not much the worse for wear, being refreshed with a bottle of champagne which was shared amongst all hands.

Next day in their grass hut on Mafia Island the R.N.A.S. officers gave a luncheon party to which came Commander Bridgeman, Colonel McKye, and the captains of the two monitors, who have all figured in our narrative; the occasion concluding with a solemn burning of the three Short seaplanes no longer required, and no longer cherished. Since there seemed no further need for aircraft, and in the future only the blockade would have to continue, stores were immediately packed and transported to Zanzibar. Here, with great relief, the news of *Königsberg's* fate was celebrated amid rejoicings, and the Sultan held a victory reception. North to Mombasa, west to Lake Tanganyika, south to Durban and Capetown the information travelled, that the Rufiji difficulty passed; there could be no more anxiety for any of its waterways, and still less for any of the Indian Ocean highways.

CHAPTER 19

From Sea to Lake

The position now to be faced off the East African coast was simple. Firstly, to prevent supplies of food, stores, guns, and ammunition arriving by sea for the German land forces; secondly, ensuring that German steamers at present inactive within certain ports should not fit themselves out as raiders with the guns and crew from *Königsberg*. In regard to these points, the *Kronberg* (ex-*Rubens*) had shown what might be expected on the one hand; whilst the presence in Dar-es-Salaam of the *Tabora, König, Feldmarschall*; in Tanga of the *Markgraf*; and in Lindi of the *Präsident*, continued potential menaces given the right opportunity. Cutting-out expeditions had therefore to be undertaken to render incapacity certain.

But whilst everyone was congratulating himself on having seen the last of the Rufiji there came a sudden setback. The *Laconia* from Zanzibar had proceeded to Mombasa, where the whole R.N.A.S. contingent was to be landed (for duties up country), together with some new airplanes that had recently arrived too late for the *Königsberg* operations. Now the month of July had not passed before the admiral entertained doubts as to whether the *Königsberg* really had been effectively smashed up. Owing to the fact that the last available machine had crashed immediately on its return from the scene, it had been impossible to make a reconnaissance, wherefore he decided that this should now be done since two more Caudrons and three seaplanes were available.

A small party of officers and men must return to Mafia Island, make a close aerial inspection therefrom, and report the actual damage visible. It fell to the lot of Flight-Commander Cull, Flight-Lieutenant Blackburn and a few mechanics, with one machine (a Caudron) that this should be done; so, "in a deep state of gloom," as the former records, by the end of July this little band were brought back. There was the same awkward job of getting the Caudron ashore athwart the ship's boats, unpacking, erecting and trying in the air. Then the weather set in badly for several days, and it was not until August 5 that a reconnaissance could be attempted.

Ascending from the aerodrome at 3.24 p.m., she flew over, and the first object to be noticed on reaching the delta was an enemy tug which was lying at the top of an elbow near the entrance on the southern side of the Simba Uranga channel with an awning aft. Then the *Königsberg* came into view, and was still in her old position but with a list to starboard of 15. Her starboard battery was under water, her quarter-deck was a bright red colour, thanks to the rust which had accumulated in little more than three weeks, for at high water it was completely submerged, and the boat davits showed up above.

The centre of the three funnels was lying across the stricken hull in a heap, and the only gun visible was that on the starboard side of her fo'c'sle still in position. Her topmasts were gone, there remained part of the fighting top, and in general (as will be seen from the accompanying photographs) she was clearly destined never to see the ocean again. All this was most satisfactory.

On reference, however, to one of these illustrations the reader will notice what Commander Cull describes as "a sharply defined road across the sand," and there was a group of huts close to the water's edge. No one was visible aboard the cruiser, but a disturbing factor was the sight of a large lighter lying on her port (*i.e.* landward) side with a small *dhow* lashed along the lighter. Astern of *Königsberg*, and very close to the western shore, were a supply ship with awning and a couple more dhows, which had been visible on a previous occasion.

In examining such historic pictures, it is not difficult to imagine the showers of shells which came down from the sky on July 11 at pretty much this angle, and one can indeed visualise the party of German survivors as they landed on the adjacent shore which shows up lighter than the neighbouring forest. The lighters and *dhows* we cannot see, but on a later page we shall find Cull's supposition that they were engaged taking guns to the beach was not very far wrong.

Such a possibility had of course been reckoned with, yet how could it be prevented? The delta was still in the enemy's control and not occupied by British forces; the time had not yet come when the freedom of the Rufiji, like the command of the sea, belonged to the blockaders. There was plenty of work in store for the monitors up and down the coast, and it was hardly worth while risking them unnecessarily at the Kikunja or Simba Uranga entrances. Even one shell from a field gun might penetrate hulls at the waterline, burst among the engines, and bring about total loss; which, having regard to the considerable difficulties in towing such delicate shallow gunboats out from England, would have caused inconvenient delay.

Therefore, it was decided to bombard from the air, blow the lighters to destruction, and thus put a stop to any transference of *Königsberg*'s guns. Orders were given to this end, the necessary bombs were being sent down from Mombasa, but before they had time to arrive came a decision countermanding the intention. Cull's party were recalled, the R.N.A.S. detachment was split up, and assigned to more pressing operations. One section under Squadron-Commander Robert Gordon was sent with seaplanes to Mesopotamia, whilst the other under Flight-Commander Cull was to take the two Caudrons (accompanied by Flight-Lieutenant Watkins and Flight Sub-Lieutenant Gallehawk) up country and work under the military. The last-mentioned officer had now definitely severed his connection with the Royal Naval Reserve, and been transferred to the Royal Naval Air Service.

We thus see no more of that plucky and enterprising band which did such bold pioneering in the Rufiji air, and made the monitors' fire fatal to the last German cruiser beyond the seas. Presently both Captain Fullerton of the *Severn* and Commander Wilson of the *Mersey* were awarded the Distinguished Service Order, as indeed were Commander Cull and Lieutenant Arnold. Captain Fullerton today is an Admiral, whilst Group Captain Cull is one of the senior officers in the Royal Air Force, and Gallehawk is a Wing-Commander. Our final African view of the two last mentioned is at Mombasa early in September 1915, leaving by train to serve under General Tighe. They were setting off for an entirely new front, and the departure was spectacular whilst not wholly devoid of humour.

To the special locomotive were attached carriages for officers and men; to say nothing of the vans which carried a couple of hangars, two Caudrons in their great packing-cases, and quantities of stores. "The whole bore a very close resemblance to a circus on the march," is Cull's apposite description, yet its personnel still retained that wonderful adaptability which is characteristic of those brought up to be sailors. For the day came when something had to be done in counteracting the German African Army's unpleasant habit of leaving in their retreat land mines on the road. The R.N.A.S. thereupon converted a Ford car into a road minesweeper that would tow astern some heavy

NO FURTHER TROUBLE

The once smart German cruiser *Königsberg* still lies miles up the Rufiji, bare of paint and covered with rust. This photograph, which was taken nine years after the action of July 11, 1915, indicates the vessel as she appears at dead low water, her bottom resting on the river bed.

ON THE LOOK-OUT

Some of the *Königsberg's* crew are seen ashore among the palm trees with their mounted telescope. This photograph was taken by a German officer.

logs, which in turn would touch off the explosives whilst not injuring the car. Surely such an ingenious contrivance for African warfare requires to be illustrated by a supreme comic draughtsman!

Now that we have seen it established beyond all manner of doubt that the *Königsberg's* career was ended, there still remains much to be told, for, whilst the ship was finished, there was considerable work ahead for her people, whose fighting spirit continued to be something real and vital. It is true that during the attack of July 11, the British monitors had been able to do more than ruin *Königsberg*.

Today we know from German sources definitely that Pemba Hill was an "*arttllerte-beobachiung*" (spotting-station), as had been surmised; that our fire, besides killing the cruiser's gun-crews and a number of signalmen, had severed the German telephone wire which connected *Königsberg* to the observation station; but such information was not available at this time. Whilst, too, one could scarcely expect the survivors to remain unemployed, it was impossible to ascertain their numbers, or whither they would next be sent. But it was a natural inference that shipwrecked sailors would sooner or later find themselves afloat once more, and somehow—somewhere—they would get hold of a vessel. Hence arose the natural anxiety as to the five steamers in Dar-es-Salaam, Tanga and Lindi.

But warfare is so full of surprises that we must not expect to find events following in strict logical sequence. The *Königsberg* 's crew, instead of being kept together as one compact company after being stranded on the river-bank, was split up in such a manner that whilst some proceeded to engage in warfare afloat, others (so to say) lost their marine personality by becoming land warriors and became merged with the German East African military forces.

So much has been written concerning the East African Armies' campaign that it is necessary for reference to be made only incidentally, and we shall be able to concentrate our attention now on the adventures of such *Königsberg's* survivors as carried their naval service through to a conclusion. At the beginning of this volume, we likened this ship's company to a gang who were being hunted by the police, and the simile still holds; for, when the pursuers were able to wreck their vehicle, the gang forsook the ship and separated, just as some miscreants when chased have been known to discard a damaged car before scattering across the adjacent country.

Our task henceforth is in fact the piecing together of many events which have an aim and motive that could not be appreciated in those

THE TELEPHONE ROAD

This was cut through mangrove swamps by the Germans at the Rufiji delta, so that the *Königsberg* might receive warning immediately British men-of-war were seen approaching the coast.

THE TROPHIES

In the foreground is the ingenious native dugout with an Evinrude motor attached; and alongside lies the cylinder fitted with dynamite that was to blow up the British ships on Victoria Nyanza. On the other side is one of the *Königsberg's* famous 4.1-inch guns mounted on a field carriage and used by the German Army.

days; and even the smallest item takes on a significance now that we have the whole truth from both German and British records. Hitherto, for the sake of clarity and directness, we have followed the *Königsberg's* own story alone, and traced the clues right up to one remote corner of the Rufiji; but German East Africa meant something more than the series of rivers pouring out through a particular delta. This was the largest and most important of our enemy's colonies, and in vastness twice the size of Germany; but here is the interesting geographical fact, that, whilst this eastern coast-line from Wanga in the north to the River Rovuma in the south measured some 470 miles, the colony also possessed at its north-west, west, and south-west boundaries a littoral of about 950 miles.

For a considerable part of the Victoria Nyanza, the entire eastern sides of Lakes Kivu and Tanganyika, and a great deal of Lake Nyasa, were all comprised in German East Africa. It so happened that the opposite shores of these lakes were British or Belgian, or Portuguese territory; therefore, that from the earliest days of hostilities there would be a clashing of wills which, on the entry of Portugal as an ally at a later date, could not be expected to become less fierce. We have, then, a most curious situation of a land war being almost ringed in by war on sea as well as lake.

This was further complicated because, (1) there was a paucity of European men in the German colony; for we have it on the authority of General von Lettow-Vorbeck that his forces of white men never exceeded 3,000; (2) very few of these (and 10 *per cent* at the most) were experienced in seafaring; (3) the colony, being so hemmed about, could not expect to be sent any reinforcements. An odd steamer or two might possibly run the Indian Ocean blockade, but that would be the best limit to further assistance. (*Vide My Reminiscences of East Africa* by Paul Emil von Lettow-Vorbeck; Leonaur 2010.)

It follows, then, that whilst von Lettow could, and did, gather to himself 11,000 *Askaris* for excellent soldiers, he was awkwardly situated in regard to white men. Of the latter some must assuredly remain to protect Tanga, Dar-es-Salaam, Pangani and Lindi; many more must be destined to march painfully and fight strenuously in the field; but not every available seaman should be sent soldiering, when there was a demand on the lakes for officers and crews accustomed to ship-handling.

At the beginning of the war, the German Defence Force (as it was officially designated) consisted of not more than 216 Europeans and

2,540 *Askaris*, plus 45 of the Police Force with their 2,154 *Askaris*. The officer commanding was Colonel (later General) von Lettow-Vorbeck who had come out to Dar-es-Salaam (the colonial capital) in January 1914. He had at an earlier date been in command of the Marine Battalion at Wilhelmshaven, and had accompanied the German Fleet on some of its cruises besides taking part in naval manoeuvres. We envisage him from August 1914 responsible for the colony's protection not merely by land but by lake, and fitted by his previous career for the dual role.

Now when the *Königsberg* cleared out on July 31 from Dar-es-Salaam in order to be at sea before the outbreak of war, and avoid being bottled up by the approaching Cape Squadron of Admiral King-Hall, there remained within the harbour not only the steamers *Tabora*, *König* and *Feldmarschall* belonging to the German East Afrika Line, but also the German naval ship *Möwe*. (Not to be confused with a different vessel of the same name which during 1916-1917 carried out two raiding voyages in the Atlantic.)

The latter was of little fighting value, and indeed looked more like a steam yacht. She was eight years old, of only 650 tons, with a speed of 10 knots, a single funnel, bowsprit and schooner bow. Her duty off this coast was surveying, but now she was entrusted with the important office of organising a supply of coal and stores for the *Königsberg*, after which she was to fit out one of the steamers as an auxiliary cruiser and then go raiding. We at once begin to perceive the danger which threatened the African sea-routes from the first, and very nearly materialised. It was part of the extensive system, arranged before the War, for attacking Allied shipping in every ocean of the world.

Lieutenant-Commander Gustav Zimmer was *Möwe's* commanding officer, and he succeeded in fitting out a couple of supply ships for *Königsberg*; but the possibility of taking a raider to sea was promptly negatived by the arrival on the coast of Admiral King-Hall's three cruisers who made the risk too great, so that on August 6 Zimmer brought the *Möwe's* crew ashore. Two days later came H.M.S. *Astraea* to bombard Dar-es-Salaam, and the Germans themselves (as we have previously noted) closed the harbour to big vessels by sinking their floating dock across the narrow entrance. On that same August 8 did Zimmer sink the *Möwe*, though much further within the port.

But why had Zimmer not taken a chance and put to sea under cover of darkness with all lights obscured? Could not a steamer fitted for raiding have set forth between the departure of *Königsberg* and the declaration of war with Britain? The answer is that, firstly, a raider must before all things be independent of the shore for long periods, and this connotes enormous quantities of coal on board; but secondly, she must be well armed. Now when Zimmer set about his preparations, he found both of these conditions impracticable of fulfilment: the requisite amount of coal was not obtainable, and the only guns at his disposal consisted of two obsolete 22-pdrs. with 400 rounds of ammunition.

In this dilemma Zimmer placed himself and crew of 106 at the disposal of von Lettow for defence of the colony ashore, and they travelled more than a hundred miles inland to a place called Morogoro, where they received their equipment and began their training as soldiers. Morogoro was one of the stations along the Central Railway which runs from Dar-es-Salaam *via* Tabora to Kigoma situated on the eastern side of Lake Tanganyika. This railway was about 787 miles long, and followed generally the old caravan route from sea to lake. The Germans had completed this locomotive road only as recently as the previous February, and it was destined to become of the greatest war utility because it made the Lake no longer in a state of isolation, but only a few hours' distance from the capital.

But what of the crews aboard those other steamers of the German East Afrika Line? Could not they be employed? Von Lettow admits that the matter was at first muddled:

"By mistake, the crews of a few ships belonging to the East Afrika Line, lying in Dar-es-Salaam, were informed, in response to their application, by the officer in command at the railway station, that there was no room for them in the Defence Force." (*My Reminiscences of East Africa.*)

As to the *Möwe's* contingent, 30 seafarers under Lieutenant Horn took train to Kigoma on August 12, went aboard the German lake steamer *Hedwig von Wissmann* (60 tons), armed her with four pom-poms brought from the *Möwe*, and settled down to naval routine once more. This small ship was commissioned as a man-of-war in miniature, though her best speed was 7 knots and the range of her guns did not exceed 2,200 yards: but we shall observe in the course of these pages how gradually this beginning was to work up into a climax of exceptional importance.

First of all, there must be a naval base, so Kigoma harbour was fortified against any attack by lake. Tanganyika is no glorified pond, but is 400 miles in length and forms the longest freshwater lake in the world.

At its narrowest, however, where its sole inlet, the River Lukuja, flows in at the western side by the Belgian Albertville, the width is only about 30 miles. Practically the whole of this lake was either Belgian or German, for the British territory at the southern end was restricted. But there was one Belgian steamer, named the *Alexandre Delcommune*, of 90 tons, which was accustomed to travel up and down, and even on August 6 she had called at Kigoma to fetch some cargo. By a curious decision the German authorities had allowed her to depart, but now Lieutenant Horn was ordered to search her out, render her innocuous, and thus make Tanganyika to all practical purposes a Teutonic sea.

Easier commanded than accomplished! Looking for a small steamer somewhere on an inland ocean of 13,000 square miles requires time and patience, and Horn did not sight her till August 25. The *Delcommune*, being off the Belgian shore and possessed of superior speed, was able to escape under the cover of the batteries of Lukuja River, but after an action of two hours the Belgian steamer received from her enemy so many hits in boiler-room and funnel that she had to be beached, whilst the Wissman had not been touched. Thus in one action the Germans obtained what von Lettow rightly regarded as "the extremely important command of the Lake."

Next day von Lettow, appreciating fully how desirable a natural defence were the waters of Tanganyika, wisely decided not to waste the other 76 of *Möwe's* men by employing them as soldiers, but ordered them up to the Lake, and appointed Lieutenant-Commander Zimmer to be in command of both the Tanganyika and that smaller Lake Kivu which lies to the north. Before August was ended, we find Zimmer with the whole of his old crew, an excellent harbour, a wide western frontier before him; and a most useful railway at his back.

Whilst he had been unable to assist the *Königsberg* any longer, the railway had in the most perfect manner provided him with special mobility, so that naval strength could be transferred with comparative facility from salt water to fresh. Not merely had he brought with him from Dar-es-Salaam every article from *Möwe* likely to be serviceable; but in particular the *Möwe's* steam-pinnaces, together with all the other boats belonging to the government which happened to be in that seaport. In effect, then, this transportation of men and small craft was the incident of naval strength making a jump from one colonial boundary to another.

But the *Delcommune* was wounded rather than destroyed, and it became Zimmer's duty to wipe her out utterly. She was lying hauled up on the beach at Albertville by the Lukuja mouth: so, reported one of *Möwe's* steam-pinnaces, whereupon Zimmer with two of his officers, Lieutenant Horn and Lieutenant Odebrecht, proceeded thither in the *Wissmann*. It was a plucky intention to blow up the Belgian steamer as She lay there surrounded by a temporary protective breakwater of sand which kept off the surf. One October night Horn with a party of men landed on the silent shore, who made their way unseen past the sentries and got right up to the steamer before the alarm was raised. There was just time to throw some dynamite into her stokehold and light the fuse before rushing back towards the *Wissmann*.

On the following night Odebrecht with seven more men landed less than a mile north of the spot, stole in to within a few yards of the *Delcommune* and by the light of the watchfires ascertained that the explosion had certainly damaged her bottom. But this was not enough, for the steel plates were capable of repair, and another effort had to be made later that same month. This was a small but quite intriguing combined expedition consisting (*a*) of the *Wissmann* and a steam-pinnace afloat; (*b*) some of *Möwe's* men and *Askaris* ashore. Now the *Wissmann*, having been built as a light passenger steamer for the lake, was too weak to carry any gun heavier than a pom-pom, so the pair of 22-pdrs, which had been brought up from Dar-es-Salaam were mounted on a raft which was towed astern of the *Wissmann*. It was an ingenious method for obtaining some sort of a gun platform, though the speed of travel under these circumstances was less than 2 knots even in smooth water. Whilst Horn took charge of the *Wissmann* and Odebrecht commanded the pinnace, Zimmer was on the raft.

The Belgian position was found to be impregnable from the land, with wire entanglements, pits and earthworks; but after the German craft steamed in to about 4000 yards of Albertville harbour they were attacked by two 12-pdrs. One of these was now silenced by the 22-pdrs., and the *Wissmann's* pompoms together with the Askaris engaged the Belgians' 3-pdrs. After the range had come down to 1800 yards, and the raft's guns had for some time been shelling the *Delcommune*, Zimmer ordered Odebrecht to enter the harbour with his pinnace. For the Belgian steamer had been repaired and launched since the last visit; she was now lying moored inshore, and the Germans proposed to take her away. The pinnace, however, got aground and came under a very hot fire. Compelled to give up the task, she retreated with her rudder damaged and her hull punctured in many places. But the shells from the raft had been so well directed that it was presently reported the *Delcommune* consisted of nothing better than a wreck.

At the southern end of Tanganyika, where British territory skirts the lake, there existed two ancient British steamers possessing neither engines nor boilers. Lest these hulls should become a threat at some later date, Zimmer sent the *Wissmann* and *Kingani*, during November 1914, to destroy them likewise. The *Kingani* is worth noting, as she deserves special attention. Built of wood, this little steamer was 55 feet long, and her speed of 7 knots made her more than useful. She had come by train from the Indian Ocean, but a sister ship (named the *Wami*) was still up the Rufiji.

With Zimmer's mixed flotilla of two small steamers, pinnaces and motor-launches, the German Navy ruled the Tanganyika waves and was keeping the Belgians from crossing the lake into East Africa. The curious development is now witnessed of the *Kaiser's* colony being blockaded by the British at its eastern side off the Rufiji, whilst German mariners at the western side were blockading the Belgians. Nor was the miniature marine content to be passive. It kept the shipless rivals in a state of suspense by repeated surprise visits and raids. On November 20, 1914, the *Wissmann* and *Kingani* co-operated in driving off a Belgian company in the bay west of Bismarckburg, and in capturing four machine guns together with over 90 miles of telegraph wire that came in most useful to the Germans. Lake stations were bombarded, landing parties assisted by spies used to make night attacks on weak garrisons, and altogether the *Möwe's* people were scouting, photographing, harrying, pinning their enemies down, and thus rendering von Lettow the greatest possible help.

So passed the first ten months of war, by the end of which von Lettow was sending up troops to Kigoma whence they had to be taken down the lake to Bismarckburg by the flotilla and some dhows. But the shipwrights at Kigoma Dockyard had not been idle and by June 9, 1915, succeeded in completing a new steamer which was a very important addition. She was of 1500 registered tons, and similar to many a cargo vessel that one sees every day of the week round the British Isles. Of the three-island type, with a funnel rather shorter than is customary at sea, she possessed a speed of 8 knots, which made her the queen of Lake Tanganyika, though she was named the *Graf Götzen*. Her immediate utility lay in respect of trooping, for she could carry about 900 men in a quarter of the time taken by the *dhows*.

Our late enemies by means of their engineers, the resources at Kigoma and Dar-es-Salaam, and the Central Railway, had certainly wasted no time: or opportunity; but, separated as they were from Germany, they had to rely entirely on their own supplies. Airplanes would have been most useful, but could not arrive. It is true that at the very beginning of hostilities one did exist. It had been brought by the S.S. *Tabora* (previously mentioned) to Dar-es-Salaam, where there was to have been a great Exhibition opened in August. Certainly, this machine was taken over for military purposes, but it was no more reliable than our early examples off the Rufiji; for it came to grief by accident, destroying both itself and the pilot.

CHAPTER 20

Establishing Command

Until the end of 1915 Lake Tanganyika continued to be dominated by the German flotilla, and we shall shortly return to watch a sudden, surprising, intensely dramatic change which came over that vast inland water.

In the meanwhile, there were several disconnected, independent, sets of naval operations being carried on which formed parts of the East African campaign yet were, so to speak, minor affairs of their own. On Lake Nyasa there had been a steamer ever since the year 1875, when the *Ilala* made her first trip, and nine years later there had come out from England thither, packed in sections, the 25-tons S.S. *Charles Janson* for the Universities Mission. She had to be taken up country in pieces so small that there were 380 cases in all and each had to be no bigger than could be carried slung on a pole by two men. The joining together of all these parts under the Central African sun, until a two-masted ship with sails and steam took shape, and the launching without any special apparatus, remind us of what pioneering was accomplished in Victorian days.

Nyasa is another huge freshwater sea, 350 miles from north to south, and in places 400 fathoms deep. At the outbreak of war, the Germans owned thereon the armed gunboat *Hermann von Wissmann*, named after their distinguished countryman who explored equatorial Africa in the 'eighties and afterwards became Governor of German East Africa. The British strength consisted of the S.S. *Gwendolen* (350 tons), armed with one 3-pdr. and a Nordenfelt quick-firer, together with the *Pioneer* (40 tons), which had one Nordenfelt. It became necessary to recall the *Charles Janson*, the *Queen Victoria* (177 tons), and the Universities Mission steamer *Chauncy Maples* (320 tons). But the *Gwendolen* was sent to search over the 14,000 square miles on August 8, and five days later discovered the *Hermann von Wissmann* at Sphinxhaven undergoing a refit. She was promptly disabled, and the crew taken prisoners, so that the control of this lake forthwith became British. A later expedition in May 1915 was made against Sphinxhaven by Lieutenant-Commander G. H. Dennistoun, R.N., when this disablement received confirmation. Thus, the experience on Nyasa was exactly the reverse of that on Tanganyika.

Even that small Lake Kivu which lies 60 miles to the north of Lake Tanganyika and likewise is about 60 miles long, did not escape attention. 'It was here that Lieutenant Wunderlich, with some of *Möwe's* men, requisitioned a motor-boat; though he was destined to be wounded and afterwards to die. The fourth of these large "backwaters," *viz.* Victoria Nyanza, affords a far more memorable lesson in the use of "sea" power, and the capabilities of little ships. The latter, without doing much spectacular fighting, were none the less the decisive factor in causing the Germans to withdraw from one of the richest parts of their colony. Although the territory surrounding the Victoria Nyanza was divided fairly evenly between Britain and Germany, the latter's naval strength thereon was weak, notwithstanding that this inland sea has an area of some 26,000 square miles.

Just as the German Central Railway connected Dar-es-Salaam with Kigoma, so the Uganda Railway from Mombasa to Kisumu joined Victoria Nyanza to the ocean coast after a journey of less than 600 miles. Kisumu is at the north-east corner of the lake and was the headquarters of the Uganda Railway steamers, with such valuable adjuncts as wharves, workshops, dry dock and building slip: in fact, there existed a splendid base not merely for the upkeep of the British peacetime flotilla but for the reconstruction of craft sent across the railway in sections. These ships were manned by native crews, under British commanding officers and engineers appointed by the Colonial Office.

Germany had two chief ports, Bukoba on the western shore and *Mwansa* on the south. At the outbreak of war Britain owned on this lake three twin-screw passenger ships; the *Clement Hill* (800 tons), the *Winifred* (600 tons) and the *Sybil* (600 tons): together with four single-screw cargo carriers, *Nyanza* (1,000 tons), *Kavirvondo* (1,100 tons), *Usoga* (1,100 tons) and *Rusinga* (1,100 tons), though the latter was not quite completed until several months after the campaign had begun. There existed also a couple of tugs, an old steamboat, a launch, a motor-boat and some steel lighters. With the exception of a 12-knot tug, the speed of this flotilla did not exceed 10 knots.

The Germans were handicapped by having no railway to this lake

MAP TO ILLUSTRATE THE NAVAL OPERATIONS ON VICTORIA NYANZA

and possessed only one small tug, the *Mwansa*, besides some lighters and launches. At first sight, then, the British "sea" strength was overwhelming: it might have been, but there were no guns available for some weeks, whereas the enemy mounted two good guns in the *Mwansa* which accordingly became a serious threat. Indeed, the slow *Nyanza* on August 3 barely escaped the *Mwansa's* attentions. Not until September did some sort of armament arrive, when a couple of French 24-pdrs. (more than twenty-five years old with an effective range of less than a thousand yards) were mounted in the *Winifred* and *Sybil* respectively, and a much older (muzzle-loading) 9-pdr. was allotted to the *Kavirvondo*. Such were the improvised and delayed preparations for a lake war.

Naturally the German land forces began by an effort to seize Kisumu, which was the Portsmouth of this "sea." The capture of such a naval base would have meant obtaining control over the whole lake and shutting it off from British East Africa, with serious results to Uganda. The enemy brought a mixed force of 560 Europeans and *Askaris* in the *Mwansa* and lighters to Karungu on the east side and landed them, so that they were able to reach a place inland, named Kisii only 30 miles to the south of Kisumu. The *Clement Hill* almost simultaneously arrived at the last-mentioned port with two companies of King's African Rifles, who on September 10 established themselves to the north of Kisii, and after a brisk action caused the enemy to retreat.

But the *Mwansa*, emulating the deeds of *Königsberg*, *Emden* and others' exploits on the high sea, now tried raiding across the lake against the unarmed steamers which were still carrying on their work, as their sisters plied their trade along the ocean routes. She was still further aided by the fact that both at Bukoba and *Mwansa* there was a German wireless station. Just as *Chatham* and other British cruisers had been sent to locate and destroy the *Königsberg*, so from October 1914 came the determination to seek out the *Mwansa* and bring her to finality; the flotilla selected consisting of the previously mentioned *Winifred*, *Sybil*, and *Kavirondo*, besides the *William Mackinnon*, which was an old-fashioned steamboat of 80 tons.

Many of the British officers in these railway steamers had previously served at sea in bigger ships and in the Royal Naval Reserve, though it is to be noted that such was the complete lack of war prevision on Victoria Nyanza that at the outbreak of hostilities there existed no plan for their employment on the lake, where their local knowledge was invaluable. These officers had therefore immediately started for the sea coast to report themselves, though fortunately the authorities recalled them and the flotilla after all was not bereft of their services. We have noticed that there was, too, no sort of war organisation for ships, guns, or ammunition, still less for administration; and the result was that during the initial weeks confusion in control was rife. It was the old story of "muddling through" and hoping for the best.

But under a Lieutenant-Commander R.N.R., as Senior Naval Officer, the flotilla of four rendezvoused preliminary to making a search of Speke Gulf, which is a rocky inlet at the south-eastern end of the lake. H.M.S. *Fox*, which we last saw off the sea coast, was able to send up by rail a 12-pdr. and gun's crew for the *Sybil* to be used in addition to her 2½-pdr. There had also arrived a Maxim gun for the *Winifred*; and, whilst the *Kavirondo* had her original 9-pdr., the *William Mackinnon* found herself with two 24-pdrs. An attempt was made by *Winifred* to bombard Bukoba wireless station, but the range was too great for her.

She and *Kavirondo* were sent to search round Speke Gulf for two days where it was deemed likely the raider might be lurking amid the islets and bays, but no benefit accrued other than the capture of three dhows and the destruction of a German rice mill ashore. The *Sybil* (senior ship) and *William Mackinnon* had remained patrolling to the west of Speke Gulf in the neighbourhood of Mwansa, which lies at the mouth of a sound with Juma Island to the north-west. There was still no sign of the German, so the investigation was transferred northeastwards beyond Ukerewe Island. Now it so chanced that just as the *Sybil* was steaming through the Majita Channel, she struck an uncharted rock and had to be beached to prevent being sunk. Everything movable was salved and her personnel got back safely to Kisumu, but she had to be abandoned where she lay in German territory.

Weeks passed, and in the first week of March 1915 another effort was made to discover the *Mwansa*, which continued a serious danger to the transportation of troops. By this time, and a curious reversion, the *Königsberg* was able to render us assistance indirectly. In an earlier chapter we saw that she had sunk the *Pegasus*, but that the latter's guns were being salved. Among these. were a quick-firer and two 3-pdrs., which were sent up by rail from Mombasa to Kisumu and mounted in the *Winifred*, whilst the *Fox* and *Goliath* (now that the *Königsberg* was bottled up) were able to contribute other small armament. From the survivors of *Pegasus* there also came a party of bluejackets to help in using the guns, and we thus have another similarity to the enemy's employment of *Möwe's* crew on Tanganyika.

For this second attempt *Winifred* and *Kavirondo* were selected, who early on March 6 reached the Speke Gulf area. The former hid herself under the hilly Nafuba Island which is to the south-east of Ukerewe Island. Now between Ukerewe and the mainland there exists a very narrow and very shallow channel called the Rugesi Boat Passage, which was not navigable by the British steamers; but for the small tug *Mwansa*, possessed of intimate knowledge, it was quite practicable and there was reason for believing she was wont to make use of this convenient short cut. If we care to think of Ukerewe as Sicily and the mainland as Italy, with the Rugesi Passage as the Messina Straits, we: have on a small scale a naval situation analogous to that of the *Goeben* and *Breslau* exactly seven months before this date. (*Vide The Goeben & the Breslau: the Imperial German Navy in the Mediterranean, 1914—The Flight of the Goeben and Breslau* by A. Berkeley Milne, Julian S. Corbett, W. L. Wyllie and Others: Leonaur 2020.)

Whilst the *Winifred* was lying invisible within reach of the southern exit, the *Kavirondo* was waiting at the northern end of the Passage, so that there existed an ambush for the enemy by either exit. Inasmuch as she was the only vessel which the Germans owned in these waters, and her services were in great demand for bringing supplies to the military forces along the shores, it was impossible for the *Mwansa* to spend in idleness such periods that were not being used for raiding. So, this was quite a good spot for her pursuers to hunt.

Nor had they long to wait, for, having entered the Passage by night, she was in the morning sighted by our observers (posted on Nafuba Island) steaming | north and towing a lighter filled with stores intended for troops further up the lake's eastern shore. Out came the *Kavirondo* at the top of the "straits," who frightened the tug into scurrying back not merely southward out of the Rugesi, but eastwards to the extreme end of Speke Gulf. Here at Guta (whence there lay communication northward by land) she hoped to leave her stores, but she had not reckoned with the well-armed *Winifred* who now slipped out from Nafuba and gave chase. The *Mwansa* cast off her lighter and headed for the beach with utmost speed and, having reached soundings of a fathom and a half, sank herself; though she continued to fire her guns until the *Winifred's* superior artillery drove the Germans ashore. She had clearly suffered heavy damage and was left as an obvious wreck.

But another of those curious twists of fortune ensued, which are always occurring during a campaign and prevent the direct application of cause and effect. Leaving the raider in a condition similar to that of *Königsberg* at her final destiny, the *Winifred* and *Kavirondo*, conscious of having at last obtained for Britain complete command of the Victoria Nyanza, steamed off northward. They halted on their way to visit the wreck of *Sybil* but found it so fiercely protected by enemy troops that rifle fire made further inspection out of the question. So, the late senior ship must remain a loss.

On the other hand, within a few days the Germans by sheer doggedness managed to salve the *Mwansa* and get her back into the port after which she was named. They then gave her a thorough overhaul so that after a few weeks she was in service again, though not once more did she go raiding or carry a gun. As a man-of-war she faded out of existence, so that in truth there was no "sea" power on Victoria Nyanza left to the Germans; but in her original capacity as tug she was still able to acquit herself creditably doing transport work in Speke Gulf—but using only the night hours. Not till the port of *Mwansa* was captured from the Germans on July 14, 1916, when the wireless station also conveniently fell into our hands, did the *Mwansa* show herself to enemy gaze.

And the *Sybil*? She likewise had one adventure following another. A few weeks after the *Kavirondo* and *Winifred* had been driven off from their examination of *Sybil*, a second call was made on her. On this occasion the *Winifred* shelled her mercilessly, inflicting such damage that it was hoped the Germans would desist from working on her. At the end of April (1915) there was yet one more transposition, when it was decided not to complete her destruction but try salving. If ever a vessel was ill-treated, her name was *Sybil*. She had been ripped open on a rock and bumped to a beach; the Germans had helped themselves to part of her upperworks; and, after the latter had dynamited her, her sister *Winifred* had struck her with two dozen shells. What a life for one whose career had begun as a peaceful passenger steamer! So now they proposed snatching her out of German hands, and fighting over her remains?

It was an imposing ceremony. Four hundred troops were transported by the *Winifred*, *Kavirondo* and *Nyanza*. The troops landed, but the enemy yielded easily and the work of reviving began. Ships and lighters went alongside, holes were plugged, pumps were set going and four days later she was floated off, and towed safely into Kisumu where she was docked. The amazing thing was that after all the above experiences neither engines nor boilers were much damaged, so the hull was repaired and she lived to go on with her transport duties. Like the *Mwanza* she retired from fighting, and rounded up an exciting period by assisting the Army. This was by no means inconvenient since now was developed an increasing demand for military transport: in fact, there was now introduced an improved organisation, under Commander G. S. Thornley, R.N., who had come out from England to act as Senior Naval Officer of the flotilla. The ships maintained a constant patrol, but their chief function was found in carrying troops. More bluejackets were sent up from the coast, as well as another 4-inch gun salved from the *Pegasus*.

To what practical use this naval domination of Victoria Nyanza could be applied is well illustrated by the incident of June 22, 1915. We have already called attention to the enemy's wireless station at Bukoba, a town on the lake's western shore where there was an important base with stores and garrison. The flotilla was able to bring a military expedition all the way from Kisumu and to cover the landing of the infantry with safety. The ships' guns likewise were able to render excellent aid in bombarding the Germans' positions, and finally Bukoba was entered, the wireless station destroyed, all ammunition and Government stores being burnt. Similarly, this command of the lake enabled the steamers to bring material and personnel to the extreme north-western corner *en route* for the Belgian forces operating from Lake Kivu district.

But we must now return south again to the Rufiji and Lake Tanganyika, which from July became mutually affected. The loss of *Königsberg* meant the release of 322 men for land or marine duties, and whilst the greater number were now absorbed as soldiers under von Lettow, fifty of *Königsberg's* crew, together with three of her officers—Lieutenants Rosenthal, Beckmann and Freund—came across to strengthen the German flotilla at Kigoma. This was a considerable addition, but it was supplemented by the arrival of Lieutenant-Commander Schönfeld, who deserves special mention. Here was one who had retired from the German Navy some time before the war, and had settled down in East Africa as a planter. Full of energy and a born leader, he had at once become extremely acceptable to von Lettow, who had known him during the preceding months, and Schönfeld soon found himself in the right sphere for his first-class driving abilities.

The reader cannot have failed to be impressed by the determined and well-placed opposition which the enemy had organised with their limited resources at the various mouths of the Rufiji delta. This was all the work of Commander Schönfeld, whose previous training as a naval officer exactly fitted him for the job. Far better than any soldier, he was able to distinguish the British units off the entrance, to discern their movements, and to send Captain Looff reliable information. Schönfeld served the interests of his country, and the *Königsberg*, with great devotion and the most commendable skill; so that not one British vessel entered either the Simba Uranga or the Kikunja without very grave risk. If only the German colony had possessed a few more powerful guns at that period, Schönfeld could have made the entrances impregnable. *Königsberg* would have remained in her lonely fastness as a continual menace, and we should have been compelled to maintain the Rufiji blockade for many more months.

The only force which Schönfeld possessed comprised a mixed assortment of naval ratings, European reservists and Askaris; having 150 rifles, a few light guns, together with the machine-guns already so frequently mentioned. This "Delta Detachment," as it was called, relied not so much on its positive numbers as on the skill with which they were employed. At a later date, when British naval and military officers were able to land and examine Schönfeld's positions, it was patent that he had taken every advantage for concealment by the local foliage and trees. Not merely were his emplacements invisible at even a few yards, but they were frequently changed as circumstances demanded.

Thus, whilst it was practically impossible for our steamboats and monitors to shell unseen targets, yet there was even less hope for the British cruisers outside who, in bombarding from a distance, had to rely on a certain amount of luck. Nevertheless, we have it on no less an authority than Captain Looff himself that such attacks on the Simba Uranga entrance were terrific; that:

> The British hurled a salvo of shells from all their guns across our outposts, beheading palm trees and filling the shore with yellow fog. For some time we thought that not one of the small detachment was alive.

Nor did Schönfeld's enterprising energy ease up when the *Königsberg* finally settled down to the mud on that fatal July 13. From various German sources of information, it is now possible to perceive exactly what happened. The total losses which our monitors had inflicted on Captain Looff's people were thus: 32 killed, 65 seriously wounded and 60 slightly wounded. That is to say, a total of 157 casualties, which represented a very high percentage, including Captain Looff himself among the seriously wounded. After the survivors had come ashore, they trekked 14 miles across country to the south-west till Kilindi was reached, whilst the sick cases were taken into hospital at Neustrieten.

In August about 150 survivors, under Commander Koch, set forth on a long march which at last brought them to Dar-es-Salaam, and were officially known as the "*Königsberg* Detachment." Those 50 who were sent to serve under Commander Zimmer on Tanganyika became part of the "*Möwe* Detachment." Whilst some bluejackets were employed on land for gunnery duties, there were about 80 invalids still confined to the above hospital in September. In that month Captain Looff recovered from his wounds and was able to take over command at Dar-es-Salaam, an order having been sent from home that he was to place the whole crew under von Lettow and come to an agreement with the latter as to how they were to be employed.

Now before quitting the *Königsberg*, Captain Looff had caused the breech-block of every gun to be thrown overboard in to the Rufiji lest his enemies should make use of his ship's armament. But this decision was somewhat precipitate. It should here be mentioned that when the monitors gradually silenced one gun after another, it was not because the weapons themselves had been—as surmised—destroyed; rather it was the guns' crews who had been blown out of existence. There now arrived at the wreck Commander Schönfeld who (as von Lettow remarks) "with great forethought" began to rescue these breech-blocks from the muddy bed, and under Schönfeld's supervision the whole of the ten 4.1-inch battery was brought ashore.

The cruiser was submerged so slightly that most of her ammunition could be reached by divers and landed likewise. Here was achieved an invaluable piece of work, for during the whole East African campaign von Lettow never had more than 60 guns, and 10 of them came from the sunken *Königsberg*. Having got them on to the beach, Schönfeld was faced with the problem of transporting them to Dar-es-Salaam across about a hundred miles of awkward country, but he got over his difficulty by obtaining several vehicles found on a neighbouring plantation. It was a great moral victory to have triumphed when despair had already set in. Of these 10 splendid guns, 5 were mounted at Dar-es-Salaam as protection against British men-of-war; 2 were sent on to fortify Tanga; 2 more travelled up by the Central Railway to the lake at Kigoma; whilst the tenth, after much travel and travail, at last reached *Mwansa*, on Victoria Nyanza, by September 12, 1915. There it remained until it was captured by British forces when *Mwansa* was occupied in the following July.

Now when the train steamed into Kigoma with such powerful modern ordnance, there was great joy. One 4.1 was mounted on shore to make this base secure from all attack, whilst the other was assigned to the newly built *Graf von Götzen*. It was placed in the bows of this comparatively big ship, and enabled her to terrorise the whole lake. Thus, thanks to fate, the monitors and Schönfeld, there were now 156 men of the German Navy on Lake Tanganyika with a flotilla consisting of the *Hedwig von Wissmann*, the *Kingani*, the *Graf von Götzen*, the steam pinnace and some quite small craft. Under the leadership of Lieutenant-Commander Zimmer there were those three Lieutenants from *Königsberg*, keen and plucky, able and daring; but in addition to all these must be mentioned three more officers, one warrant officer and 40 naval reservists from the ships of the German East Afrika Line sent up from Dar-es-Salaam.

Let us now see how the marine campaign on Tanganyika worked up to its crisis and conclusion; its comparison with the operations carried out along the waters of Victoria Nyanza may be studied with no usual interest.

CHAPTER 21

Tanganyika Tactics

All this neat little Lake Navy, with its miniature dockyard, its convenient rail communication for supplies from Dar-es-Salaam, and the *Tabora* wireless station situated between the two coasts, had one great lack during almost the rest of the year 1915.

There were no big British or Belgian vessels to be fought: they did not exist on Tanganyika.

It must not thereby be imagined that inactivity reigned: on the contrary, there was an extremely busy period for ships, officers and men. News filtered through from the opposite shore that the Belgians would not have to wait very long before the *Alexandre Delcommune* was replaced by a steamer of 1,500 tons similar to the *Graf von Götzen*, and would be named the *Baron Dhanis*. The Germans accordingly made it their business to find out where the construction was taking place, in order that steps should be planned for her destruction. The *Wissmann* and *Kingani* were ordered to reconnoitre along the Belgian side, and they paid careful regard to Lukuja which seemed the most likely site: but no signs of a slipway could be found.

Presently, however, the Belgian wireless imprudently made a free gift of information: intercepted messages proved that Lukuja was, after all, the spot. It was important to know from time to time how the *Götzen*'s intended rival was progressing, and when she was likely to be launched; so, it was this desire for knowledge which led to some thrilling adventures. First came Lieutenant Odebrecht, who stole ashore one night just to the southward and crept up till he could clearly define a building slip being constructed. It was 250 feet long, and that was a confirmatory fact of their rivals' intentions; for, whilst the *Baron Dhanis* had not yet taken shape, it was within probability that she would be not smaller than the *Götzen* which measured 200 feet in length.

This officer and Lieutenant Rosenthal (late of *Königsberg*) specialised in a series of risky raids, which for downright courage and cool determination stand out among the best stories of the war. Not once, but repeatedly, these two either together or independently courted death after landing from one of the flotilla and trying to evade the alert Belgians. On a certain night Odebrecht came off in a dinghy to make his way up the Lukuja River; on another occasion Rosenthal went disguised as a native, hoping to get through the sentries unsuspected. Both these attempts failed, but Rosenthal had scarcely better luck when he chose a particularly dark hour at a later date. He was just foiled from arriving at Lukuja close abreast of the building slip, but he captured an open patrol-boat manned by Africans whose testimony still further corroborated the Germans' intelligence.

And now came the climax of Rosenthal's exploits. It was the first of December 1915, and before the night vanished, he had brought the *Hedwig von Wissmann* within 200 yards of Lukuja. Dawn broke, and at this distance he had just time to get a good photograph of the building slip, though there were not even minutes to spare. With the coming of light burst around this ship a hot squall of Belgian shells, yet somehow there was no damage done and she got away. The photograph was developed, and proved that the building slip was now completed, but it seemed as if the new ship had already been begun. Further details were imperative.

So, Rosenthal steamed down here on the next night, and then transferred to a boat, whence he would at the right moment take to the water and swim to the beach. It was an undertaking of which the very bravest might think twice before attempting. An iron nerve and great power of physical endurance were essential, but the difficulties were cumulative, in that they needed a man with almost superhuman valour to meet them willingly. Firstly, these raids had become so frequent that the Belgians had never relaxed vigilance, and were ready to kill instanter.

If the *Königsberg's* late officer was to reach the shore, make his way through the sentries to the slip, and then escape, he would have to dart like a javelin. But as a preliminary to this he would have to contend with his body against the surf which was hitting the strand, whilst crocodiles of uncertain size and numbers intensified the suspense. Altogether Rosenthal had set before him a pretty full plan.

He started out, got within 300 yards by boat, took to the water, reached soundings, stumbled ashore and ran dripping inland without being noticed. There was the slip! And after another 50 yards he would be alongside. Yes, he would soon find the information: he was progressing excellently.

But now came the check! Sentries! They were moving about in alarm—looking with lanterns, expecting to pounce on him at any moment.

Rosenthal, who had spent so many monotonous weeks in Rufiji boredom, seemed to have changed into a totally different existence that was a sublime contrast to life in a cloistered cruiser. He could advance no further, but turned and scurried back. Plunging into the surf, he swam away from the land and was picked up by the boat in a state of exhaustion after a mighty narrow escape. Did it damp his ardour? Not the smallest. For on the following night he went through the same proceedings, except that he took with him a lifebelt, tied his boots on his head, wearing nothing except shirt, trousers and cap. This time he deserved to succeed, and actually did reach the slip, where he found a couple of motor-boats but no steamer.

That was enough. Regaining the water, he swam for the boat, but could not find her. He kept swimming, and still he failed to meet her; so, crocodiles or no crocodiles, there was not an alternative between keeping afloat and drowning. Morning came and found him still working his weary limbs, whilst away to the north he caught sight of the *Hedwig von Wissmann* steaming off home, having given him up as lost. It was enough to break even Rosenthal's stout heart, and now there was every likelihood that the Belgians would open fire on his head. He therefore tore his way a couple more miles to the south, came ashore at 8.30 a.m. and hid himself.

But such a succession of perils must certainly come to an end some time, and today his luck was clean out. Some Belgian *Askaris* discovered him and took him prisoner, yet even now he still felt the pressing urge to complete the task which had been entrusted to him. The news about those two motor-boats? It must reach Commander Zimmer—yet how? He asked and obtained permission for sending a letter to Kigoma, with the natural request that some of his clothes be forwarded; but on the back of this letter, he wrote an invisible message with his urine.

It was a time-honoured method which many a spy has employed with success, and the intelligence would have been welcomed. Unfortunately for the Germans, this letter never reached Zimmer for another two months, and during that period—came the sudden, dramatic alteration which was suggested at the beginning of our last chapter.

Rosenthal was a very gallant fellow, whose failure was more brilliant than the successes of many others whose praise is in the histories; and one can extend to this intrepid enemy sincere sympathy that he was compelled to spend many more months of galling inactivity before being released. So, during that December of 1915 another officer of similar calibre was sent from Kigoma to raid Lukuja, and blow the place into air. Commander Schönfeld seemed just the right selection, and he was given a free hand to act as he deemed best. But not even he could get near the slip, though he brought back news of the two motor-boats.

This intelligence likewise arrived too late. Incidentally the 53-ton *Kingani* (commanded by Sub-Lieutenant Junge of the German Naval Reserve) had been assigned to co-operate with Schönfeld.

But whoever could those two motor-boats be? Whence and how had they reached Kukuja, or rather Kalemie, which was a small adjacent port specially built under the guns of Lukuja; for there was a shallow bar where the Lukuja joined the lake?

In answer we must lift our imagination for a while from Central Africa to the Admiralty in Whitehall. It was the spring of 1915, and many weeks before the *Königsberg* had been knocked out. The Germans indisputably were in command of Lake Tanganyika, whereas on the other lakes it was otherwise. What, then, was to be done? Send out some craft that would be superior to any of the enemy's flotilla! But naval predominance can be of two kinds: (*a*) speed, (*b*) armament. Given the former, a craft can choose its own range: and, moreover, such superiority provides the invaluable element of surprise.

Hitting an enemy ship is dependent primarily on closing to such a range as will make the fire decisive. Contrariwise it avails but little a much heavier armed, though slower, ship if the latter cannot bring her guns to bear. Thus mobility, when properly applied, may enable a fast, light vessel to hit another at a "blind" spot, so that the heavier craft cannot reply; however she may twist and turn, there is always her rival altering course more swiftly.

The decision was made, accordingly, to send out two very light motor-boats whose 15-knots speed would far exceed that of the *Hedwig von Wissmann* or the *Kingani*, and the armament was to consist of one 3-pdr. plus, one Maxim for each. But what route was practicable for their transport? Here was a problem of the first magnitude. Certainly, the whole of German East Africa, being still in our enemy's hands, could be ruled out at once, though geographically it would have been the shortest way. If only the Central Railway and Kigoma had been in British control at this time, and Dar-es-Salaam had fallen, the matter would have presented no difficulty.

Under the existing circumstances there was only one route feasible; yet this demanded boldness and patience, immense determination to overcome obstacles, and months of preliminary preparation. The two boats selected were necessarily of small displacement, and of a type that one sees running along peacefully with a pleasure party past river banks, or gliding over a sunlit bay at the height of summer: but essentially, they were in no sense of the word "sea" craft. Designed with fine lines and a transom stern, they drew only a foot or two of water, but had a raised deck for'ard. Each of these motor-boats measured 40 feet long with 7-foot beam, and weighed not more than 44 tons, thus being of such a size that they could readily be handled at a quay or railway siding.

But their ultimate advantage of excellent speed, developed through first-class motors and twin propellers, and the temporary convenience of easy weight, overcame the obvious drawbacks in regard to seaworthiness no less than vulnerability. Had they been bigger or heavier, this Tanganyika plan could not ever have been attempted, and in any case it was a gamble of no ordinary character, the pessimists prophesying that the boats would never reach their destination. The names given to these tender little vessels were appropriate to their frailty, and suggested fanciful prettiness rather than the war-like strength usually associated with a man-of-war.

Mimi and *Toutou* were lying up the Thames at Teddington, and could easily run down to the London docks, whence they would be carried through the submarine zone by steamer and risk meeting any German raider in the Atlantic. At Capetown their transference to the railway and their journey as far north as Rhodesia need cause no anxiety, but that was only the first phase. On June 12 they left Tilbury, and reached Capetown early in the following month without adventure. The train then departed on July 19, so that they began now an overland journey of some 3,500 miles and many vicissitudes.

After Bulawayo and Livingstone, it became necessary to rely mostly on such primitive ways and means as belong to the days preceding rails, or even rough roads. Their progress now was akin to that of explorers hewing along through virgin country, and it was surely one of the strangest freaks in a complicated war that through the bush, across

African mountains, and down tropical valleys two modern speed boats should be trundled.

Ahead went the pioneering party, where roads had to be made, nearly 200 bridges constructed, trees felled and desert tracks indicated. It is true that a couple of traction engines and trailers were also detrained, but these brought their own difficulties with them. Bridges collapsed under their ponderance, and they needed water for steam even when neither well nor river was at hand; so the crew had to sacrifice their thirst-quenching to the boilers' greater need. Under the scorching sun and over the irksome "roads" the cavalcade swung forward painfully, the day's run being logged at from 2 to 6 miles! On one special occasion they even did 14 miles!

Never once could anxiety be relaxed, for what with the heat attacking the wooden hulls, and the innumerable narrow escapes of the boats being capsized or struck, there was the ever-haunting fear of irreparable damage—of the long trek failing suddenly. Even a bent propeller, a strained shaft, or a tree-puncture below the waterline, was very likely and not less serious a threat. Each boat was settled in its cradle, but a certain amount of rough usage could not be avoided, and there were crises when traction engines and even oxen had to be discarded for the seamanlike method of hauling by blocks and tackles.

Sometimes the expedition had to climb with their precious burdens up to 6,000 feet, and later on the boats were allowed to float down streams so shallow that barrels had to be lashed alongside the hulls, whilst natives bodily lifted each craft clear of the sandbanks; for the projecting shaft-brackets always seemed to be courting injury. At another stage the river would deepen, allowing *Mimi* and *Toutou* the privilege of using their own engines and towing the store-laden barges. Having got well into the Belgian Congo area and come once more to a railway, they were placed on trucks and in this fashion were brought to Tanganyika's lakeside at Lukuja.

It was now October 28, and three months of unrivalled toil had thus been rewarded by the sight of this huge freshwater sea lying in front of them. Had the boats immediately perished now by accident, or by the raids of the enemy, it would have been a sad loss: yet the persistent tenacity of that naval party, who sweated their advance through countless embarrassments, would still be remembered with admiration.

Now it was following the arrival of these motor-boats that the Belgians resolved to build the small port of Kalemie, previously mentioned. It was close to the Lukuja mouth, and after soundings had been taken as well as piers constructed, there remained not a great deal of work. Such liveliness, however, had intrigued the Germans and kept both Odebrecht and Rosenthal busy with their nocturnal raids. But there was a further reason which motivated all this inquisitiveness on the enemy's part. Post-war histories have repeatedly emphasised the statement that Germany from August 4 onwards was kept in a state of ignorance regarding our plans and movements. Spies were arrested and shot; the whole Teutonic system of secret agents fell down when hostilities broke out.

But the unsettling truth has to be faced that the Germans in East Africa, as far back as March 1915, were warned that a British naval expedition with motor-boats was about to set forth. Von Lettow knew of it, though he scarcely took the news very seriously. Zimmer heard of it, and never rested till a successful raid should settle the question once and for all. Why were the Belgians so busily employed by day at Kalemie? The *Wissmann* had reported that they seemed only to be strengthening fortifications. But Zimmer had reason to suspect—what he never knew definitely unto too late—that all this activity by the water's edge was for a more definite object. Natives have a way of their own for gathering and transmitting information, especially when it is worth their while.

Both the British and Germans found such agents more than convenient. It was impossible for traction engines, ox-waggons, boats in cradles, and the whole cavalcade of men with stores, to pass slowly across Africa without the news penetrating to Kigoma. Zimmer claims, indeed, to have traced their anabasis right up to the day when they were traversing their last stage through the Belgian Congo.

Looking back on the past, one can now see that the greatest peril which *Mimi* and *Toutou* experienced was not the submarines, nor the Atlantic raiders; not the improvised African bridges, nor the mountainous declivities down which the boats' trollies threatened to hurl themselves. The real crisis was on the night of December 2, when Rosenthal actually gained the slip and saw the two motor-boats with his own eyes, yet was never able to hand on this confirmation before he was taken prisoner. Nothing but the most efficient vigilance prevented the enemy thereafter from blowing the craft into flames and smoke, and that would have made all the difference to future events: so narrowly poised is the fortune of war.

November had passed, Christmas approached, and the new harbour at Kalemie was just about finished. On December 23 behold *Mimi* and *Toutou* tuned up so that they were being launched from the slipway on to the Lake. Next day they went on a trial run, and in spite of all their land buffetings were not much the worse, for a speed of 13.4 knots—or nearly twice that of any other craft on Tanganyika—was attained. Christmas Day came and went, but next morning happened to be a Sunday. In charge of this British expedition had come Lieutenant-Commander Geoffrey B. Spicer-Simson, R.N., with a party of 28, who included some officers of the R.N.V.R. as well as regular naval ratings. It was just before 9.30 a.m. when all hands were assembling for Divine Service, and the lake was sparkling with choppy waves caused by the freshening south-east breeze.

This was the period when Commander Schönfeld, and a party well experienced in raiding, were at large bent on blowing up the slip. Today we know that they happened to be not far from this scene, and the reader will remember that the *Kingani* was working with him under his orders.

Suddenly the church party ashore had a surprise. Down the lake was coming a steamer. Not a very big one, nor apparently very fast; slightly longer than the *Mimi*, and about twelve times her tonnage. She was on a course which would enable her to pass Kalemie at a distance of 7 miles, and Commander Spicer-Simson allowed her to continue till she was not merely abreast, but well to the southward, his intention being to cut the stranger off from her Kigoma base to the north. It was quite obvious that this steamer was heading for the Belgian coat just below, for she was steering about south-west, and presently she showed herself to be the *Kingani*. It was about 11 a.m. when the time came to shove off from Kalemie in pursuit, and the Teddington toy warships were to have their long-deferred opportunity. This was the day!

In the *Mimi* went the commander; in charge of the *Toutou* was Sub-Lieutenant A. Dudley, R.N.V.R., whose expert knowledge of African country had been so important that the transports were entrusted to his care. This morning, however, found him as captain of a man-of-war going into action. Motor-boats such as these consume large quantities of petrol when run at full speed, and the vast extent of Tanganyika, with 1,500 miles of coastline, was very different from a narrow river, with all facilities for refuelling. No one could tell how long this chase might last, so a small Belgian motor-boat called the *Vedette*, with a crew of British naval ratings, followed out from the shore carrying more petrol supplies and took up a position so as to be at hand if the chase came north.

These British boats had been built for the Greek seaplane service, and drew only 2¼ feet. Neither in design not construction were they originally meant for knocking about exposed waters, yet on this very first cruise they were put to the severest of tests which might prove overwhelmingly unfair. They had come 10,000 miles from Teddington without damage; hot and thirsty men had dragged and cursed them through one long furnace with only half a pint of water daily for parched throats. Through villages silent with sleeping sickness, through thunderstorms and tropical rains; attacked by mosquitoes, scorpions, rhinos; threatened by snakes and lions, 26 officers and men besides their commander had plodded on to deliver their own tiny flotilla—yet today the weather seemed to mock at their efforts.

By the time Commander Spicer-Simson had finished reading prayers, ordered his men into clean shirts and shorts, and taken his two boats out of harbour, the weather began to change for the worse. Heavy rain squalls swept down, and soon there was a nasty sea running. The width of Tanganyika hereabouts is not less than the distance from Portland Bill to Torbay, so that no protection could be expected from the shore. The wind gradually veered from S.E. to S.W. and increased to force 6-7 (Beaufort scale) rousing such seas that were endurable by the S.S. *Kingani*, though they bullied motor-boats which were only partially decked and had little grip on the water. For these diminutive ships the conditions were the equivalent of a healthy gale, as every yachtsman will appreciate; whereas it might have been hoped, and expected, that when the day of battle should arrive the setting would be suitable for high speed over a smooth surface.

Two facts were very manifest: the enemy had given Kalemie such a wide berth that he had not sighted the motor-boats, and he was making for Tambwa Bay, which was much frequented when the Germans wished to begin a reconnaissance of the Belgian base. But he would have to come out and fight to a finish, or else be driven ashore: more than likely he would try to escape back to Kigoma.

What were Commander Spicer-Simson's battle plans? What were the limitations? In a sea fight between ordinary men-of-war, able to use their guns on either broadside and thus to bring the maximum concentration of artillery into action, the fight soon resolves itself into steaming along parallel courses. But these were no ordinary warships. The *Kingani* carried only one gun—a pom-pom with a range of

2,600 yards—and that was mounted forward. Each motor-boat carried a 3-pdr. mounted forward, but the decks were so weak that they would not tolerate the gun being fired abeam: therefore, it must be fired ahead. By such reasoning it was requisite that the two boats must attack from a position astern of *Kingani*, which would have the additional advantage of preventing the latter's gun from being used. For it would be masked by the funnel and deck hamper.

It was decided, then, that *Mimi* and *Toutou* should not steam in line-ahead, but in line-abreast; and this formation would be convenient if the enemy began running away. In that event *Mimi* would take up a berth on *Kingani's* starboard quarter, and *Toutou* on her port quarter.

At 11.40 a.m. picture this pair bumping over the waves bound south, whilst the *Kingani* was away on the starboard bow but some distance off, and stopped in Tambwa Bay. The motors were warming up to their work, the fine bows were throwing the spray to either side, the men were ready with guns and ammunition. Suddenly the *Kingani* saw these craft racing so rapidly towards the bay that she would presently be trapped. She got under way, steamed out, turned eastward and went off at full speed, being now only 5,000 yards due south of her opponents. By 11.47, just as she was swinging gradually round to N.E., and the motor-boats were only 2,000 yards astern, fire was opened by the latter, though very slowly at first. Why? Partly because the rough sea made these boats so lively that good gunnery was difficult; partly because only a limited amount of shells could be carried, and economy must be studied.

Kingani could not bring her gun to bear on *Mimi*, but she had a shot at *Toutou* as the latter was the inner side of the circle and at the moment of turning N.E. By 11.52 both motor-boats were so placed that the enemy's gun was completely masked, and the range was down to 1500 yards. They were now running before the sea instead of against it, which was all to their advantage, and their gunners had found the target perfectly. Every shell registered a hit, so the Commander ordered lyddite to be used instead of common, increased the rate of fire, and fairly deluged the steamer with destruction. One projectile went through *Kingani's* armoured screen that shielded her gun, blowing Sub-Lieutenant Jung in two and killing likewise a petty officer. Another shell wiped out a warrant officer; yet another blew three natives overboard.

There now survived only a couple of European seamen of whom

one was the helmsman and the other was the Chief Engineer. The former was so dazed that he remained steering mechanically, yet still heading up more or less straight towards Kigoma. But the Chief Engineer took over for a few moments till he realised that escape was hopeless. He stopped engines, hauled down the German flag, and now it was 11.58. Thus, within eleven minutes the action had been begun and ended, thanks to the right employment of clever tactics and superior speed.

It was now time to go aboard and take the prize into Kalemie, but the sea had been increasing from bad to worse. Three times did *Mimi* come alongside the steamer, and thrice did she fail to transfer a man. The waves were so considerable that during the attempt *Mimi* received such a nasty nudge from the heavier vessel as to begin leaking. Under these conditions the only possibility was to order *Kingani* to steer N.W. for Kalemie which was now the weather shore. It was desirable for the steamer to reach shallow water without delay lest she should founder from the hole which had been made on her port side abreast of the boiler.

Escorted by *Mimi* and *Toutou*, she was brought into Kalemie harbour, where she took the sand and grounded with a heavy list. Not one British casualty had occurred today, but both motor-boats had suffered severely from the shock of their own guns. *Toutou* eventually fared the worst and later on became a loss during bad weather; but she had accomplished that for which she had left the Thames, and had helped to provide a more seaworthy vessel in *Kingani*, which was now repaired and commissioned as a British man-of-war with the name *Fifi*.

When the *Kingani* failed to appear at Kigoma, the loss could only be surmised, and next day (December 27) Commander Schönfeld's party were recalled after no success. Not till early in February did Zimmer learn definitely that *Kingani* had been lost to the Germans, and even then, the information lacked accuracy. By means of native spies it was learned that she was lying in shallow water off Kalemie, and that her funnel was visible. All this was fairly true—but only for a time. Apart from the news being out of date, it erred in reporting that she had been sunk by means of a battery newly placed on the shore. Hitherto these spies had always brought trustworthy intelligence, but this time they mystified Zimmer by no reference to British craft the senior German officer had no definite knowledge that the motor-boats were using the lake; and, indeed, when a second German ship failed to return, he still believed she had approached too near the

Belgian battery. For we have seen that Rosenthal's scribbled message had not yet come through, and the Schönfeld expedition had failed to get near Kalemie.

Such uncertainty as to what exactly was happening; such accidental secrecy; such absence of reliable details, made Zimmer's outlook blurred, whilst shrouding Spicer-Simson's activities and future intentions. And we shall now watch the sequel.

CHAPTER 22

Victors on the Lake

Whilst the Germans on Lake Tanganyika were still wondering and guessing as to the fate of *Kingani*, she was again steaming about the lake but with a British naval crew. The *Fifi*, as we must now call her, did not remain long disabled, for she proceeded south on January 20 (1916) in order to collect fuel. These lake steamers, like the locomotives of the Central Railway, used to burn wood, though a certain amount of oil could be consumed when required to give extra heating; and it was necessary now that suitable wood depots be arranged. But so ill-known was the change of fortune which had occurred on December 26, that when this very familiar craft approached southern land, she was promptly fired at by Belgian and British posts alike. Fortunately, no damage was incurred.

The *Toutou* suffered her disaster by the storm which raged at the end of January, but the loss was not permanent. She was salved, and was now being repaired. Similarly, the *Delcommune*, which had received about forty enemy shells several months ago and was in such a bad condition that an intercepted Belgian wireless had reported her as "*complètement détruit*" was rising again to life, though as yet she had no propellers. This still left our allies with no real serviceable ship. True, they had the small motor-boat *Vedette*, and another called the *Dix Tonnes*, but neither was particularly seaworthy though they could be employed in fine settled weather. On the occasion of December 26, the *Vedette* had managed to keep afloat, and she might be risked again.

So, we come to February 8, by which date Zimmer in his uneasiness determined to locate his long-lost *Kingani* and, if those British motor-boats really had reached the lake, to capture them forthwith. His plan was thus. There remained at his disposal the two steamers *Hedwig von Wissmann* and *Graf von Götzen* together with the steam-pinnace. On this evening, he despatched the first two, who were to reach the shore opposite Lukuja. Leaving the pinnace at the eastern side, the *Wissmann* was to steam the 40 odd miles across to the western land in order to approach Kalemie at dawn. Native spies were on board, who would point out leading marks for use at night. This knowledge having been obtained, the *Wissmann* must return east to the pinnace, where they would be joined at noon of February 9 by the *Götzen* in readiness for a combined nocturnal raid. Lieutenant Odebrecht was in the *Wissmann*, and Zimmer in the *Götzen*.

Now daylight on February 9 came at 5.45, and just then the lookouts on the Belgian coast reported to Kalemie that over in the northeast was a vessel steaming slowly south. Such tidings were enough for Commander Spicer-Simson to give immediate orders for his flotilla to get ready, and the *Fifi* began raising steam for full speed. At 6.15. a.m. the stranger was identified as the *Wissmann*, and at 7.45 a strange miscellaneous collection of craft put to sea. Forming line-ahead, they proceeded across the lake with the *Fifi* (flying the commander's pennant) in the van, followed at 100 yards interval by the *Mimi*, after which came the *Dix Tonnes*, together with the *Vedette* carrying supplies.

It was an ideal day for frail, fast, motor-boats. The surface of the lake was like polished glass, with a long easy swell that could hardly hinder good shooting. Gloriously fine and not yet too hot, there was an absence of wind, but the atmosphere was hazy; the reflection and refraction making it difficult to define the exact position of any object. For the purpose of preserving a good head of steam in the *Fifi*, and of retaining the flotilla together, the speed was kept down to 6 knots. It was 8.55 when the *Wissmann* was seen to the N.N.E. about 6½ miles distant, and approaching on a S.S.W. course.

Odebrecht evidently experienced the shock of his seafaring life when the curious procession from Kalemie showed up, so he put his helm hard over, put oil on his fires, and began retreating to the N.E. just as quickly as his engines would revolve. His speed had been 6 knots, but he tried desperately to improve on this when he witnessed the old *Kingani* flying the White Ensign, accompanied by the *Mimi*. Nominally the *Wissmann*'s maximum speed was 7 knots, but the application of oil in the furnaces soon gave him speed for 2 knots more. On the other hand, *Fifi*, having solely the wood fuel, could not raise such a good head of steam as was desirable, for no draught this windless day came up the funnel, and the best she could do was an 8-knot gait. At 9.10 she fired a couple of rounds with a recently mounted 12-pdr., *Kingani*'s original gun having been sighted only to 2,600 yards.

Commander Spicer-Simson now found himself confronted with an interesting problem in tactics, ordered the fast *Mimi* to get dead astern of the enemy, and attack from a distance of 3200 yards. It was known that the German steamer carried a 14-inch revolving gun for'ard and another aft similar to that which had originally been placed in the *Fifi*'s bows, so that the difference of 600 yards should be adequate to prevent the *Mimi* from being hit. If, however, the *Mimi* kept shelling, the *Wissmann* would most likely turn aside to port or starboard for the purpose of concentrating both guns on the motor-boat, in which case the *Fifi* would have time to come up and fire her gun.

It now became a battle not merely of guns and ammunition, but of wits. The *Mimi* dashed in up to about 3,800 yards, sent a hot fire, and with her second shot destroyed the port side of *Wissmann*'s bridge. The latter then yawed, as expected, but before Odebrecht's guns could get the range sufficiently low, the *Mimi* was too far astern. At 10.5 the *Fifi* had advanced, but her shells were reported by *Mimi* as falling "over." At 5,000 yards the commander hit the enemy with a second and third shot, insomuch that he now began firing rapidly sixty, of which about forty-five struck the *Wissmann*, the time now being 10.30.

Repeatedly did Odebrecht endeavour to get within range, but he was inferior to the *Mimi* in regard to speed and to the *Fifi* in regard to gunnery; so that it was now only a question of time before a very clear result would show itself. Nevertheless, no action is finished until it is won, and it needed just one shell from *Wissmann* to settle the motor-boat's fate for all time. But there could be no question that Odebrecht would need a large slice of luck if he was to extricate his ship from so difficult a position; and help could only come with the arrival of Zimmer in the *Götzen* who ought now to be steaming down the lake and not very far away. The latter's 4.1-inch gun, that had once been *Königsberg's*, would make all the difference—outranging all the British armament.

Matters developed quickly, eager German eyes looked up the lake in vain for a sight of the *Götzen's* upperworks, and the crisis soon came. One shell shot down into the *Wissmann*'s engine-room, killing the Engineer and bursting the tank which contained the oil fuel. Another turned the engines into twisted metal, pierced a boiler, opened a big hole in the ship's bottom, set alight the oil-soaked firewood, and turned the ex-passenger steamer into a mass of flames. She stopped going ahead, and Odebrecht gave orders that she was to be abandoned. One apparently seaworthy steel lifeboat remained into which the natives jumped, whilst the European survivors put on lifebelts and then jumped overboard, being afterwards picked up by Commander Spicer-Simson's flotilla.

The lifeboat was so full of shot-holes that she sank. By 10.47 the *Wissmann* was doomed and the attack on her ceased: less than ten minutes later she disappeared beneath the surface. There were no British casualties of any sort, but the enemy lost 7 killed and 3 wounded. The survivors having been rescued, nothing now remained but to make for Kalemie after one of the most instructive naval engagements of modern times.

Some months later Commander Spicer-Simson (to whose account I acknowledge my indebtedness) delivered a lecture before the Royal Colonial Institute in London, and on that occasion Admiral Sir Henry Jackson summed up the achievement thus:

> "I doubt whether any one tactical operation of such miniature proportions has exercised so important an influence on enemy operations.

For, practically, the British and Belgians were now in command of the Lake's waters, which was exactly the object intended. The expedition had been sent out from England in order to assist the military, and on the expert advice of a Mr. Lee (who, as a famous big-game hunter, pointed out the way to travel across dark Africa from the south) the improbable had been accomplished.

Nevertheless, we can appreciate nowadays that the result might have ended very differently: in fact, another two hours would have introduced the heavy reinforcement for Odebrecht. Zimmer arrived at the rendezvous, 40 odd miles opposite Kalemie, not till after midday, by which time the British-Belgian flotilla were out of sight and heading for home. The *Götzen* knew nothing of this engagement, and the steam-pinnace (which was found waiting at the appointed spot) was equally ignorant. Where was the *Wissmann*? Why was she late? The only information which the pinnace's people could offer was that between 9 and 10 a.m. heavy gunfire had been heard in the direction of Lukuja.

More uncertainty for Zimmer! Two of his three steamers gone, and still no satisfactory explanation respecting either! He began searching the lake, and even advanced towards Lukuja, yet found no evidence. Most annoying! Belgian wireless reports were intercepted announcing the destruction of *Wissmann* "off Lukuja"; but since Zimmer even now knew nothing definite of the Allies' "flotilla in being," he could only assume that the Belgian shore batteries had sunk the *Wissmann* when she approached incautiously. The element of suspense was welcomed no more by the Germans on Lake Tanganyika than it ever has been in any campaign, and (omitting the pinnace) there remained only the 8-knot recently built *Götzen* to contend for inland sea supremacy.

The chances were that, in spite of the *Königsberg*'s gun, a third defeat might be suffered, so our enemies were compelled at this juncture to act on the defensive. Kigoma was converted into a fortress, and the *Götzen* instead of making raids remained within harbour. Nor was that all. Military matters were affecting lake strategy, so that the German Army could no longer afford to do without her 4.1-inch and 22-pdr. guns. These were required urgently in other parts of the colony and had to be taken away from her. She was left with one pom-pom for defence against aircraft, and a wooden dummy gun was mounted as well. Under this condition she was hopelessly inferior to the *Mimi* (although the latter had again suffered from her own gunfire), in respect both of armament and speed.

Lieutenant-Commander Spicer-Simson was promoted to Commander from the date of his first victory, December 26, 1915, and awarded the D.S.O. Six of his officers were given the D.S.C., and most of his men the D.S.M. Apart from the fact that this naval party had been able to add enormously to the Allies' prestige, and to make the lake safe for the transportation of troops, such decorations would have been well earned for having brought the boats through the bush when the temperature mounted to the intolerable figure of 180°. But, whilst the complete control of all the lakes was now secured to the British and Belgians, we have yet to narrate a very fine effort on the part of the Germans.

In previous pages the reader will remember that we mentioned the 250-ton tug *Adjutant*; how that this enemy vessel was captured at sea by H.M.S. *Dartmouth* in the Mozambique channel, and afterwards commissioned as a British naval unit; but that early in February 1915 she was shelled and damaged when making a reconnaissance off the Rufiji so that she was compelled to surrender. The enemy then kept her for a short while just inside the Simba Uranga; but one dark night before the end of that same month a party of Germans bravely took the risk of steaming her out of the river, through the British blockading ships (with which she had till recently served), up the coast for most of a hundred miles, till she finally got safely into Dar-es-Salaam. There she remained for about a year.

****

Even in May 1915 the British naval forces were still unaware of the *Adjutant's* escape from the Rufiji. It was considered possible that she might have been repaired by the *Königsberg* to come out and attack the whalers, especially in order to drive off the latter if *Königsberg* were about to emerge. Whalers were therefore ordered to keep a good look-out, and to report her movements at once by wireless.

****

Now among those vessels in the Rufiji, when the *Königsberg* was bottled up, there has been mentioned the collier *Somali*, which had been with her at sea; but two much smaller steamers must now be noted. The *Rovuma* never came out again but was scuttled, though it is interesting to remark that she remained undiscovered until the year 1921, by which time she had decorated herself with the tropical growth of seven years' accumulated foliage. She was not much bigger than a river steamer or small tug. The second craft was not wholly dissimilar, and named the *Wami*. She was in fact sister ship to the 53-ton *Kingani* of Tanganyika fame.

Anxious to follow the example of the *Adjutant* and make herself of some use, the S.S. *Wami* waited for a ripe opportunity after the *Königsberg* had been deserted, as a hopeless wreck. On the night of September 26, 1915, she also rushed out of the Rufiji and found her way into Dar-es-Salaam; so that, in spite of all the boats and pinnaces which had been long since removed to Tanganyika, there now remained a couple of useful little steamers snatched from British vigilance. As the days passed, it became patent that both *Wami* and *Adjutant* would be of more value on the lake than on the ocean. Before the *Wissmann* was sunk, but after the loss of *Kingani*, Commander Zimmer had arranged for the *Wami* to be sent up by Central Railway to Kigoma, where she arrived in February 1916, and was commissioned early the next month, though her armament consisted of nothing better than a pom-pom.

Soon after the *Wissmann* failed to reach her base, Zimmer requested Dar-es-Salaam to let him have the *Adjutant*; yet this was a much more serious proposition, being five times the *Wami's* tonnage and too big for any railway trucks. Under the direction of the engineer who had constructed the *Götzen*, the railway company's staff now took the tug to pieces and thus she travelled to Kigoma. The beneficial result was hardly in keeping with this fine effort, though there are few such vessels which can claim to have served under both flags, to have been men-of-war on the ocean, up a river, and about to be launched on an inland lake all during the same campaign.

During June 1916 the *Götzen* was bombed by Belgian airplanes which flew over Kigoma; on July 26 Kigoma was evacuated because the Belgians had captured the railway; so, the *Götzen* was filled with cement by the Germans who then sank her, and *Adjutant* was blown up on the stocks. Next day the *Wami* took on board what remained of Zimmer's detachment and landed them at the southern end of the lake by the mouth of Malagarassi River, luckily unseen by the motor-boat which was patrolling off Kigoma. The *Wami*, having fulfilled her function, was now sunk by the Germans, whilst the motor-boat opened fire at long range. And with this incident the *Königsberg's* crew became a spent force insofar as they were mariners.

Commander Zimmer's Tanganyika force (known officially by the Germans as the "*Möwe* Detachment" even till the end) consisted of 106 men from his *Möwe*, 53 officers and men from the *Königsberg*, 44 reserve officers and men from the German East Afrika liners at Dar-es-Salaam, or about two hundred in all. That they persisted pluckily cannot be denied; that they were beaten in fight by superior tactics on the lake is equally true. But what with fighting and starving and sickness, only about half of them ever reached Germany again. War is an ugly business, yet throughout history it has been the means for the finest expressions of fortitude, and it is but just that brave deeds performed by our late enemies should be remembered in perpetuity.

Even during the few years that have elapsed since the War, mechanisation has still further transformed the relationship between Central Africa and Europe, so that things can never find quite the same environment as they did, and German East Africa could not any longer suffer from isolation: consequently, a sea blockade, whether locally on Tanganyika, or generally off the Indian Ocean coast, has recently lost much of its power.

Today all these lakes are within a week's flying distance from London and Germany: the Tanganyika operations would be carried out by flying boats, who would take about as many days to reach the Lukuja as *Mimi* and *Toutou* needed months. Medical supplies, spare parts, ammunition—even crews or troops—could travel direct to Kigoma regardless of what was happening in the Zanzibar neighbourhood. If only the enemy had possessed seaplanes on Tanganyika, definite information as to the arrival and location of the two British motor-boats would have been made possible, so that Zimmer's steamers could never have suffered disaster through surprise.

CHAPTER 23

Dénouement

We began our story as if it were some mystery that had to be solved, a chase that had to be made for the culprits of a deed, and we have seen that, after loss of their transporting vehicle, the party had split up so that a compact capture was impossible. But there yet remain several knots to be untied, more than one loose thread to be joined, ere we can get the final explanation full and perfect.

For years after these operations were concluded there existed many essential points that were annoyingly intriguing, whilst no solution was forthcoming. Hitherto we have followed the problem chiefly from the pursuer's point of view: it will now be our pleasure to take a glance at the chase as regarded by the hunted. For only during the last three years has it become possible to know the "why," the "how," the "where" certain things occurred. No longer need we suggest theories or express wonderment at this or that enemy decision: we have the plain facts, and can see into the mind of *Königsberg's* captain. In short, the problem at once ceases to be a riddle, whilst simultaneously we notice how near one can get to another man's motives through intuition and deductive or inductive reasoning.

Now, primarily, we insist on knowing why Captain Looff committed himself and ship to such a blind alley as the Rufiji? Why did he not keep at sea, instead of allowing himself to be trapped?

Here is the answer, and it is not without its illuminative lesson. I have shown elsewhere (*The Sea-Raiders*), that Germany's preparations for war included a very thorough organisation for attacking British ocean routes not merely by means of naval cruisers, but by liners of her various steamship companies, to whom a *Cruiser Handbook* had been given indicating a list of secret rendezvous, together with other instructions requisite at the outbreak of hostilities; and Zimmer (for example) had been charged with the impracticable duty of fitting out at Dar-es-Salaam one of the D.O.A. Company's liners as auxiliary cruiser.

The *Königsberg*, after leaving Dar-es-Salaam at the end of July, steamed north-eastward so as to be at a spot where she could be very sure of finding British vessels. She chose that focal district of the Aden Gulf because (theoretically, at least) failure would seem to be impossible. Past here comes a vast amount of valuable shipping, rich with cargoes, bound from Europe through the Suez Canal and Red Sea to the Orient. Hither, too, converged the trade routes from Karachi, Bombay, Colombo, the Dutch East Indies, China, Australia, East and South Africa and Mauritius.

It was scarcely surprising, then, that on August 6, when cruising about athwart this route convergence, the *Königsberg* made a capture of the 6,600-tons British S.S. *City of Winchester*, which was bound up the Red Sea from Colombo. The exact position was 280 miles east of Aden, and the *Königsberg's* track shows that the next area visited was further northward, off the South Arabian coast. Hither she brought the prize: hither came also the German liner *Zieten*, which happened also to be bound along the Colombo route, to whom the *City of Winchester* was entrusted whilst the *Königsberg* went off to seek more victims. A few days later the *Zieten* helped herself to some of the British steamer's coal and took off most of the latter's crew. The *Zieten* afterwards steamed south to land the prisoners at a neutral port, thus being next heard of on August 20 at Mozambique in Portuguese East Africa. This being accomplished, the German crew proceeded north along the coast in boats and reached Lindi, where they joined up with the colonial Defence Force, the *Zieten* remaining in neutral territory.

The *Königsberg*, for some reason, had absolutely no further luck when raiding but came back to the *City of Winchester*, took a few hundred tons of coal, sank this steamer, went south likewise, and spent some time off the north end of Madagascar, being conveniently placed on the flank of British traffic coming up from Capetown and Durban, as well as French steamers coming south to Madagascar. On August 31 she forsook this area and went into the Rufiji, where the D.O.A. Steamship Company's *Somali* was ready to give her the much-needed coal. On September 20, as the reader is well aware, *Königsberg* arrived off Zanzibar about 5.30 a.m. and bombarded H.M.S. *Pegasus*, after which she returned to the Rufiji.

Her maximum draught of water was 17½ feet; there were several feet on the bar of the Simba Uranga entrance even at dead low water;

but at spring tides there are at high water another 14¾ feet; so that, by choosing the right part of the month and the right time, the *Königsberg* would have no difficulty either in leaving or arriving. Especially would this be the case seeing that she had been on the East African station some time, and could rely on local knowledge. Admiral H. P. Douglas, hydrographer of the Royal Navy, has been courteous enough to tell me that on September 20, 1914, it *was* spring tides; that high water off the Rufiji today occurred approximately at 4 a.m. and 4.15 p.m. respectively. We can thus perceive how easy to enter it was, with no British warship watching off the coast; yet why ever did the German want to advertise her presence in such a blatant manner as bombardment?

It is the simple truth that Captain Looff's scheme went all wrong after the bombardment: almost it seemed as if the German cruiser were now to receive perpetual punishment for having sunk the *Pegasus*. Obviously the *Königsberg* would not be so foolish as to remain in the neighbourhood longer than was necessary: she meant to do her job and then clear out to a totally different sphere, so that she had really not the slightest intention to tarry hereabouts. Having once left the Rufiji, Captain Looff contemplated never entering the delta again except she should receive serious damage: it would always be a handy place where, as a last resort, he might temporarily hide and make a few repairs after engagement with a British ship.

His plan was to avenge the bombardment of Dar-es-Salaam by surprising the impotent *Pegasus*, thereby making it certain that the missing *Königsberg* had come back to East Africa. Full of enthusiasm and flushed with victory, the German cruiser was next bound south, hoping to get coal from any steamer she cared to hold up on the way. Captain Looff had laid out 'on the chart his course round South Africa, and in accordance with secret orders received from home was to try making his way up the Atlantic back to Germany. This was the period when our ocean patrols and Northern Blockade were far from completely organised, so that there was quite a good chance of *Königsberg* winning through.

Suddenly her hopes were shattered. We have not failed to notice that the engines of a fast light cruiser, regardless of nationality, require continuous attention or inefficiency follows. Now the *Königsberg* during August did considerable steaming at high speed, with the result that she could endure the effort no longer. Whilst scurrying away from Zanzibar, she developed such dangerous engine defects that South Africa was not to be considered: she must re-enter the Simba Uranga and go back to Salale. Nor was it just one of those breakdowns which can be set right in a few days by the skill and patience of the ship's engineers. Much worse than that, parts of the damaged machinery needed to be taken ashore to a foundry. Foundry? In loneliest Africa? What a perfect instance we have of the contrast between a frigate of the sailing age and the cruiser of today! The former could have made any repairs to her hull or gear, and then carried on. She could remain for years away from dockyard and workshops, relying on her own crew to refashion spars and sails.

Not so the turbine 23-knotters that have been hard driven for weeks in all weathers. Now the *Königsberg's* dilemma was both ludicrous and pathetic. A more annoying situation for a captain so early in the war is hard to imagine; for he had roused at Zanzibar the greatest fury, and now had stumbled into terrible lameness. The only available foundry was at Dar-es-Salaam, to which his engines could not take him; where, moreover, his own countrymen had closed the entrance by the sunken dock.

There was but one thing to be done. The damaged machinery must be carried all the way to Dar-es-Salaam. So, the heavy casting was taken out and brought ashore at this most inaccessible Salale. Thanks to Commander Schönfeld and some German planters scattered over the Rufiji neighbourhood, wheels and sledges, together with hundreds of negroes, were obtained, after which the dead weight was dragged painfully through deserts and thornbush, rivers and burning heat, to the broad highway whence the journey was continued up to Dar-es Salaam.

That was the reason for *Königsberg's* protracted stay and the lengthy operations which shortly afterwards began outside the delta; and the irony of this situation is not hard to notice. Captain Looff's ship, with her engine all adrift, now found herself in just that predicament which had characterised the *Pegasus* immediately before bombardment. But he was to suffer a much longer period of suspense, that was in no way lessened by such incidents as the *Newbridge* incursion; the airplane visits; the long-distance shelling by the cruisers; and the first attack by the monitors. As a protection against surprise, Captain Looff landed some of his crew, whose 3-pdrs. and Maxims were posted at the Kikunja and Simba Uranga mouths because these were the two most important.

Very soon communication was established between ship and these stations by heliograph, and the reader will recollect that on a certain occasion the *Königsberg's* light was seen working at night. A kind of basket crow's-nest was erected in tree-tops whence a clear look-out was maintained seawards. Pemba Hill, where a lieutenant was placed to observe how the *Königsberg's* shells were falling, is about 450 feet high, and was connected with the ship by means of a telephone before the monitors arrived on the scene. Thus, on July 6 the officer informed his ship:

"Hit bows of monitor lying to west." "Smoke issuing from bows and amidships." "Her fire silenced." "Monitor steaming away at slow speed." "Monitor ashore." "They tow her off."

Elsewhere have we seen the difficulties under which the British cruisers approached the Rufiji delta owing to inadequate cartographical knowledge at the time; and we have noted the extreme range of their guns which had, however, the effect of driving Captain Looff further and further up river until he was safely out of the danger zone. Today we realise that the *Königsberg's* 4.1-inch guns were ineffective beyond 12,760 yards, so that a kind of stalemate inevitably existed until the monitors arrived. In those days we possessed a moderately, though not wholly, accurate idea of the *Königsberg's* hiding-places, but the chart in Chapter 7 now provides a comprehensive view of the seven successive stages along her *via Dolorosa*.

Thus, at first, she was brought up close to Salale, after which she was like a scared animal not knowing which way to turn. It is interesting to observe that her sixth movement suggested that she might have had hopes of trying to emerge by the Msala mouth; but she doubled back and eventually came to her final anchorage as indicated. If these repeated retirements were to prove nothing else, they assuredly indicate how hopeless did Captain Looff consider his chances of coming out to sea again: he had at last shifted his ship so far inland that she was virtually no longer a cruiser but an immobile battery of which only half the guns could bear seawards

Nevertheless, the *Königsberg* was far from forgotten by the German Admiralty, and the sending forth of *Kronberg* (ex-S.S. *Rubens*) from Hamburg was not wholly unconnected with the former's plight. It seemed that here was quite a new chapter of hope beginning, and the *Königsberg's* engineers might take new encouragement that even the most defective machinery parts should presently be replaced by new. It was a bold conception to think of succouring her so effectively, and it would have been a tremendous triumph if the warship had got back home after assistance from *Kronberg*. During the first days of March mysterious signals in cypher were received in the *Königsberg's* wireless-room which read as follows:

> In the middle of March an auxiliary ship, the *Rubens*, will arrive from home off the East African coast. She will have on board all the necessary materials and supplies in order to enable the *Königsberg* to return home. Medicine, arms, and ammunition for the colony will be brought too. (*Kreuzerfahrt . . . mit S.M.S. "Königsberg,"* by Vice-Admiral Max Looff.)

Thus, the primary intention of this relief steamer was not for the German troops. Looking back on events, one can see that if the *Adjutant* and *Wami* were able to escape out of the Rufiji, the *Kronberg* might possibly have escaped in, notwithstanding our blockade. The fact that she got to Manza Bay shows that Lieutenant Christiansen, her commanding officer, was a brave and successful blockade runner. Although the *Hyacinth's* shells prevented him from going further, it did not make the voyage a complete failure. There could no longer be any possibility of dramatically steaming up alongside the *Königsberg*, but von Lettow in that April was not less surprised than grateful for the cargo which was brought ashore by boats and dug-outs. Here are some of the items:

There were salved enough Mauser rifles to re-arm the entire German land forces; numbers of machineguns, together with large quantities both of small arms ammunition and shells for the big guns. Von Lettow adds that although during the ensuing weeks:

> We salved almost the whole of the valuable cargo, we found that the cartridges had suffered severely from the seawater. The powder and caps deteriorated more and more, and so the number of misfires increased. There was nothing for it but to break up the whole of the ammunition, clean the powder and replace some of the caps by new ones.

But the moral effect through this steamer's arrival was of even greater worth. It aroused among the hard-pressed Germans:

> . . . tremendous enthusiasm, since it proved that communication between ourselves and home still existed. All of us listened to the stories of the captain, Lieutenant Christiansen, when he arrived at my headquarters at New Moshi after his wound was healed. . . . Many who had been despondent now took courage once more, since they learned that what appears impossible can

be achieved, if effort is sustained by determination. (*My Reminiscences of East Africa*.)

This sentence deserves to be noted; and one begins to sympathize with the British naval officers who felt that *Königsberg* must remain a perpetual menace until the day of her destruction should be attained. It was well that the monitors escaped so miraculously since several more months must have elapsed ere other shallow men-of-war could be sent to this station, and they might have been too late. Why? Because that next winter the Germans once more took advantage of the long dark nights off the north of Scotland, so that they were able to send out a second relief ship. This was the S.S. *Marie* which likewise arrived with something more than a few kind wishes. In March 1916 she got to Sudi Bay, which is at the southern end of what was then still German East Africa, between Lindi and Mikindani.

She succeeded in landing 4 field howitzers, 2 mountain guns, a quantity of small arms, several thousand rounds for the *Königsberg's* guns then being used in different parts of the country; together with other warlike stores. It was a smart bit of work to have run in to the coast and then disappeared off to sea without being caught. Most of these items were then transported by land to the Central Railway, but there were a few dozen smaller articles of a more personal interest. For the *Marie* had brought her emperor's appreciation of the *Königsberg's* efforts; one Iron Cross of the first class arriving for Captain Looff, whilst there was a Cross each for half the cruiser's company.

It is a suitable subject for debate whether, after the *Königsberg's* loss, the German General and Captain Looff between them acted wisely in dissipating the latter's crew over several enterprises, rather than preserving in one well-knit force a body of men who had been together through so many months. A seaman is more of a specialist than an infantryman, and his training is longer. The whole of his environment and mode of expression belong to ships and water, so that when he takes to the field, he cannot be expected to make the best possible soldier.

Would it not have been better to have concentrated the whole, and not merely a part, of the *Königsberg* personnel on Tanganyika? To have taken most of the 4.1-inch guns thither? Could not arrangements have been made to have sent the land detachment with a couple of these guns aboard the *Marie*, and allowed her to go raiding round the world, having landed her cargo? Surely both officers and men could have been far better employed performing such brilliant voyages as were made by the other *Möwe* (commanded by Korvetten-Kapitan Count zu Dohna-Schlodien) and the *Wolf* (commanded by Korvetten-Kapitan Karl Nerger)? (*Vide Wolf: Raider! Three Accounts of the Imperial German Navy Armed Commerce Raider, SMS Wolf, During the First World War* by A. Donaldson, F. G. Trayes & John Stanley Cameron: Leonaur 2017.)

One has a feeling that it was a pity to waste such fine material, which could have been so dangerous to our trade routes in the Orient; for instance, off Australia and New Zealand where British naval forces were not strong. And in an unexpected source I find this opinion confirmed by a distinguished German military officer. Writing in the *Army Quarterly*, (Vol. XI, "Random Recollections of East Africa, 1914.1918,") Colonel G. M. Orr remarks:

> Two years later (*i.e.* after *Königsberg's* loss) Tafel, who had been Lettow's Chief Staff Officer in 1916, and who commanded the Western forces of 1917, told me that he thought it was a fatal and unnecessary policy on their part to let the *Königsberg* put itself out of action in the Rufiji. . . its speed and armament. . . would have caused more damage and been of more help to them (*i.e.* the German military) than were its crew and armament acting with their land forces. From other things Tafel said, it was evident to me that he had small opinion of the representatives of the Imperial Navy in East Africa.

Even allowing for a certain amount of possible professional jealousy between the two German services, there remains a fairly controversial point for discussion.

Conversely, the *Königsberg* was not always assisted by the German soldiers. The reader will not have forgotten that in a previous chapter we saw H.M.S. *Chatham* sending her steamboat inside Lindi on October 19, 1914, and receiving no opposition, so that Commander Fitzmaurice was able to penetrate some distance up Lukuledi creek and visit the German liner *Präsident*. It will be further remembered that this was a fateful day, since the *Präsident's* documents definitely established the fact that *Königsberg* was up the Rufiji. Had the Germans at Lindi attacked the steamboat and shot everyone dead, as they swung round the corner out of sight from the *Chatham's* guns, this key to the Rufiji riddle would not have been there obtainable.

Until after the war one marvelled that the enemy put up no more opposition than by words; but today one knows that the local Defence Force happened to be away from Lindi. Leaving this important colonial harbour unprotected, they had gone to repel an expected British landing at Mikindani, which is a little to the southward. Actually, no such invasion occurred that year in this locality, but it was not till eighteen days after the monitors finished off the *Königsberg* that on July 29, 1915, some of our whalers were sent up the Lukuledi creek to damage *Präsident* sufficiently by explosives that she could not leave harbour. And the *Severn* paid a visit to her in June 1917.

If only the *Rubens* had been able to bring *Präsident* coal and guns, there would have been a further chance for enterprising seamen to go raiding.

CHAPTER 24

The Final Phase

We have left till now the relating of an incident which occurred at Dar-es-Salaam five weeks after the *Chatham* paid her call in October of 1914; and because we have not interrupted the *Königsberg's* story from discovery to destruction we must needs stay to clear up an issue before the last act is presented. This exciting affair not merely concerns some of the very craft which did such dangerous work off the Rufiji, but the sequel clears up the fate of more than one officer whose life or death has yet to be accounted for.

When the *Chatham* made the mistake of identifying a steamer in Dar-es-Salaam as the *Königsberg* and sent in a few shells, without damaging the town itself, the date was less than a fortnight before the real fugitive was definitely located in the Rufiji; but, in spite of the sunken dock across Dar-es-Salaam's S-shaped entrance, there still lurked in the British naval mind a sense of uncertainty—a fear that the *Tabora*, *König* and *Feldmarschall* might none the less find a way out. So, on November 28, whilst the *Chatham* was fully engaged off the Rufiji shelling the *Somali*, collecting information, capturing *dhows* and so forth, there arrived at anchor 3 miles off Dar-es-Salaam's mouth H.M.S. *Goliath* and *Fox*, together with our old friends the ex-German tug *Helmuth* and the antiquated cable ship *Duplex*.

In response to a signal, the German governor came off in a motorboat and was informed that boats would presently be sent in to inspect the three liners, and even to disable them (for at that time they were still suspected of communicating with the *Königsberg* a hundred miles away). The deceit practised at Lindi of pretending the *Präsident* was a hospital ship remained uppermost in the mind, and there was no sort of proof that the *Tabora* was genuinely a Red Cross vessel. Seeing might perhaps banish disbelief, so a visit was highly advisable. After the Governor had been warned that any hostility shown to the inspection parties would be punished by bombardment, he returned to harbour. About 11 a.m. the *Goliath's* steam picket boat and the *Helmuth* started for the shore that seemed so peaceful in the brilliant sunshine. The first awkward occurrence was at the harbour entrance when the picket boat hit the submerged dock and was so damaged that she had to be sent back, but a steam pinnace came off instead. In command of the *Helmuth* went Commander H. P. Ritchie, R.N., whilst Lieutenant-Commander J. C. S. Paterson, R.N. (previously mentioned in connection with the sinking of *Newbridge*), was in charge of the pinnace, which also contained Surgeon E. C. Holtom, R.N. All these three officers belonged to the *Goliath*, of whom the first-mentioned was second-in-command, the next was a torpedo expert, and the third was the ship's doctor.

Paterson was to make any demolition that might be requisite aboard the German liners, whilst Holtom was to satisfy himself that the *Tabora* really was a hospital ship; for she had certainly not been registered as such at the beginning of War. She was lying nearest to the harbour mouth, whilst the *König* and *Feldmarschall* were lying some distance further up, above the wreck of Zimmer's *Möwe*.

Against a background of palm trees waving in the breeze, the *Tabora* was a conspicuous object flying the hospital flag from her masthead, having on her side the painted Red Cross. But when the surgeon went aboard, he found there was a Sister in nursing uniform and also a Dr. Weiss; but there was little else to indicate the *Tabora's* bona fides. A patient had certainly been thought of, but just in time only. When Holtom began his rounds and was shown the sick man lying in bed, the British officer deemed it well to throw back the nice clean sheets; whereupon the "invalid" was found still to be wearing his trousers. It was perfectly true the "sick man" had once undergone an operation, but that was some time ago, and now he was already convalescent. The *Tabora* began to justify the suspicions.

But now the external peacefulness was suddenly interrupted by the rattle of machine-gun fire. Down the harbour came the *Helmuth* steaming as hard as she could go for the open sea, followed by showers of bullets. What had happened this sunny noon? Holtom could not know all that had been occurring, though it was briefly as follows. After an explosive charge had been placed so as to disable the *König's* engines, the demolition party under Lieutenant-Commander Paterson were still on board, whilst Commander Ritchie had taken the pinnace temporarily further up the harbour.

There seems to have been some misunderstanding as to who was to bring off the demolition party, but at any rate the *Helmuth* was towing a couple of *König's* boats full of the latter's Lascar crew, whose German officers were mysteriously absent. As Commander Ritchie came down harbour with some lighters in tow, he could see no one aboard either the *Feldmarschall* or *König*, so presumed Paterson's party had been taken off, though actually the latter expected that the pinnace would come. In spite of the fact that the Governor still had two white flags flying at the harbour entrance, the Germans had permitted a gross act of treachery, troops had opened fire from the shore, and Paterson wisely kept his people below decks in the *König*, hoping for the best.

Surgeon Holtom managed to borrow the *Tabora's* skiff manned by four natives, and shoved off into the stream to meet the approaching pinnace. Commander Ritchie saw him and was just slowing down when the enemy sent a storm of bullets, wounding mortally one of the natives in the skiff. Then another contretemps happened, for whilst the skiff's crew were seized with alarm and began rowing hard across the tide back to *Tabora*, the pinnace, much hampered by her lighters, was difficult to handle and eventually had to carry on. It was by this time dark and she had a thrilling time as she made her way seaward through the narrow gauntlet.

Attacked by shot and shell from the land, with several of her complement wounded, including Commander Ritchie himself, she just managed to get out and reach the *Fox*. He had received eight wounds and, at the crisis, had the wheel in his hands, though there had been a terrible interval when the pinnace slithered up on a shoal and remained for a brief spell. For his gallantry Commander Ritchie was eventually awarded the Victoria Cross.

Surgeon Holtom regained the *Tabora* with difficulty, but he had the satisfaction of hearing the *Goliath* bombarding Dar-es-Salaam for fifteen minutes, though at following dawn the two ships steamed away. He therefore found himself a prisoner together with Paterson, two of the latter's officers and eight men, who were presently removed up the Central Railway to Kilimatinde, about half-way to Kigoma. On November 30 Dar-es-Salaam was punished by another naval visit when official buildings were carefully selected as targets, shelled and turned into rubble.

Now, during the month of January who should come in to the prisoners' camp at Kilimatinde but Sub-Lieutenant Cutler, that enterprising young aviator who had been the very first, see Chapter 11, (with Gallehawk) to make a flying reconnaissance over the Rufiji, yet in the end had crashed and been taken captive. He was able now to clear up the mystery. It appears that his unsatisfactory engine had failed him just at a critical moment, so that he was forced down on to the water close to the river entrance. As his was a seaplane, he hoped the delay would not be protracted and that after some adjustment he might resume; but unfortunately, the spot was just opposite a position where some of Schönfeld's detachment were posted with machine-guns, and they opened a hot fire.

The miracle is that Cutler—the young adventurer with half a dozen lives—was not instantly killed; but with the first few shots his petrol tank was hopelessly punctured and further flight was prevented. Unfortunately, too, the tide happened to be flooding, so it carried him with the machine shorewards, where he was finally compelled to wave his handkerchief in token of surrender. A German seaman waded out and carried him off; though the seaplane itself was not destined to fall into enemy hands. Still, for one who had shown so much disregard of his own life, and performed such gallant pioneering during the first few weeks of war, it was bad luck to spend the ensuing years a prisoner whilst better and more reliable airplanes, worthy of his skill, were coming into use.

Then towards the end of February 1915 there came to Kilimatinde yet another British officer to whom the Rufiji had brought misfortune. This was a lieutenant, R.N.R., who on the 6th had been sent into the river in charge of an armed launch to test the strength of Schönfeld's defences. The test was made speedily enough, for the launch had not gone very far ere the enemy opened such a hot fire as to make further progress impossible. In accordance with previous orders, the lieutenant, having put his helm hard over, was in the act of retiring.

Just then one of Schönfeld's shells struck her and jammed the steering gear. She was placed in a predicament of the greatest embarrassment whilst the crew worked desperately under a terrible fire to free the locking. In this they failed, and had the situation been less serious one might have been reminded of the celebrated episode in one of W. W. Jacobs' humorous stories concerning the Thames tug which steamed round and round between London bridges. Whilst the armed launch was making circles in dangerous proximity to the enemy, she was given a merciless reception, yet was unable to reply effectively since Schönfeld's guns were perfectly concealed.

So, at last the launch ran aground, and in this helpless condition had to suffer a concentrated storm of lead that made further resistance out of the question. Several of the crew had been wounded and one was killed. The white flag was then hoisted and surrender was made. The dead comrade now lies buried on the river bank, with a little wooden cross to mark the site and remind future traders that here fought sailormen in small craft during minor operations requiring great bravery. The launch was veritably riddled with shots, but the enemy made her tight and she was afterwards taken up to swell the German flotilla on Lake Tanganyika. It is such an incident as this which makes one realise how perilous were the other expeditions that came in, as well as out of, these river mouths alive.

By many people at home the East African campaign, whether in regard to its land or marine operations, was generally considered merely to be a side show. Public attention was too centred on what was happening in Europe to divert much interest further south; yet there is an immense amount to be learnt from the difficulties met and overcome, and the mistakes which inevitably were bound to be made by both contestants. The low-lying swamps, the fevers, the heat, the rains, the deadly monotony varied by sudden spasms of excitement, were common to either rival; but the loss of *Königsberg* really marks the climax, and the British naval forces at least were freed from one anxiety.

Thus on August 15, 1915, the *Hyacinth*, assisted by the two monitors and whalers, was able to make an attack on Tanga, which resulted in the port being bombarded and the German liner *Markgraf* being destroyed; so one more of these single-funnelled steamers was wiped out from the list of possible raiders; a month later the *Severn* was to have the interesting experience of steaming into the Simba Uranga and having a look at Salale which had been made historic by the *Königsberg's* visitation. She had no difficulty in getting past the blockship *Newbridge*, and von Lettow's claim that the latter never did close the fairway may today be accepted as the truth. Nevertheless, like the blockships in the Zeebrugge canal, it did have a fine moral effect; and there is no record of the Germans sending demolition parties to blow up the *Newbridge* in preparation for any nocturnal emergence by the *Königsberg*.

Early in 1916 a number of changes came over the campaign. Admiral King-Hall departed and was succeeded by Rear-Admiral Charlton, who came out from England after being in charge of the minesweeping organisation. One of his first acts on reaching East Africa was to present on *Severn's* quarterdeck the decorations that had been earned by the monitors during the preceding July. In the field General Smuts took over, and a general advance followed: in March the geographical situation was simplified by the entry of Portugal on the Allies' side, so that the neutral frontier north of Cape Delgado no longer existed and such a port as Mozambique would be of no assistance to the enemy. (*Vide* also *General Smuts' Campaign in East Africa: Military Operations Against German Forces, February 1916-January 1917* by J. H. V. Crowe: Leonaur 2017, and *With Botha and Smuts in Africa* by W. Whittall: Leonaur 2012.)

By June the German forces had been driven out of British East Africa, yet the coast towns, such as Tanga, Pangani, Bagamayo and Dar-es-Salaam, all remained occupied. The essential point is that so long as these ports were uncaptured, they would be gates for other relief ships of the *Rubens* and *Marie* species to bring stores and ammunition for von Lettow. If, however, the gates disappeared there would be still less demand on the British blockading squadron.

Tanga was therefore taken on June 7, 1916, Pangani on July 23, and Bagamayo on August 15, when another of *Königsberg's* 4:1 guns was captured; the *Severn, Mersey* and *Helmuth* all being present at this occasion. A week later Dar-es-Salaam began to be bombarded, and on September 3 it surrendered, so that the final picture includes German liners lying on their sides burnt out, and British naval prisoners presently arriving from Kilimatinde after their release.

Before the end of September, the remaining coastal towns of Kilwa Kivinji, Mikindani, Kilwa Kisiwani, Sudi, Kiswere and Lindi were all in British hands, so that with one exception the whole sea front of German East Africa had passed away from the enemy. The only coastal territory not yet captured was that pestilential swamp of the Rufiji delta.

After the evacuation of Dar-es-Salaam, Captain Looff proceeded first to the Rufiji district, which still suggested memories painful to soul and body; after which he went further south still to take over command of the Lindi area. With three newly raised companies of *Askaris*, he entrenched himself in front of the British positions and was able by means of a *Königsberg* 4.1 to inflict damage on the Portuguese. But he brought with him no happy recollections. Not merely was the *Königsberg* a wreck, the *Tabora* lying on her beam ends, and the *König* beached at the mouth of Dar-es-Salaam, but he was destined to learn that the *Feldmarschall* had been taken over by the British who also raised the floating dock.

There existed no German ships, no crews, no ports. The lakes had been taken away from them, and the German land forces were retreating to the southward hopelessly. The food supply had become so bad that they were only too pleased when prisoners could be released: but there could be no longer any expectation or optimism of further replenishments by relief steamers, or of stores coming up the Central Railway. So, all the bridges thereon were blown up, and the rolling stock capsized.

****

It is worth noting, however, that when the raider *Wolf* (ex-Hansa Liner *Wachtfels*) left Germany in the autumn of 1916 for a raiding voyage of 451 days, steaming 64,000 miles, she carried a field gun below, and stores, in case she could aid in East Africa.

****

Commander Schönfeld during this year was busy directing a *Königsberg* 4.1 and other naval guns from the heights of Kanga mountain. The reader will notice in the accompanying illustration a photograph of the former type, mounted on a field carriage, but attention is also called to the strange coffin-like affair by its side. Here we have one of the most ancient forms of human skill united to what in 1916 was one of the most recent inventions. The Germans on Victoria Nyanza designed an ingenious torpedo intended to be launched against our improvised gunboats, whose experiences were discussed in an earlier chapter. The torpedo consisted of that most primitive kind of boat, a native dugout, with an Evinrude outboard motor affixed to the stern. In order that its approach might not be heard, the exhaust pipe was led into a silencer which lay within the dugout.

There was a detachable false bow with a cylinder full of dynamite. This cylinder was in effect the torpedo's warhead, but actually was an old flask such as used for storing CO^2. It is shown in the photograph by the dugout, and the motor is clearly discernible. The exhaust was allowed to escape through the deck by a bunghole, the whole hull being covered over with sheet iron, whilst inside was a lining of reinforced concrete. Altogether this was an extremely ingenious arrangement, which might have been efficacious in destroying certain of the British lake steamers and handing the marine command to our enemies. But it was apparently never employed, and not till June 1916 was the dugout discovered, with the various parts scattered near the reeds of Victoria Nyanza's southern shore.

The fact is worth noting that during the Cameroons campaign, many hundred miles to the westward, the Germans employed an almost identical principle in the expectation of torpedoing H.M.S. *Dwarf*. In that case two such cylinders filled with dynamite were prefixed to the bows of a motor-boat. (An illustration can be found in my *Gallant Gentlemen*.)

It was early in 1917 that British land forces reached the Rufiji River valley, and in order to assist by the transport of military stores the Royal Navy were requested by the General Officer Commanding to make a survey of this inland water. For this purpose, H.M.S. *Mersey* again demonstrated the value of her light draught. It was real exploration work among unknown creeks, shoals and twisting channels; though one associates such practical scientific activities rather with the time of peace, and freedom from interruption. Soundings were carefully made, a current of 3 to 5 knots was ascertained, and it was evident from the numerous shifting bars that the *Königsberg* during her steady retreat must have been literally driven through the mud in certain places. |

During this surveying under difficulties, precautions had first to be taken each day against surprise attack from the banks, and occasionally a spy would be captured; but all this detailed experience, this intimate knowledge of the Rufiji's peculiarities with its floating "islands" of trees and muddy weed fouling the propellers, helped to complete the picture of the *Königsberg's* difficulties. One does not envy Captain Looff's problem of having kept his men alive in spite of malaria and mosquitoes through ten hard months. For half of the *Mersey's* crew succumbed now to that fever.

The German cruiser must have taken full advantage of the rainy season (beginning about January); otherwise, there were some bends and narrow shallows where a ship of her size could not have been piloted. Thus, more and more does it become manifest that her chiefest anxiety was to withdraw from the range of British naval guns: she was little concerned with the danger of being "neaped," and she was too intent on the defensive for any anxiety lest she might never float off when the rainy season passed away.

The holding ground was found to be indifferent up this river, so that the tide would suddenly take charge of a ship and send her broadside bumping on to a sandbank dragging her anchor with her. The furthest south (marked K6 on the accompanying chart in Chapter 7), to which the *Königsberg* attained during her inland peregrination was at a village named Batja, where the Buma River meets the cross channel that joins with the Kiomboni River. She had thus managed to withdraw a distance of 12 miles from the sea, and was still in tidal water. It looks as if Captain Looff was endeavouring to get still further inland—to Kilindi—but the conditions turned him back, and he took up his final position as previously described.

There can be no doubt that Kilindi (where, after his ship's defeat, Captain Looff's crew mustered) would have been the ideal spot for *Königsberg* to remain, had the pilotage been practicable. Attack by monitors would have been far more difficult, and the latter could have received no assistance from ships bombarding off the coast. The narrowness of the river and the well protected banks; the facility for minefields and use of torpedoes, to say nothing of the *Königsberg's* own 4.1-inch guns, could have delayed her destruction indefinitely.

Only troops and aircraft with bombs could have settled her fate. The *Mersey* with a length of 269 feet and a beam of 49 feet got within 7 miles of Kilindi during February 1917. She was the biggest vessel which had ever pushed up so far, and the natives were consequently panic-stricken. The *Königsberg*, however, drew considerably more water and was 90 feet longer, although 3 feet less wide. Had she needed 8¼ instead of 17½ feet, she could certainly have found herself at Kilindi, whence there was a land route to the German headquarters at Dar-es-Salaam.

It was from above Batja that conditions of life and scenery would have been less irksome; for signs of habitation and 'cultivation, rice fields and villages, sugar and rubber plantations, make a more pleasant effect than the uninteresting environment lower down. On May 13, 1917, the fortunes of war had so far become modified that H.M.S. *Severn* was able to send up the Rufiji a party in motor-boats who went alongside the *Königsberg*, stepped aboard, and took photographs. The final picture which we reproduce of this wreck was taken, however, as recently as the year 1924, at low water spring tides. Not only does this illustration indicate the dense high trees behind which the *Königsberg* sought to hide herself from her opponents' gaze and guns, but we see how very narrow was the river and how extremely shoal for a vessel of that size.

A strange experience it was, too, for the *Severn's* visitors as they passed the *Newbridge* lying submerged as to her hull, with funnel and upperworks all above water—a relic and reminder of a very gallant effort. Three miles above Salale, lying on the ground, with a conspicuous list and foremast missing, lay the battered, burnt-out hull that was once *Somali*. These three wrecks are war memorials wrought in steel, left by the Europeans as grim presents to the African race.

CHAPTER 25

Down the River to Death

In recent years the word epic has become one of the most abused of all within the vocabulary; yet it were never more applicable than to the following story which closes the long list of adventures whereof the *Königsberg* was the central motive. The last scene of many a drama permits the reappearance of certain leading characters, and in this final act we view again some of the people and ships—the winding Rufiji, the wrecks, the Simba Uranga mouth, the Kiomboni peninsula, the German outposts that had been once created by Schönfeld; and, not least, the insatiable mosquitoes, the heat, the bullets that sting to death.

It was January 6, 1917, and the Rufiji delta still remained in the enemy's hands because it was not worth the trouble of taking; though, before the year should end, the East African campaign would have come to a close. But it was necessary to keep in touch with this area, and to make occasional reconnaissances. On January 5 Flight-Lieutenant Deans flew over from one of H.M. ships anchored off Niororo Island and made his inspection. He returned safely, though his seaplane was not undamaged; for, whilst he was swooping over the *Königsberg* wreck there was a fusillade from German rifles, and a bullet struck one of his wings. His departure from the river's mouth was greeted by another discharge. Thus, it was quite certain the enemy had not forsaken the neighbourhood.

So, on the following day a further reconnaissance must be made, but with a different seaplane. As Pilot went Flight-Lieutenant E. R. Moon, who had come out from England the previous February; but as observer there accompanied him this morning Commander the Hon. Robert Bridgeman, that keen Flag-Commander whom we have seen on previous occasions taking the air in order to espy the German cruiser. The flight began at 7.30 a.m., and all went well as they crossed the strip of ocean, flew over the delta, examined the familiar river branches, and made a thorough inspection of the *Königsberg*.

At about 8.30 a.m., fully satisfied with the information obtained, the seaplane from her inland limit turned for home, but as she sped on it was painfully noticeable that the engine revolutions were dropping almost to nothing. Moon therefore had no alternative but to alight on the water where he might adjust the trouble. The creek he chose for this purpose was to the south-east of *Königsberg*: it was in fact that branch which joins the Suninga with the Kiomboni River, and had been navigated by the *Königsberg* during her penultimate stage. (Represented on the map immediately south of K5.) It was near to the spot from which Deans had been fired at the previous day, with thick vegetation on either side shutting out the rest of the world. A few moments soon disclosed the predicament, for the after magneto drive was gone, but unfortunately pressure in the petrol tank was allowed to drop, and the engine failed altogether, utterly refusing every effort to be restarted.

Bridgeman decided that the only course now was to destroy the seaplane and make for the river mouth, where sooner or later they hoped to find a boat from a warship, or at least a native dugout. In the meanwhile, they were expecting every minute to be surrounded by the enemy from out of the vegetation, or else to be attacked by water. For surely the Germans could not have failed to notice the seaplane falling.

Having flooded the machine with petrol and fired it with Very's lights, the pilot and observer left a useless wreck, started to walk down by the river bank, then covered their tracks by swimming across it and reached the Suninga River, which of course led past Salale village, the *Somali* and *Newbridge* wrecks, down to the Kiomboni peninsula facing the sea. It may be mentioned that on starting off this morning, Moon had partaken of no more breakfast than a cup of tea, but he was a good swimmer. The commander was a moderate swimmer and wore an inflated belt, which unluckily leaked.

On gaining the Suninga River, progress by land was most difficult through such dense bush, but it happened that the tide was out and they flopped along through the mud. The brilliant sun had reached its zenith when, across its glare, was sighted Deans' seaplane that had come to search: for Moon's craft carried only three hours' petrol and that meant he should have been back not later than 10.30. The pathos here lies in the situation that the two pilgrims could see their friend and waved their arms to the burnished sky, yet understanding all the while that Deans could never see them separated from the background: the tragedy becomes more pitiful because today we know that Deans presently sighted the seaplane lying upside down, that he alighted on the water, noticed there had been a conflagration, stood by some time, fired off Very's lights to announce his presence—till he could imagine no other conclusion than one. His friends must have been burnt to death. He took off again and raced back to the ship.

On and on for mile after weary mile the two officers sweated their way seawards along the Suninga bank till they were abreast of the point where the Somali was lying. By this time, it was about 6 p.m. and the tide had come up, making it impossible any longer to use the mud; but the bush still continued impenetrable. The commander was becoming exhausted after the heavy going, and his safety belt was deflated. But Moon, full of pluck and vitality, though empty of stomach, thought that several hundred yards across the river he could see a green dugout lying close to the *Somali*. It was now dark and he decided to swim thereto, hoping also that aboard the *Somali* he might find at least some rainwater, for their throats were dry as leather, and the river was salty with the flood-tide.

Leaving Bridgeman on the southern shore, Moon got across, and landed near the channel which runs N.W. and S.E. joining the Suninga with the Simba Uranga. He had the disappointment to find that the dugout was not a boat: it was merely a tree branch. He then climbed up the *Somali's* hull, found that steel deck had not been indented by the act of her burning (when shelled many months ago by the *Chatham*): it had buckled upwards like a watershed, so the rains had fallen back into the sea leaving no cavities for a well. The most he discovered comprised a few drops which wetted the tip of his tongue.

With this lack of encouragement Moon started to swim back to the southern shore, but everything was dead against him. The set of current in these Rufiji rivers is somewhat abnormal, as was discovered (*a*) when the *Newbridge* party were trying to get exactly athwart stream, and (*b*) when the monitors were being moored for their first attack. Moon was to become acquainted with this same irregularity, for the tide, instead of flowing parallel with the banks, took rather a northerly twist. He had reached the *Somali* vicinity, therefore, more easily than expected, but now that same odd turn was to thwart him when going back. Twice he essayed to stem the stream, but could make no headway. Three times—four—five! He gave up the attempt till slack water should return with the dawn, but with black night came the torment of mosquitoes in myriads, driving him back into the water till nothing below his lips could be pierced by their poisonous injections.

After such a night Moon did manage to swim across, but there was no sign of Bridgeman. Whither had he vanished? As it was again high water, making it impossible to hug the edge of the bush, Moon went swimming downstream with the young ebb till he was abreast of Salale's deserted village. On the southern bank, just opposite, he sighted a lonely hut, which evidently had been used by the *Königsberg* when she first moored herself in the river. A human figure was now seen to move, and it was Bridgeman hungry but alive. Moon joined him, and together they went off looking for food; but the search concluded with only a few coco-nuts gathered from some palm trees, and a couple of empty bottles found in the hut which German sailors had evidently discarded. Not much of a breakfast after twenty-four hours' fasting and toiling, but the bottle came in handy for sorting the coconuts' milk.

Progress in future should be made by raft. The *Königsberg's* people had left behind three wooden poles, which were now lashed together by means of dried grass, across which were secured old window frames; and, fortunately, a broken paddle that once belonged to a native dugout was discovered. It was less a raft than a submersible, and the travellers sitting astride it found such slight buoyancy that nothing was out of the water except shoulders and head. In this manner, driven down with the ebb and up with the flood, they spent the hours between noon of January 7 and the following dawn optimistically joking about the future, notwithstanding the massed onslaught of mosquitoes.

There now loomed up another real vessel with funnel and masts. It was the blockship *Newbridge*. Perhaps there might have been left a pint or two of drinking water? A few bits of canned food might have survived two years' neglect? Go alongside!

But the strong tide swept the raft past, till a landing had to be made a little to the east, that is to say not far from those mangrove-hidden positions wherein German guns had been so busily employed against the blockship expedition. Moon and Bridgeman were accordingly in dangerous territory, and might expect to be shot dead any moment; but it was two days since either traveller had eaten a meal, the salt water had got into the bottles, and there was only one coco-nut left. Food and drink must be sought and obtained from the natives, who might be bribed into lending a boat from the Kiomboni peninsula to the aviators' ship. What a relief might thus be at hand!

Fate, however, chose otherwise; and the mosquitoes drove the fatigued pair from out of the mangroves back to the river facing the *Newbridge*. At slack water the raft was again launched, but the blockship's upperworks were unable to yield anything at all: even rest was denied them. For with night once more came the mosquitoes, who made existence such a buzzing hell that, without waiting for the return of day, the officers took to their improvised raft.

On January 9 heavy-handed doom dealt them a cruel destiny. They were still intending to land at a suitable patch on the south-western side of the peninsula; still hoping to find off the mouth a dugout, or better still a naval boat steaming in from the sea. Now the bank was no real distance away in terms of measurement, yet in terms of tide and time it was unattainable. Upstream was the raft swept by the flood, and all control was lost. Down with the ebb, past the *Newbridge*, past the entrance, past everything, the turning tide carried them next. Where once machine-guns had crackled and pom-poms had coughed, there was complete silence. Not a shot had been fired. It was goodbye to the dreaded delta and all its swamps; to the inhospitable wrecks, the mosquitoes, the mangroves and sniping Germans.

But something worse awaited them than hunger or thirst, a sting or a bullet.

They were rushing out to sea at the rate of knots; the peninsula's high trees over which the *Chatham* had shelled the *Somali* were fast receding, but it was all wrong: a nightmare, a mad ride into death on a crazy raft. Here was the Indian Ocean, and the wind was kicking up a nasty lop which speedily developed into ugly waves that kept capsizing their two victims and twisting the grass-tied spars into a meaningless mess. Time after time the two men, worn out beyond all endurance, broken in body and almost in spirit, clambered back to their impossible perch, only to be washed off again. There is a limit to the suffering of such terrors, coming hard upon prolonged fasting and utter helplessness. In itself the sea is Nature's greatest bully, merciless, dominant, without discrimination; yet it was brutal beyond all reckoning to smite two men at such a crisis.

They were losing all grip on life, fading into unconsciousness, and Bridgeman was in the worse condition. Moon did his best to encourage; to uphold with words of optimism and tenacious hands. But, after keeping the latter's head above water for what seemed an interminable time, Moon likewise flopped into that state where a man can contend no more: he must submit and relax. His strength was gone, the sea had robbed him of all purpose.

It was evening when the incoming tide carried the raft back to Kiomboni beach. One body had been washed off: that of Commander Bridgeman, a brave warrior, whom the air had not dared to destroy and the ocean had claimed for itself. He had simply disappeared, and the end came as the last item of physical strength parted. Somehow Moon, dazed, almost dead yet not quite gone, was thrown without knowing it into shallow water and struggled through the surf, whence he staggered a few steps and must then have collapsed. He next walked mechanically a little inland, met a native, tried to bribe him for a passage in his dugout; but a second, and older, native came up who took Moon by the wrist within a grass hut, where a couple of mangoes were given him to eat: the first solid food the aviator had consumed since the night before he left his ship.

Moon was treated not unkindly: in fact, a primitive tenderness and simple sympathy were expressed in action. There sat the sad object, with his clothing torn to shreds and sea-stained, his stockings all tattered and slipped down to his tired feet. But these *Askaris* were part of the German war organisation; so, having put on their uniforms, they conducted the British officer for one and a half hours southward till they came to one of the German observation posts, where Moon fell into a faint. When he regained consciousness, it was to find himself a prisoner of German sailors, who likewise behaved with kindness.

But the rest of this officer's experiences after being taken to a prisoners' camp further inland, his suffering fever during the ensuing months, being moved on from place to place for several hundreds of miles as the enemy retreated before the British Army, were not marked by excessive consideration. Finally, when the Germans were compelled to leave behind not merely their sick prisoners but their own invalids, Moon at last was a free man. Out of great tribulation had come great joy, for now had arrived the victorious troops who had helped to drive the enemy clear of what once was called German East Africa. Few would care to have suffered the agonies of mind and body which tortured this flying expert, and modern warfare has scarcely any parallel instance of this extraordinary adventure which developed from what one may regard as an error of judgment.

If Commander Bridgeman had been not quite so anxious to prevent the seaplane from falling into enemy hands, that gallant fellow might be alive today, (1932). The Germans certainly espied the machine in its descent and realised it was in difficulties. A search party was despatched, but quite reasonably they failed to estimate the exact position where the seaplane stopped, and imagined the spot to be in the Kiomboni River. This clears up the question as to why the two officers were not speedily surrounded and arrested. Deans, in his seaplane, would have been able to rescue at least Bridgeman, before returning for Moon, had they both remained a few hours hidden by the vegetation yet in close proximity to the burnt aircraft.

The episode concludes, however, with the satisfaction that, after all, the Indian Ocean claimed the Flag-Commander only for a time. One of the flood-tides brought his body back to the delta, deposited it on the shore, and there released it for committal to mother earth. With full military honours our late enemies gave him a Christian burial, and there he lies home from the sea where the African palms rock to the onshore breeze.

By the end of 1917 the East African campaign had passed into history. The last flight of the R.N.A.S. was made on November 17, and it was two days later that Moon, with Lieutenant-Commander Paterson, ended his captivity. Some of the still surviving members of the *Königsberg's* crew succeeded in reaching the water again, and got back to Germany *via* Arabia and Turkey; following the example set by some of the *Emden's* people who started off from the Cocos Islands in the *Ayesha*. By January 1918, General Smuts was already in London lecturing on a war that had terminated so favourably; in spite of the heat, the fever, the hardships that were common to both sides. "In the story of human endurance," he remarked, "this campaign deserves a special place."

For us who have watched the *Königsberg's* vicissitudes, and even noted the criticism of a German military officer, it is not devoid of interest to conclude with the generous appreciation which General Smuts extends to Captain (now Vice-Admiral) Looff's vessel:

> The *Königsberg*, though destroyed, yet made her voice heard over all that vast country, for her ten big naval guns, pulled by teams of 400 stalwart natives each, accompanied the enemy armies in all directions; and with other naval guns and howitzers smuggled into the country made the enemy in many a fight stronger in heavy artillery than we were.... Although we had complete command of the sea, it was not found to be a

sound military proposition to invade the country from the sea: partly because of the difficulty of landing; partly because of the extreme heat and unhealthiness of the swampy coastal belt. . . where in a very short time an invading force must have disappeared from malaria; and partly because of the great difficulty of properly timing and co-ordinating large operations in which military and naval forces have to co-operate,

The Destruction of "Königsberg": A Synopsis

The war on the trade routes came to a final end with the destruction of *Königsberg*. Although this was only accomplished in July, 1915, the incident can be given here before returning to events nearer home. *Königsberg* played an even more passive part than *Dresden*. Her station was the eastern side of Africa, based on the German colony there. It seems likely that her inactivity was occasioned by her lack of supplies. If this is so, it once again throws an interesting light on the question of German cruisers being able to exist with the help of neutrals, and unable to operate from their own distant or ill-placed bases. In naval war we, as a seafaring nation, possess the priceless advantage of well-chosen stations in every part of the world.

Our entire garrison of regular troops was removed from South Africa and sent home, other troops coming from India to carry out the invasion of German East Africa. *Königsberg*, therefore, had a fairly free hand, but she failed to make good her opportunities. Her only real success was against *Pegasus*, which she found at anchor, repairing her machinery on September 19, off Zanzibar. She sank her without difficulty, holding her from the first at her mercy. After this exploit *Chatham* and *Weymouth* were dispatched to hunt down and destroy *Königsberg*. *Goliath* and *Dartmouth* arrived a little later, to cover the wide area in which she might be found.

Leaving Aden on September 22, *Chatham* arrived at Mombasa in four days. Nothing was known of *Königsberg's* movements here. *Chatham*, therefore, took aboard all necessary supplies and left the next day for Zanzibar. The inhabitants had been considerably relieved to see her, as it was not known whether a further attack might not be made on the town itself. *Königsberg* had not fired at the place when she sank *Pegasus*, except at a dummy wireless installation—the real one being

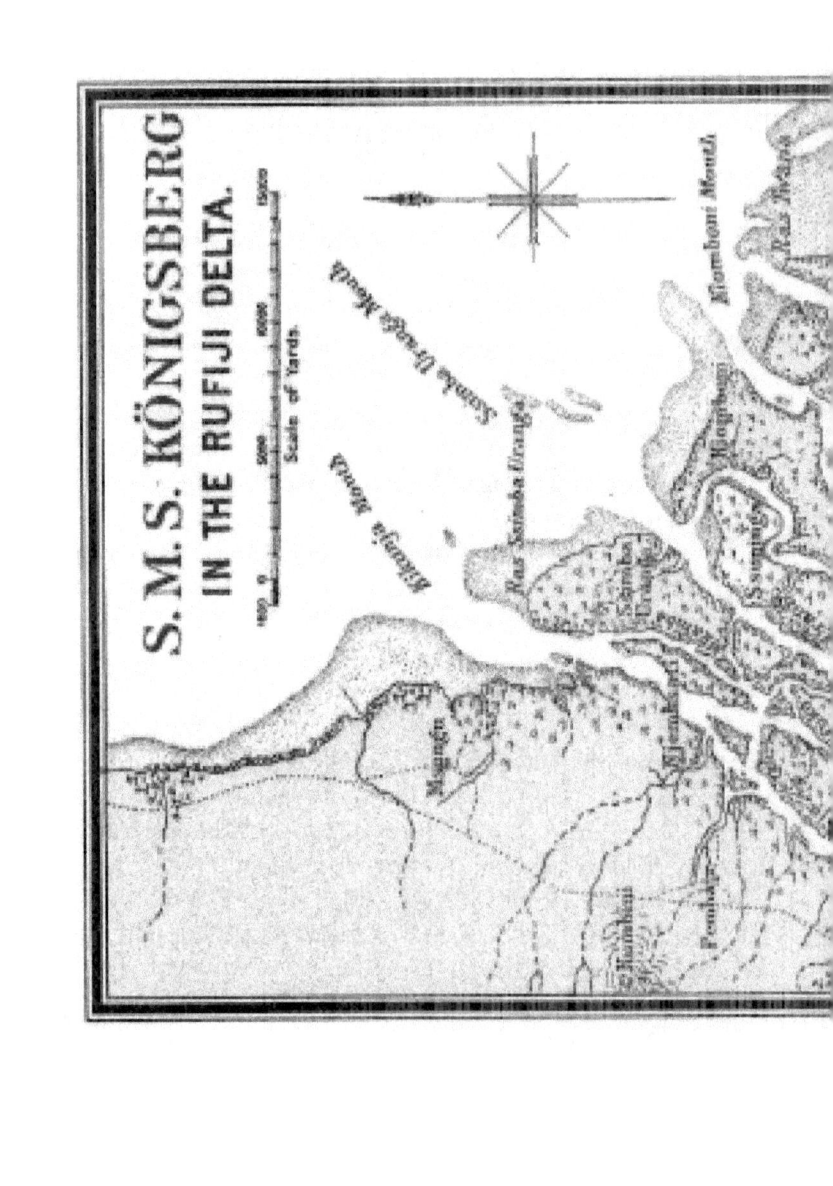

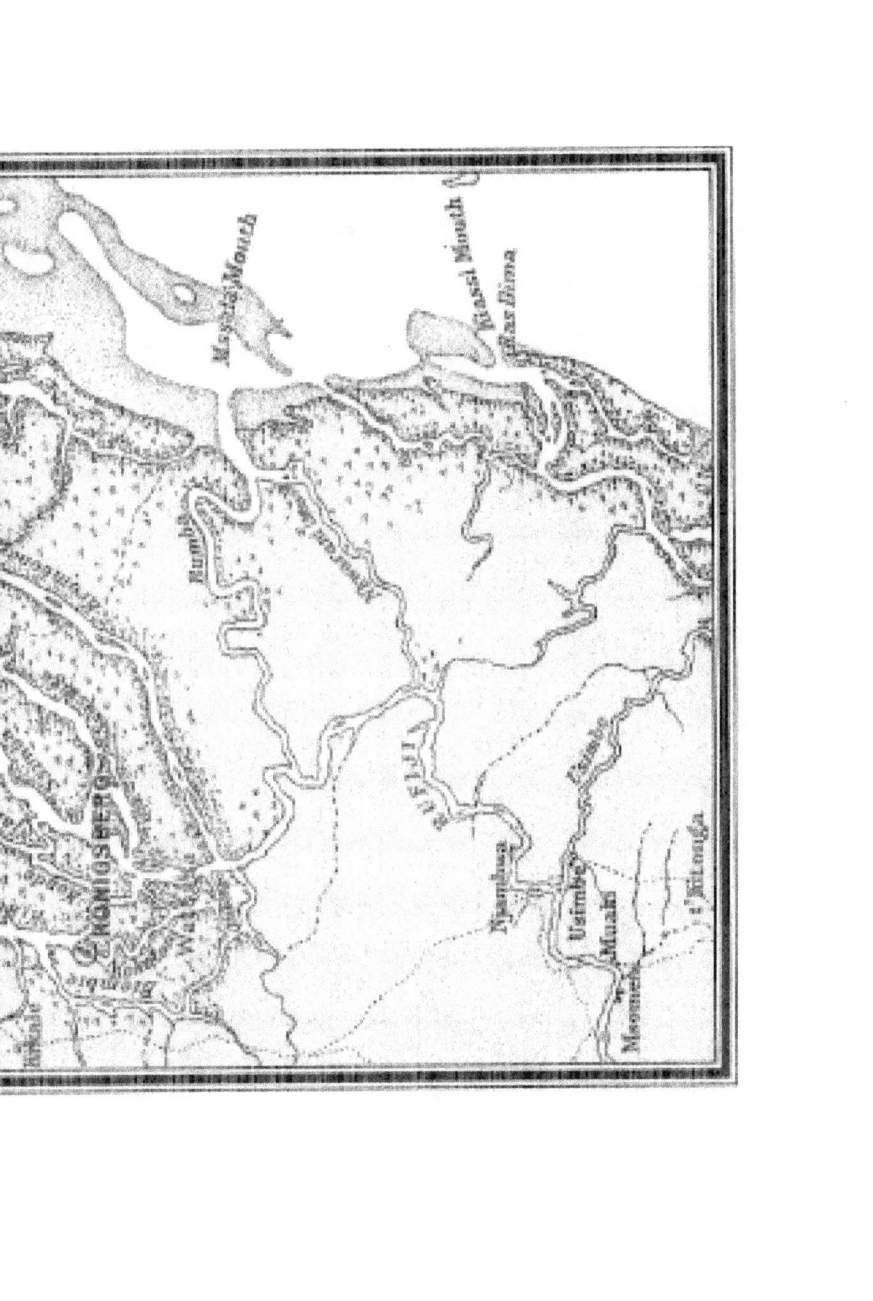

concealed in the bush. It was empty pretence of humanity at the best, though. The crew of *Pegasus* were still ashore, and had been salving the guns.

These had fallen clear of their ship as she turned over and sank, and were reached more easily in consequence. *Königsberg* had also been seen laying what looked like mines in the south channel, and had wirelessed *en clair*—"keep clear of southern entrance," but the mines turned out on investigation to be zinc cases used in the German Navy for cordite charges. It was a German *ruse de guerre*, palpable and easily discovered.

The search for *Königsberg* was now planned with deliberation, and was carried out systematically. The area to be searched was between Cape Guardafui on the north and Delagoa Bay on the south, including all the islands between. The coast of East Africa offers a large number of hiding places—bays, inlets, unknown anchorages. The Germans had established a very efficient system of signalling along the coast, so the movements of our ships within sight of land were all promptly reported. A telegraph line ran along the shore, and this in turn connected with wireless stations which could communicate with *Königsberg* at any moment.

As a start, the area to be searched was divided up, and a number of rendezvous fixed. *Weymouth* and *Dartmouth*, based on Comoro, were to search the Mozambique Channel and to southward. They had also to protect the trade. *Chatham* was to search between Mombasa and Cape Delgado—a special duty never lost sight of.

By the end of October all the coast had been thoroughly accounted for except the Rufiji delta. It was thought unlikely that the German cruiser would be in hiding there, because, as far as was known, the water was too shallow for a ship of *Konigsberg's* draught. At last, a clue was obtained of her unexpected presence there through the capture of the steamer *President*, of the German East Africa line, which had been working in secret with *Königsberg*. This ship is of interest, as she throws a typical side-light on the case of *Ophelia*, which the Germans fitted out as a hospital ship, and which was condemned as a prize because she was obviously out, reporting our movements. She had never done any hospital work.

The German colonial authorities claimed that *President* was also a hospital ship. She had had a red cross painted on her sides, and flew a Geneva Cross flag. Those were her misleading insignia—an attempt at meeting the requirements of war, but a subterfuge. In reality she was not fitted as a boat on the errands of mercy. She had no medical stores or appliances, and carried no doctors. Most of her important papers had been destroyed, but among those left was a receipt for supplying coal to *Königsberg* in September at Salali, a village up the Rufiji delta. A new German chart was also found, which showed channels up which *Königsberg* could be taken at certain states of the tide, which had a rise and fall of fifteen feet at spring tides and nine feet at neaps. That was the trade that *President*, with pretended innocence, was systematically plying.

The delta is formed by the mouths of the Rufiji and Mohoro Rivers. It extends for about forty miles along the coast, and is split up into creek after creek. The shores are all thickly wooded by mangroves, and as a great deal of the ground is high, it is impossible to spot even the mast of a ship from seaward, except from certain places. The three most important entrances are the Kikunja, the Ssimba Urunga (which joins with the Ssuninga at its mouth), and the Kiomboni. The Ssimba Urunga had been used by the Germans, but no Englishman had been known to go there for at least ten years before the war. We took little trade interest in this impossible region. Still, Mafia Island lies off the mouth of the delta. It was known the Germans were in force on the island, and also on the shores at the entrance to the delta. That was to be their first line of defence.

So right at the end of October *Chatham* arrived off the Kiomboni mouth just after dawn. The ship was compelled to anchor some way off shore, but the voyage had been made at night as it was known that the alarm would be given to the land forces as soon as she was sighted from Mafia Island. Her plan was to send an armed boat, with an interpreter, ashore to capture some of the natives in order to obtain information. This was done; the party met with no opposition, and a headman and two intelligent natives were brought back triumphantly to the ship. These men frankly stated that German sailors were among the troops in the vicinity, and that *Königsberg* herself lay off the village of Salali, which was some six miles up the Ssimba Urunga, and nine miles from the nearest point *Chatham* could reach.

At any rate she was run to earth, though she was safely moored out of sight. Anchor was therefore weighed, and *Chatham* took up a position at the mouth of the Ssimba Urunga, being forced to keep over six miles out to sea on account of the shoals. On the way there the masthead look-out reported the topmasts of ships up the river, one obviously belonging to a man-o'-war—later proved to be *Königsberg*, while the other was *Somali*, a merchantman once more acting as store ship. At one time it was thought the former was under way and coming out, but it was soon seen she was definitely at anchor. *Chatham*, therefore, stood guard about eight and a half miles off the entrance, and wirelessed to *Dartmouth* and *Weymouth* to close on her in support.

The last day of October and the forenoon of November 1 were taken up sounding towards the entrance. In the forenoon of the latter day *Chatham* was able to close to within four and a half miles of the shore, and was just 14,500 yards (her maximum range) from *Somali*, *Königsberg* being one and a half miles beyond that station. Fire was opened on *Somali*, but no result could be observed, as even from *Chatham*'s highest observation point only *Somali*'s masthead could be seen.

The next day *Weymouth* and *Dartmouth* arrived, and as the latter had her bunkers nearly empty, it was decided she should stand in as near as possible at high water (3-9 p.m.). All three ships closed on the entrance shortly before, and *Dartmouth* got to within two miles of the bar. *Königsberg* was not visible at all from that position, but *Somali* was again shelled until the falling tide necessitated our withdrawal. On the following day spring tides reached their maximum height at 4 p.m., and *Chatham* managed to approach to within two miles of the entrance, at a point from which *Königsberg's* lower masts were visible. She had housed her topmasts, and placed branches of trees at her mastheads. The range was 14,800 yards, and by listing the ship five degrees the starboard guns could be brought to bear. Fire was kept up for half an hour, until the ebb made it necessary to go out again.

A boat attack was made on November 7. One of *Goliath's* picket boats had arrived from Mombasa, where that ship was undergoing repairs, and this boat led the attack, supported by three steam cutters from the cruisers. Orders were to the effect that the attack was not to be forced if the banks were found to be held in strength, and because a very heavy fire was opened on them as they approached the shore they returned to the ships, their venture unaccomplished. While this was being done, *Chatham* stood as close in as possible and shelled *Somali* at 13,000 yards range. This caused a fire which, it was afterwards heard, completely gutted the vessel.

It was now evident that neither the ships nor the boats could reach *Königsberg*. It was therefore decided to block the entrance to prevent her exit. The only channel she could navigate was the Ssuninga, and the chart showed that the narrowest part of this lay just within the first bend from the entrance. A collier, *Newbridge*, 3,800 tons burden, was procured from Mombasa and prepared for the needed operation. The fore-bridge and positions fore and aft, from which cable parties were to work, were covered in with protective plates and sandbags. Explosives were placed in the engine-room and lashed outboard under the bottom. The crew manning her were men from aboard *Chatham*. *Newbridge* was to be taken up to her position at daybreak and anchored. She was to be sunk when the flood tide swung her across the channel, as it should do at 8 a.m.

All arrangements were carried out as planned. *Newbridge* started at 4 a.m., *Chatham* and *Weymouth* closing in to her support, and at 5.15 the cruisers opened fire on the entrance. *Newbridge* passed up with the attendant boats and was soon lost to sight in the bend. From the time our blocking ship got into range from the shore until the boats returned, all were subjected to a very heavy fire from maxims and rifles. Three killed and nine wounded were the only casualties, thanks to the protection erected on board and to the accurate return fire from our boats. *Newbridge* was successfully sunk exactly in the place arranged, the tide assisting as expected, and the boats all returned safely to the ships.

After this *Weymouth* and *Dartmouth* left, being no longer needed. *Chatham* remained, to be joined by the auxiliary liner Kinfauns Castle, which arrived from the Cape with a Curtis seaplane. *Königsberg* was located by the seaplane a very long way up the river. She must have been got up there at the top of successive spring tides, possibly by warping.

The operations to destroy *Königsberg* for a time came to an end. On January 7, 1915, Mafia Island was captured with the help of a military force. In the meantime, the coast was blockaded, and *Chatham*, helped by three small steamers—*Adjutant, Dupleix* and *Halmuth*—was kept on this duty throughout.

The next attacks on *Königsberg* were made in July, 1915. At the beginning of the war three monitors, which were being built in England for Brazil, were taken over by the Government and named *Mersey, Severn* and *Humber*. The ships were quite small and were built for river work. They displaced 1,250 tons, and had an overall length of 265 feet and 49 feet beam. The draught was only 6 feet. The armament consisted of two 6-inch guns, two 4.7 howitzers, four three-pounders, and machine-guns. The 6-inch guns were mounted fore and aft, behind shields of the pattern usually supplied for guns of that size mounted on deck.

The monitors had taken part in the bombardment of the Belgian coast in October, 1914. They had done various duties since, and later were ordered to proceed to Mafia Island. The ships were specially fitted for an ocean voyage. *Mersey* and *Severn* were towed by tugs out to East Africa. (*Humber* only went as far as Malta and was left there.) The crews of the monitors were accommodated on board *Trent*, which was fitted out as a parent ship and accompanied them.

The voyage out naturally took some time. Malta was reached on March 30, and a long stay was made there. It was June 3 before the ships, having passed through the Suez Canal, finally arrived at Mafia Island. Work then commenced in earnest. The baulks and strengthening shores, which had been put in to enable the monitors to make a long sea voyage, were quickly removed. Plates and sandbag protection were erected on deck, and all the exposed parts of the ships, especially the propelling and steering gear, were guarded. Some 4,000 kerosene tins, made watertight, were stowed in all available compartments on each ship to provide buoyancy in case they were hulled below the water-line. The twins were painted green in various shades to harmonise with the colour of the shore; the crews wore khaki—the whole attack being camouflaged.

In the meantime, more seaplanes had been obtained, but they were not very successful, owing chiefly to atmospheric conditions. They could, as a rule, only rise about 1,000 feet above the sea, and they came down to 700 feet as soon as they crossed the land, a height which was too low for safety. Finally, an aerodrome was made at Mafia Island. More aeroplanes were obtained—strange and monstrous birds in a strange land. No further trouble was experienced. The aeroplanes were not weighed down by floats, each two hundred-weight (as in the case of seaplanes). They rose at once to 3,000 feet, a height from which observations could efficiently be carried out.

Photographs were taken of *Königsberg*, and her position was accurately located. A system of signalling from the aeroplane to the ships was arranged, and for some days practice was carried out at the southward of Mafia Island, the monitors firing over the land at dhows anchored out of sight on the other side, the aeroplanes signalling the result of the shots. It proved a successful experiment, prophetic of disaster to the German cruiser.

At the beginning of July all was ready for the carefully planned attack. On the 5th a demonstration was made at Dar-es-Salaam, with cruisers and transports together, to contain the enemy as far as possible in that direction.

At 7 p.m. on July 5 the monitors weighed anchor and closed on the mainland, anchoring off the Kikunja mouth. The next morning the crews went to general quarters at 3.45, and at 4 o'clock anchors were weighed and the ships stood in to pass up the mouth of the river, *Severn* was leading. At the same time, to distract attention, the cruisers set to work to make a big demonstration off each of the other entrances. *Weymouth* was engaged with the monitors off the Kikunja mouth. The Germans had placed field guns on the left bank of the river at a point where they could fire across the channel, while any "overs" would fall into the sea, and not on the opposite shore. The narrows at the entrance were defended by rifles and maxim guns.

As soon as the monitors began to pass up, fire was opened on them, but in the dim light of the early dawn it must have been difficult for the Germans or any riflemen to take good aim. At any rate the shooting did little damage. The fire was returned by the monitors, and the heavy guns must have caused great execution at the short range of a few hundred yards. Practically nothing could be seen of the enemy. As on all similar occasions, there was far less firing from the bank.

The devastating effect of big guns at point-blank range has already been noticed, and the monitors continued to fire at all objects seen as they passed up. *Severn* destroyed a torpedo innocently attached to a log, and also sank a dhow moored up a side stream. *Mersey* hit a service cutter, which blew up with a great explosion as if it contained torpedoes or mines, or both combined.

At 6.30 *Severn* and *Mersey* had reached positions near an island in the main stream from which the attack was to be made, and moored bow and stern in line ahead. An aeroplane had already arrived and was flying with buzzing whir overhead. It was a fine clear morning, with very good atmospheric conditions for the work in hand. Distant objects were clear cut and easily observed.

At 6.50 *Severn* opened fire at a range of 10,600 yards. *Mersey* followed suit soon afterwards, both ships firing alternately. *Königsberg* returned the fire promptly, and soon straddled the monitors, aiming principally at *Mersey*. Her spotting was done from a hill in the vicinity, and her shots were very accurate. *Weymouth* bombarded the hills from outside the entrance in the hope of finding the spotting station, but the effect could not be seen.

At a little after 7.30 *Mersey* found the fire too hot for her. A shot hit the fore 6-inch gun shield, smashing it and putting the gun out of action. Two more fell just alongside. Numbers of shells were peppering the water all round and quite near the ship. Her captain therefore decided to shift his position, and slowly dropped another 1,000 yards downstream. *Königsberg* immediately turned her attention to *Severn*, blazing salvos of four guns at the rate of about three a minute. Soon after eight *Severn* found it necessary to shift, and moved to a berth where she hoped to be out of sight of *Königsberg's* spotting station. She fired at what she took to be the Spotting station, and, although she could not tell the result *Königsberg's* fire was not so accurate afterwards.

Two aeroplanes were overhead, each flying at a time for two and a half hours. Spotting was well reported at first, but later the reports became confused, as there was no proper discrimination to show which ship was being signalled to. Our fire consequently became very wild, a ship firing over, for instance, lengthening her range on the strength of a message meant for her consort and *vice versa*. Occasional hits were secured and *Königsberg* was seen to be on fire, but not out of action. At midday there was a pause of about an hour, as the aeroplane at work had to leave. *Severn* tried to carry on, doing her own spotting, as she could see the enemy, but without success. *Königsberg* still kept up her venomous return fire, but was using three guns instead of four.

By 3.30 it was obvious little good was being done, and the ships withdrew, dropping down the river over the course they came up and letting fly at objects as they slowly passed by, receiving always far less in return than on their way up. By 4.45 the open sea had been reached, and the "Secure" was sounded. It was quite time, for the crews had been at general quarters for eighteen hours, and eleven hours had been spent under fire. This was a pretty severe test, considering the climate, especially in the engine-rooms, where the temperature was somewhere in the neighbourhood of 130 degrees, so that the stokers sweated ceaselessly. Considering the nature of the fire received, they were very little damaged. The hit on *Mersey's* fore 6-inch gun shield was the most serious. *Königsberg* fired approximately eight hundred rounds, showing how active an enemy she still was.

It was difficult to determine the damage done to *Königsberg*. She caught fire, but did not burn seriously. The aviators reported that they believed the foremost port 4.1-inch gun had been hit, a probable injury. Several hits had been scored early in the action, but after about 8.15 a.m. the firing had been erratic, owing to confusion in the spotting messages received from the aeroplane. The net result was that *Königsberg* had been damaged, but not destroyed. She could sting, might be

Cruiser "Königsberg" trapped by sinking of an English ship in the mouth of the Ausidji River

repaired and escape to sea. *Severn* had fired about four hundred rounds, and *Mersey* about three hundred. The aeroplanes flew about nine hundred miles during the day, a record in such a climate. The Germans made no attempt to jam the wireless signals during the attack. Perhaps they were, while left free, more useful to them than to us.

The second attack in this drawn-out duel was made on July 14. The time between the attacks was spent refitting the monitors and making good such damage as had been done. *Mersey's* 6-inch gun was repaired, destroyed parts being made good from other ships.

The plan of attack this time was as follows: The monitors were to leave their anchorage at 8 a.m. in tow of tugs, hoping to give the impression they were returning to Zanzibar. Off the river the tugs were to cast off, and the monitors were to proceed to their old positions. The river would be reached between 11 a.m. and noon (the time of the attack was probably fixed to suit the tides). *Severn* was to moor under the bank, out of sight of the troublesome spotting station, if possible, while *Mersey* showed herself in the stream, and was to try to draw *Königsberg's* fire off *Severn*. *Mersey* might begin, but the aeroplanes were not to spot for her while she was thus engaged. As soon as she was ready *Severn* was to open up, with the aeroplane spotting, and to continue incessantly for one hour.

In the meantime, *Mersey* was to proceed 1,000 yards higher up and attack with her guns after *Severn's* activity was completed. The ships were to take attacks in turn after that, to prevent any confusion in the spotting. The proceedings were to be carried on until *Königsberg* was destroyed. Simultaneously, the cruisers were to make a feint, as they had done on the previous occasion.

The tugs cast off at 11.10, and the monitors were at the entrance at 11.30 and were at once fired at, as before. There was little result, though the field gun battery scored some hits. Only one shot did real damage. These pieces (apparently 5 centimetres) were very well handled, and got home accurately whenever occasion offered. (Ou ships returned the fire, but failed to silence the battery, which was now actually sighted. Otherwise, the Germans' defence of the entrance was much less effective than it had been on the first occasion.

Before the monitors attacked the aeroplanes flew over *Königsberg* and dropped twelve bombs. As arranged, *Severn* took up her position about 9,800 yards from the enemy. *Königsberg* commenced firing at 12.21 at *Mersey* and changed over to *Severn* shortly before the latter opened fire and very soon straddled her. *Severn* began in earnest at

End of *Königsberg* in the Rufiji Delta.

12.30, and got on her target after the third spotting report was received, and after that continued to hit. *Königsberg* replied with salvos of four guns, but soon dropped again to three only. *Severn* was hitting forward, and, in accordance with instructions, shifted her fire a little aft. The aeroplane had been flying a good deal lower than during the first attack.

At about 12.50 she suddenly signalled, "We are hit; send boat," and she began to plane down. In spite of her unpleasant position (she had to land on the water, although not fitted with floats) she continued correctly spotting and reporting *Severn's* shots. Both the monitors sent boats, and the plane alighted about one hundred and fifty yards from *Mersey*. She turned a complete somersault as soon as she struck the water. Luckily her crew received nothing worse than a shaking and a ducking. As *Severn* had the range correctly, she continued to pour in shots without the spotting, firing one salvo a minute.

At 1.15 an explosion occurred on *Königsberg*, causing a bad fire which was never extinguished. She never fired again after that. The second aeroplane now arrived, and *Mersey* proceeded to her prearranged station and opened on her enemy at 8,200 yards. At this time *Königsberg's* foremast was leaning heavily over. The top part of the mainmast had been shot away, and smoke was pouring out from its socket as it would from the mouth of a chimney, evidently coming from a fire below decks. Her central funnel had gone. *Mersey* got to her position and blazed away twenty salvos, getting on the target at once. Then the aeroplane signalled, "Target destroyed." *Königsberg* now had a list of twenty to thirty degrees to port and was burning furiously from her foremast aft, and she was also on fire slightly forward.

Signal was therefore made to return, and the monitors again passed down, firing at, and receiving fire, from the banks as before. The tugs towed them back from the mouth of the river.

The attack had been most successful. The monitors were not injured, while *Königsberg* was destroyed. The difference in hitting was chiefly due to the relative sizes of the targets. Allowing four feet more freeboard than *Königsberg's* normal, as she was aground and had probably been lightened to get her up the river, she presented a target of some 5,600 square feet, while the monitors, small ships with low freeboard, presented a target of 1,400 square feet each. Hence, while the monitors were scoring regularly, *Königsberg* was only drenching the monitors with spray. *Königsberg* was hit from thirty-five to forty-five times in the second attack, and about fifty to fifty-five times in all.

The aeroplanes flew about 950 miles during the day. Each could stay up for three hours, fifty minutes of which were occupied going and returning.

The destruction of *Königsberg* completed the doom in foreign waters of all the German warships which did not succeed in reaching home at the outbreak of the war. Excepting the captain of Emden, the German officers as a whole do not seem to have fully grasped the conditions, or to have understood when they could best force the pace and when they should efface themselves. It is hardly too much to say that English officers would have done more under the same circumstances, even if they did not hold out so long. The traditions of the two navies are, after all, totally different. Germany has probably tried to pay us the compliment of imitating us at sea. Her only success has been the mimicry of a venomous and unscrupulous ape, which had, when she so ambitiously began to dispute our sea power, neither the prestige of victories nor even of great defeat. Her attempt will go down to history and be judged by future generations of all noble and brave peoples on its merits. History never errs in its final judgments.

ALSO FROM LEONAUR
AVAILABLE IN SOFTCOVER OR HARDCOVER WITH DUST JACKET

THE FALL OF THE MOGHUL EMPIRE OF HINDUSTAN by *H. G. Keene*—By the beginning of the nineteenth century, as British and Indian armies under Lake and Wellesley dominated the scene, a little over half a century of conflict brought the Moghul Empire to its knees.

LADY SALE'S AFGHANISTAN by *Florentia Sale*—An Indomitable Victorian Lady's Account of the Retreat from Kabul During the First Afghan War.

THE CAMPAIGN OF MAGENTA AND SOLFERINO 1859 by *Harold Carmichael Wylly*—The Decisive Conflict for the Unification of Italy.

FRENCH'S CAVALRY CAMPAIGN by *J. G. Maydon*—A Special Correspondent's View of British Army Mounted Troops During the Boer War.

CAVALRY AT WATERLOO by *Sir Evelyn Wood*—British Mounted Troops During the Campaign of 1815.

THE SUBALTERN by *George Robert Gleig*—The Experiences of an Officer of the 85th Light Infantry During the Peninsular War.

NAPOLEON AT BAY, 1814 by *F. Loraine Petre*—The Campaigns to the Fall of the First Empire.

NAPOLEON AND THE CAMPAIGN OF 1806 by *Colonel Vachée*—The Napoleonic Method of Organisation and Command to the Battles of Jena & Auerstädt.

THE COMPLETE ADVENTURES IN THE CONNAUGHT RANGERS by *William Grattan*—The 88th Regiment during the Napoleonic Wars by a Serving Officer.

BUGLER AND OFFICER OF THE RIFLES by *William Green & Harry Smith*—With the 95th (Rifles) during the Peninsular & Waterloo Campaigns of the Napoleonic Wars.

NAPOLEONIC WAR STORIES by *Sir Arthur Quiller-Couch*—Tales of soldiers, spies, battles & sieges from the Peninsular & Waterloo campaigns.

CAPTAIN OF THE 95TH (RIFLES) by *Jonathan Leach*—An officer of Wellington's sharpshooters during the Peninsular, South of France and Waterloo campaigns of the Napoleonic wars.

RIFLEMAN COSTELLO by *Edward Costello*—The adventures of a soldier of the 95th (Rifles) in the Peninsular & Waterloo Campaigns of the Napoleonic wars.

AVAILABLE ONLINE AT **www.leonaur.com**
AND FROM ALL GOOD BOOK STORES

ALSO FROM LEONAUR
AVAILABLE IN SOFTCOVER OR HARDCOVER WITH DUST JACKET

ESCAPE FROM THE FRENCH *by Edward Boys*—A Young Royal Navy Midshipman's Adventures During the Napoleonic War.

THE VOYAGE OF H.M.S. PANDORA *by Edward Edwards R. N. & George Hamilton, edited by Basil Thomson*—In Pursuit of the Mutineers of the Bounty in the South Seas—1790-1791.

MEDUSA *by J. B. Henry Savigny and Alexander Correard and Charlotte-Adélaïde Dard*—Narrative of a Voyage to Senegal in 1816 & The Sufferings of the Picard Family After the Shipwreck of the Medusa.

THE SEA WAR OF 1812 VOLUME 1 *by A. T. Mahan*—A History of the Maritime Conflict.

THE SEA WAR OF 1812 VOLUME 2 *by A. T. Mahan*—A History of the Maritime Conflict.

WETHERELL OF H. M. S. HUSSAR *by John Wetherell*—The Recollections of an Ordinary Seaman of the Royal Navy During the Napoleonic Wars.

THE NAVAL BRIGADE IN NATAL *by C. R. N. Burne*—With the Guns of H. M. S. Terrible & H. M. S. Tartar during the Boer War 1899-1900.

THE VOYAGE OF H. M. S. BOUNTY *by William Bligh*—The True Story of an 18th Century Voyage of Exploration and Mutiny.

SHIPWRECK! *by William Gilly*—The Royal Navy's Disasters at Sea 1793-1849.

KING'S CUTTERS AND SMUGGLERS: 1700-1855 *by E. Keble Chatterton*—A unique period of maritime history-from the beginning of the eighteenth to the middle of the nineteenth century when British seamen risked all to smuggle valuable goods from wool to tea and spirits from and to the Continent.

CONFEDERATE BLOCKADE RUNNER *by John Wilkinson*—The Personal Recollections of an Officer of the Confederate Navy.

NAVAL BATTLES OF THE NAPOLEONIC WARS *by W. H. Fitchett*—Cape St. Vincent, the Nile, Cadiz, Copenhagen, Trafalgar & Others.

PRISONERS OF THE RED DESERT *by R. S. Gwatkin-Williams*—The Adventures of the Crew of the Tara During the First World War.

U-BOAT WAR 1914-1918 *by James B. Connolly/Karl von Schenk*—Two Contrasting Accounts from Both Sides of the Conflict at Sea During the Great War.

AVAILABLE ONLINE AT **www.leonaur.com**
AND FROM ALL GOOD BOOK STORES

ALSO FROM LEONAUR
AVAILABLE IN SOFTCOVER OR HARDCOVER WITH DUST JACKET

FARAWAY CAMPAIGN *by F. James*—Experiences of an Indian Army Cavalry Officer in Persia & Russia During the Great War.

REVOLT IN THE DESERT *by T. E. Lawrence*—An account of the experiences of one remarkable British officer's war from his own perspective.

MACHINE-GUN SQUADRON *by A. M. G.*—The 20th Machine Gunners from British Yeomanry Regiments in the Middle East Campaign of the First World War.

A GUNNER'S CRUSADE *by Antony Bluett*—The Campaign in the Desert, Palestine & Syria as Experienced by the Honourable Artillery Company During the Great War.

DESPATCH RIDER *by W. H. L. Watson*—The Experiences of a British Army Motorcycle Despatch Rider During the Opening Battles of the Great War in Europe.

TIGERS ALONG THE TIGRIS *by E. J. Thompson*—The Leicestershire Regiment in Mesopotamia During the First World War.

HEARTS & DRAGONS *by Charles R. M. F. Crutwell*—The 4th Royal Berkshire Regiment in France and Italy During the Great War, 1914-1918.

INFANTRY BRIGADE: 1914 *by John Ward*—The Diary of a Commander of the 15th Infantry Brigade, 5th Division, British Army, During the Retreat from Mons.

DOING OUR 'BIT' *by Ian Hay*—Two Classic Accounts of the Men of Kitchener's 'New Army' During the Great War including *The First 100,000* & *All In It*.

AN EYE IN THE STORM *by Arthur Ruhl*—An American War Correspondent's Experiences of the First World War from the Western Front to Gallipoli-and Beyond.

STAND & FALL *by Joe Cassells*—With the Middlesex Regiment Against the Bolsheviks 1918-19.

RIFLEMAN MACGILL'S WAR *by Patrick MacGill*—A Soldier of the London Irish During the Great War in Europe including *The Amateur Army*, *The Red Horizon* & *The Great Push*.

WITH THE GUNS *by C. A. Rose & Hugh Dalton*—Two First Hand Accounts of British Gunners at War in Europe During World War 1- Three Years in France with the Guns and With the British Guns in Italy.

THE BUSH WAR DOCTOR *by Robert V. Dolbey*—The Experiences of a British Army Doctor During the East African Campaign of the First World War.

AVAILABLE ONLINE AT www.leonaur.com
AND FROM ALL GOOD BOOK STORES

www.ingramcontent.com/pod-product-compliance
Lightning Source LLC
Chambersburg PA
CBHW031624160426
43196CB00006B/267